LEE PFEIFFER AND PHILIP LISA

THE INCREDIBLE WORLD OF 007

A Citadel Press Book
Published by Carol Publishing Group

ACKNOWLEDGEMENTS

To Janet, Nicole and my mom Shirley — for their inspiration and support for my interest in all things Bondian — and to Cubby for all the memories —
For my mother, Mary Ann, who always supported my enthusiasm for James Bond 007, and my father Philip, who always tolerated it! — P.L.

Carol Publishing Group Edition, 1995

Copyright © 1995 Lee Pfeiffer and Philip Lisa
Cover design by Martin Lovelock
Pages designed by David Goodman, Millions Design
Typeset by Litho Link, Welshpool, Powys
Origination by Fotographics, Hong Kong
All rights reserved. No part of this book may be
reproduced in any form, except by a newspaper or mag-
azine reviewer who wishes to quote brief passages in
connection with a review.

A Citadel Press Book
Published by Carol Publishing Group
Citadel Press is a registered trademark of Carol
Communications, Inc.

Editorial Offices: 600 Madison Avenue
New York, NY 10022. Sales & Distribution Offices: 120
Enterprise Avenue Secaucus, NJ 07094.
Queries regarding rights and permissions should be
addressed to: Carol Publishing Group, 600 Madison
Avenue, New York, NY 10022
Manufactured in the United States of America
ISBN 0-8065-1698-4 (pbk.)
10 9 8 7 6 5 4 3 2
The Cataloging-in-Publication Data for this title may be
obtained from the Library of Congress.
Published by arrangement with Boxtree Limited, London
England.

We are very appreciative of everyone's kind comments and suggestions. If Agent 007 isn't p
neither are we. Several errors had been pointed out by readers and we have tried to
corrections for this edition. The most mail we received concerned our "bloopers" sectio
we hope to include the amazing additions noted by astute fans in future editions of the book.

We extend our thanks to those individuals who helped contribute to the first edition of *The Inc
World of 007*: our former editor at Boxtree, Elaine Collins. Dave Worrall of "The James Bond Coll
Club", Graham Rye of "The James Bond Fan Club and Archive", Kevin Doherty, John Griswold, Tim an
Greaves, Gert and Anne-Marie Albers, Kate McMahon of the New York Daily News, Mary Ann Lisa
Ohlinger's Movie Memorabilia Store in New York City, the late Mark Ricci of the famed Memory Shop,
Corsini, Joe Fredericks, Bill Blumdetto, Corrine Tkao, James Linder, Mary and Ted Paterek, Paul Norr
Criterion laser discs, Eric Spitzer, John Ewaniuk, Steve Oxenrider, Jim Mishler, Roger Moore's agent Jerr
Joe Stachler, Doug Redenius, and special thanks to Walter Brinkman for his superb photography. We ar
thankful to the following individuals, formerly of Eon Productions: Saul Cooper, Linda Brown, Liz Ihre ar
late Mike Beck. Special thanks to Lee Pfeiffer's wife and daughter Janet and Nicole and Phil Lisa's wife
for good-naturedly enduring our neverending passion for all things Bondian. (Although we haven't
reached the point where we actually wear the *Licence to Kill* boxer shorts.)

For this revised edition of the book, we extend our sincere thanks to the staff of Boxtree Ltd in Lo
for their support and enthusiasm: Sarah Mahaffy, Susanna Wadeson, and all the talented designers;
Citadel Press in the U.S.: Steve Schragis, Bruce Bender, Allan J. Wilson, Gary Fitzgerald, Bill Wolfstahl,
Brower and Mike Lewis. From Eon Productions: Barbara Broccoli, our good friend John Parkinson, wh
continued to champion this book over the years; Gordon Arnell, Director of Marketing and Public
GoldenEye; Geoff Freeman and Amanda Schofield.

We remain most grateful for all the actors and "behind the scenes talent" who have given their tir
make this book a success: Pierce Brosnan, Roger Moore, George Lazenby, Timothy Dalton, Michael G. W
Ken Adam, Desmond Llewelyn, Lois Maxwell, Rose Alba, Jimmy Dean, Honor Blackman, Molly Peters
Clifton James. We also mourn the passing of two valued veterans of the Bond Series who helped cont
to this book: Maurice Binder, a man who was truly a legend in his field and the wonderfully talented V
Sheybal. We also would like to pay our respects to three other prominent contributors to the Bond l
who passed away recently: Harry Saltzman, Terence Young and Arthur Krim.

We remain deeply indebted to Cubby and Dana Broccoli, without whom this book would not have
a reality. With *GoldenEye*, Cubby has entered his fourth decade as the producer of the James Bond serie
other producer has provided a continuous string of high quality motion pictures over such an extended p
of time. Working with the talents of Barbara Broccoli and Michael G. Wilson, Cubby has insured that the
legacy will continue to thrive well into the next century. Cubby and Dana's enthusiasm for the first editi
this book made us eager to do this updated version. We hope it brings the Broccoli family — and fan
world over — fond memories from the truly incredible world of 007.

ABOUT THE AUTHORS

LEE PFEIFFER grew up in Jersey City, New Jersey and his proximity to New York City invoked an
interest in the arts, particularly motion pictures. In addition to writing about the cinema for va
publications, Lee has also written several books examining the careers of legendary screen stars
previously published works include *The Films of Clint Eastwood, The Official Andy Griffith Show Scrapbook*
films of Harrison Ford, and the forthcoming *The Films of Tom Hanks* (the latter two as co-author with
Lewis). He and Phil Lisa also co-authored *The Films of Sean Connery*. (All of the above are published in
U.S. by Citadel Press.)

In 1994 Pfeiffer and his partners, Mark Cerulli and John Cork established T.W.I.N.E. Entertainm
which is producing documentaries for Eon Productions and MGM/UA about the making of the James Bc
films.

PHILIP P. LISA is also a lifelong resident of New Jersey, and an avid student of the cinema, He attrib
his interest in film to the influence of his parents, who took him to drive-in theaters while s
toddler. The James Bond films proved to be addictive to Phil at an early age, and like many other
aficionados, he found himself acquiring rare 007 collectables from around the world. His collection of Bon
novelties is arguably the largest in existence, and Phil's expertise in the world of Agent 007 made
authorship of a Bond related book almost an inevitability. *The Incredible World of 007* is his first published w
and he has since collaborated with Lee Pfeiffer on *The Films of Sean Connery*.

CONTENTS

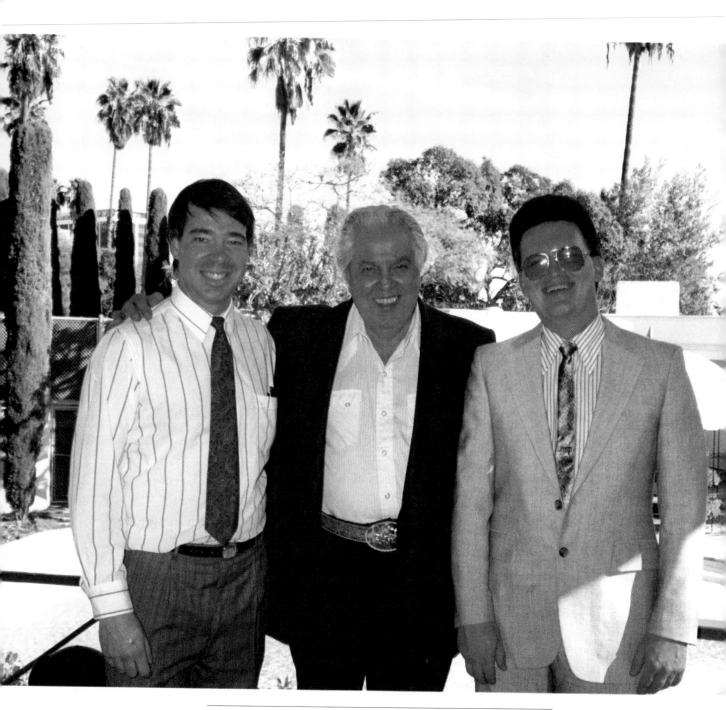

Authors Lee Pfeiffer (left) and Philip Lisa (right), with Albert R. Broccoli at the producer's home in Beverly Hills (photo by Dana Broccoli).

FOREWORD
BY ALBERT R. BROCCOLI

As this book goes to press, James Bond will be celebrating his 33rd anniversary as the most popular hero in motion picture history.

Did I know that this would happen when I decided to bring Ian Fleming's novels to the screen? Frankly, no. Those of us involved with the production of *Dr. No* in 1962 always felt confident, though our distributor was reluctant to release this "British subject" in the United States.

I'm not aware of any "top secret" formula for the success of the Bond films. However, as a producer I've always tried to give the audience full value for the price of a movie ticket and put every penny of the budget on the screen.

I am very pleased that the capable authors of this book, Lee Pfeiffer and Phil Lisa, have dedicated their intelligence and energy to assembling this comprehensive scrapbook on the career of James Bond. They have strived to pay tribute to 007 in an original manner. This volume deserves a unique niche on the sturdy bookshelf devoted to the subject.

As the book makes clear, there are many people responsible for the success of the James Bond films. This publication will help recognize their individual contributions. However, the ultimate thanks must go to the audiences themselves, who have been so appreciative and loyal for so many years.

CUBBY BROCCOLI

INTRODUCTION: GROWING UP WITH JAMES BOND

As James Bond enters his fourth decade onscreen, he remains the most enduring and remarkably successful movie hero of all times. Hundreds of books and magazines have analyzed the 007 phenomenon, both praising and damning the series along the way. To critics, Bond will always be the epitome of sexism and materialism – a living embodiment of selfish excesses. To the faithful, Bond is the quintessential capitalist, who works hard and rewards himself with every earthly pleasure imaginable. When the wine, women and song begin to become excessive count on Bond to eliminate the song!

Ian Fleming's secret agent is no longer a center of controversy. The sexual revolution he helped usher in now makes 007's erotic encounters appear to be downright conservative. Similarly, the violence displayed by today's cinematic heroes renders laughable the earlier condemnations (including those from the Vatican!) of 007's methods of dispatching his foes.

In an ever changing world, Bond remains a relatively fixed point. People still flock to 007's films because he is alternately a link to the past and a contemporary action hero. When one considers the amount of social change that has transpired since *Dr. No* premièred in 1962, the fact that 007 is still alive and well is a tribute to the filmmakers' creative instincts. He has survived seven presidents, Vietnam, civil rights marches, the Beatles, Hippies, Yippies, Yuppies and punk rockers; as well as numerous imitators, some good (*Get Smart, The Man From U.N.C.L.E., I Spy, Our Man Flint*), others – well, the less said the better. (Remember *Operation Kid Brother* with Neil Connery, Sean's brother, in his simultaneous big screen introduction and farewell?)

Bond has also survived five different actors with varying interpretations of the role. Each of the onscreen 007s – Sean Connery, George Lazenby, Roger Moore, Timothy Dalton and Pierce Brosnan – deserve praise for insuring the success of the series. James Bond is like an old reliable friend. We know what to expect of him, and how he will generally react within a given situation. For him to deviate too far from the formula would be considered a sacrilege by moviegoers throughout the world.

Yet, he is always contemporary and on the cutting edge of technology and style. Somehow, good taste has never had to be sacrificed in order to maintain the series' popularity. Bond may bed a dozen women in each film, but nudity will not be shown. Bond may eliminate any number of adversaries, but there will not be gratuitous bloodletting. For the most part, the Bond films have kept a tradition intact: they are suitable family entertainment.

Like many admirers of the Bond films, we were first introduced to agent 007 during family outings to the cinema. Indeed, both of us were virtually weaned on James Bond movies. Lee Pfeiffer first became acquainted with Mr. Bond in 1964 after persuadi[ng] mother and father to take him to see the inimitable Vincent P[rice] *Twice Told Tales*, which was playing on a double feature with [From] *Russia With Love*. He has long since forgotten the details of Mr. [Price's] effort, as the impression left by 007 on an eight-year-old bo[y was] indelible enough to make him return to the theater several tim[es to] marvel at his new-found hero, despite his father's protestatio[ns at] spending 50 cents per ticket!

Phil Lisa entered the world of Bondmania at age two with *D[r. No]* and saw each successive Bond entry during their initial runs, alt[hough] he admits his tender years prevented the films from havin[g any] significant impact. One day in the summer of 1967, his mom an[d dad] allowed seven-year-old Philip to choose between a showing of [Doris] Day's spy spoof *The Glass Bottom Boat* or the latest Bond film [*You*] *Only Live Twice*. Fortunately, Phil chose the latter, as one w[ould] shudder to think of him today harbouring a stash of Doris [Day] collectibles! Like so many others, we became hooked on Bond, [thus] placing us on an irreversible, yet quite delightful course that ha[s led] us to view these films hundreds of times.

For many fans, however, addiction to James Bond does no[t end] there. It also entails a shameless obsession with obtaining any[thing] Bondian, regardless of how impractical it may be. For exa[mple,] collectors will part with obscene sums to acquire that elusive O[ddjob] handpuppet, and while it's doubtful any sexual conquests have [been] achieved through wearing the *Licence to Kill* boxer shorts, the[y are] prized on the collector's circuit. Lest you think the author[s are] immune from these symptoms of Bond addiction, we confe[ss to] having our share of collectibles. We are also unashamed to admi[t that] our relatives know that if they *really* want to give us a memo[rable] holiday gift, then cancel the cologne or the soap-on-a-rope and g[et us] that mechanical 007 scuba diver which was sold only in Japan in [1967!]

The origin of this book is rather unusual. In 1989, Lee Pf[eiffer] wrote a favorable review of *Licence to Kill* for a New [Jersey] newspaper. Several weeks later, he returned home to be told b[y his] wife that legendary Bond producer Albert R. ("Cubby") Brocco[li had] just phoned, and would be calling again to speak with him. "Sure[," Lee] replied with disbelief, "and I suppose he wants me to be the [next] James Bond!" Lee promptly began to mow the front lawn. True [to his] word, Cubby phoned again, not to offer Lee the role of 007, b[ut to] thank him for the kind review. Learning that Lee had an upco[ming] book about John Wayne, Cubby asked why he had not consid[ered] doing a book about 007. "Because I was afraid you'd sue me," re[plied] Lee. Cubby chuckled at the candor and immediately gave permis[sion.]

To a 007 afficionado, the opportunity to do an analysis of the [Bond] phenomenon represented a responsibility only slightly less sa[cred] than transcribing the Dead Sea Scrolls. Lee immediately called [his]

d friend Phil Lisa, whose knowledge of the Bondian universe is
dary among fans, to co-author the book.

gnizant of the wealth of literature written about James Bond,
ave tried to examine the films through a fresh perspective. We
to appeal to those who are not so familiar with the series, such
e Pfeiffer's wife or Phil Lisa's father who still ask: "Is *Goldfinger*
lm with the razor-brimmed derby or the guy with a mouthful of
teeth?" Yet, we assume the reader will have at least a limited
vledge of Bond's cinematic exploits. Therefore, we have
nated formal plot synopses of the films and have concentrated
e stories behind the productions. We also hope to entertain
e hard core Bond fans who feel they have read it all about agent

e book has also been written with candor, and cannot be called
rified press release. If a scene doesn't work for us, we say as
. Thanks to the artistic freedom granted us by Eon Productions,
e been able to write an account that is enthusiastic, critical and
ctive – depending upon just how objective two writers can be
n they have full size, 007 arcade pinball machines sitting in their

e've also tried to design the book to be as visually appealing as
ible, and we can promise that readers have seen very few of the
os. They have been meticulously chosen for their rarity, and it's
otful that even the most ardent fans possess these in their
ctions.

e book incorporates many major elements of the Bond film
omenon. The word "world" in the book's title refers not only to
many aspects of Mr. Bond's cinematic success story, but also to his
national appeal. Within these pages, we display rare collectibles
around the globe, as well as some amusing title translations of
films from various countries e.g. what 007 epic is known as *The
of a Corpse* in Japan?

would be presumptuous to say that this is the definitive James
d book. The world of 007 is so vast that no one could truly
ure every aspect even in encyclopedic volumes, and someone
inevitably be disappointed that a certain aspect of the Bondian
erse has been overlooked. To that we say, if this book is
essful, there is always "Son of the Incredible World of 007"!

or now, however, sit back, fix yourself a Martini and enjoy this
ount of the greatest film series of all time. Hopefully, unlike Bond's
urite cocktail, it will leave you shaken *and* stirred.

Lee Pfeiffer
PISCATAWAY, NEW JERSEY

Philip P. Lisa
AVENEL, NEW JERSEY

Albert R. ("Cubby") Broccoli and his
wife Dana.

JAMES BOND IN

HARRY SALTZMAN E ALBERT R. BROCCOLI PRESENTANO
JAMES BOND IN AGENTE 007
AL SERVIZIO SEGRETO DI SUA MAESTA'
DI IAN FLEMING
CON GEORGE LAZENBY · DIANA RIGG
TELLY SAVALAS NEL RUOLO DI BLOFELD

AGENTE
007

AL SERVIZIO SEGRETO
DI SUA MAESTA'

GABRIELE FERZETTI E ILSE STEPPAT
PRODOTTO DA HARRY SALTZMAN E ALBERT R. BROCCOLI
REGIA DI PETER HUNT
SCENEGGIATURA DI RICHARD MAIBAUM
MUSICHE DI JOHN BARRY
PANAVISION® TECHNICOLOR®
UNITED ARTISTS, Entertainment from Transamerica Corporation

HARRY SALTZMAN et ALBERT R. BROCCOLI présentent

AMES BOND
007 CONTRE
Dr. NO
(Dr. NO)

CONNERY URSULA ANDRESS JOSEPH WISEMAN
JACK LORD et BERNARD LEE

HARRY SALTZMAN E ALBERT R. BROCCOLI presentano

Sean Connery
James Bond
nella parte di IN

Agente 007
Una Cascata Di Dian

DI IAN FLEMING CON JILL ST. JOHN NELLA PARTE DI TIFFANY CASE · CHARLES GRAY E LANA WOOD NELLA PARTE DI PLENTY O'TOOLE
PRODOTTO DA HARRY SALTZMAN E ALBERT R. BROCCOLI REGIA DI GUY HAMILTON SCENEGGIATURA DI RICHARD MAIBAUM E TOM MANKIEWICZ DIRETTORE DELLE SCE
PANAVISION® · COLORE DELLA TECHNICOLOR®
United Artists | UNITED ARTISTS, Entertainment from Transamerica Corporation

THE FILMS

DR. NO

It has been many years since a film whose nervous distributors commented "All we can lose is $1 million!" premièred in theaters throughout the world. That controversial film was *Dr. No*, the first of Her Majesty's Secret Service agent James Bond's amazing motion picture adventures. Today, with Bond in his fourth decade on movie screens, old 007 still packs a wallop with his unique blend of action, danger and excitement. It is doubtful that when Ian Fleming sat down to pen the words to the first Bond novel *Casino Royale* in 1952, he could have foreseen that his literary hero "with the most plain sounding name I could find", would spawn a loyal following of mill Just as incredulous is whether Bond film producers Albert R. Bro and Harry Saltzman could ever have envisaged that *Dr. No* woul such an enormous success.

❝ All we can lose is $1 million! ❞

In the spring of 1961, Canadian film producer Saltzman acqu the rights for filming 007's exploits, purchasing an option from Fleming. The author's fees included a handsome lump sum amo but, more lucratively, a percentage of all future box-office reven Fleming's recent bout of poor health prompted him to market property to provide security for his family. Saltzman did strive to financing for the Bond films, but could not interest investors.

Simultaneously, producer Cubby Broccoli tried to option stories, only to learn that the rights rested in Saltzman's ha

CREDITS	
YEAR OF RELEASE	1962
CAST	Sean Connery
	Ursula Andress
	Joseph Wiseman
	Jack Lord
	Bernard Lee
	Anthony Dawson
	John Kitzmiller
	Eunice Gayson
	Zena Marshall
	Lois Maxwell
DIRECTOR	Terence Young
PRODUCERS	Albert R Broccoli
	Harry Saltzman
SCREENPLAY	Richard Mabaum
	Johanna Harwood
	Berkley Mather
PRODUCTION DESIGNER	Ken Adam
EDITOR	Peter Hunt
MUSIC	Monty Norman

Above: Cubby, Harry and their "better halves" pose with Connery on "Dr No's lair".

Right: Connery and Andress in action and on the set.

Broccoli, having recently ended a production partnership with Allen, was reluctant to enter another joint venture. He prop[osed] buying the 007 franchise outright but Saltzman refused to con[sider] anything but a deal in which both men would co-produce the fil[ms as] partners. Reluctantly Cubby agreed, convinced there exist[ed a] golden future onscreen for 007.

Broccoli and Saltzman formed a producing unit called [Eon] ("Everything or Nothing"), yet still could not arouse studio intere[st to] finance the films. On June 20, 1961 the two men flew to New [York] to meet with Arthur Krim, President of United Artists. In less [than] one hour, Krim and the producers fashioned a deal for UA to fin[ance] the inaugural James Bond screen epic for a budget of $1 m[illion.] *Thunderball* was originally scheduled to be the first film; howev[er a] high profile court battle developed, with Fleming being sued [for] incorporating elements of a screen treatment previously written [by] Kevin McClory and Jack Whittingham into the novel. The prop[erty] was obviously too "hot to touch" and *Dr. No* became the ch[osen] vehicle to launch James Bond to film audiences.

> ## " *A photo of Andress, in a wet T-shirt[,]*
> ## *had left the producers more than impresse[d]*
> ## *with her assets.* "

Appropriately, Fleming's "home away from home" – the [sunny] tropical island of Jamaica – would be the locale for *Dr. No*'s prin[cipal] photography. The producers signed Terence Young – a dap[per] Englishman who possessed striking similarities to the Bond chara[cter] – to direct. An impressive supporting cast had been hired, highlig[hted] by Joseph Wiseman who would set the standard for future B[ond] villains with his chilling and acclaimed portrayal of the sinister [title] character. Interestingly, author Fleming originally suggested his is[land] neighbor Noel Coward for the role, but Coward declined. Ber[nard] Lee signed to portray Bond's crusty superior "M" and Lois Max[well] would make her first appearance as his love-starved secretary [Miss] Moneypenny. Unknown actress Ursula Andress was cast as na[tive] girl Honey Rider, the first of the legendary "Bond Girls". Not re[ally a] surprising choice as a photo of her, in a wet T-shirt, had left [the] producers more than slightly impressed with her assets.

The one missing link was the actor to portray the famed Br[itish] agent. Many aspiring thespians were screen tested, but n[one]

A rather garish representation of Sean and Ursula, clad in the bikini which launched her career.

Need anyone wonder why Sean is smiling?

possessed that special combination of ultra sophistication and animalistic sexuality. Contrary to other reports, the producers decided upon Sean Connery after Cubby Broccoli and his wife Dana saw him in Disney's *Darby O'Gill and the Little People*. Connery refused to screen test, and his subsequent aggressive outburst, especially for such a little known actor, so impressed the producers, that he was issued with a "Licence to Kill". Connery later confessed: "This was like asking a boy who was crazy about cars if he'd like a Jaguar as a present. I had never actually visualized myself as playing Bond when the rights to the books were sold, but when the chance to play Bond came along, I hardly slept for days."

" *When the chance came along, I hardly slept for days.* "

Initially, however, there were misgivings on the part of Ian Fleming and Terence Young regarding the casting of Sean Connery as Bond. Fleming thought Connery too uncouth and Young, who earlier directed Sean in *Action of the Tiger*, was convinced audiences would never buy Connery as a bon vivant. However, Connery's suitability as Bond was immediately confirmed with his first screen close-up, wherein he identifies himself with the now immortal introduction: "Bond. James Bond". Despite a few scenes in which his Scottish brogue is quite apparent, the role fit Connery like a glove. His commanding physical presence, rugged good looks, and unique ability to display charm and ruthlessness made Connery an international star overnight. His Bond was a true "anti-hero", inheriting precious few of the conventional values held by more traditional screen idols. He bedded women for his own selfish, sexual pleasure and exercised his "Licence to Kill" without remorse. This is particularly exemplified in his cold-blooded killing of Professor Dent, despite the fact that the villain is wielding an unloaded weapon.

Among other unique characteristics defining Bond was his unabashed snobbishness. He wore individually tailored suits from Savile Row; lacked interest in the less glamorous aspects of his job; teased the admiring Miss Moneypenny with almost sadistic innuendos of erotic encounters they would never share; and drank specially concocted Martinis that had to be shaken; not stirred. Connery had difficulty assimilating to these idiosyncrasies, as he grew up poor and had nothing in common with Bond's lifestyle. To get him to identify with the character, Terence Young forced Sean to sleep in a Savile Row suit complete with shirt and tie.

Although the production went considerably over budget by the then alarming amount of $100,000, filming went relatively smoothly. As entertainment, *Dr. No* is a classic which redefined the action adventure genre. Broccoli and Saltzman wisely chose not to cut corners and the budget was utilized with such creativity that the film has the feel of a genuine epic.

Dr. No remains one of the more violent Bond films, although, unl[ess] many of the epics to follow, it remained quite faithful to Flemin[g's] novel. The plot – centering on Dr. No's grandiose plans to wreck t[he] U.S. space program – is rather mundane and dated today, y[et] amazingly, nothing else about the film has lessened its impact [or] entertainment value over the years. Many of the movie's k[ey] sequences are powerful even by contemporary standards, althou[gh] in 1962 they were also innovative and, occasionally, shocking. In [his] debut film appearance, Bond is not quite the superman he wou[ld] become in the succeeding films. Lacking the sophisticated hi-te[ch] hardware later to become a staple of his adventures, Bond w[as]

Connery with the man who would(n't) be Dr. No.: Noel Coward.

Right: Joseph Wiseman as Dr. No – an immortal screen villain.

Far right: Bond disposes of a guard on Crab Key.

required to rely solely on his wits and fists to escape jeopardy. Indeed, when he finds himself in bed with a tarantula crawling up his naked flesh, he succumbs to pure fear, and we see him become physically ill after escaping the predicament. (Bob Simmons, the stuntman extraordinaire who would be affiliated with the Bond films for many years, actually had the dubious honor of performing this stunt, which he later deemed to be the most frightening moment of his career.)

Another unique element of the film was its then innovative blending of danger and humor, much of it of a self-spoofing nature. Bond inevitably relieved the tensions of an ultra-violent encounter

with an ironic but humorous throw-away line designed to "send up" audiences weaned on more traditional behavior. Not everyone got the joke. Even Ian Fleming grumbled that the film contained much more humor than did his novels. According to Terence Young, Fleming initially did not realize that the films were to be regarded as intentionally funny.

Contributing mightily to the film's success was the unforgettable supporting cast. Ursula Andress became the male-fantasy incarnate in her first scene, rising goddess-like from the ocean clad in a then shockingly brief bikini. Yes, by today's standards it looks like an overcoat, but that doesn't overpower the eroticism of one of the most memorable of all screen entrances. Andress represented the archetypical Bond girl — lustily beautiful and vulnerable; yet quite self-sufficient and courageous. Andress ironically assumed the role

Bond meets the first of the screen's Leiters – Jack Lord.

Right: Between takes, Connery and Andress get advice from director Terence Young.

Far right: Quarrel makes his point – with a switchblade.

ly because she desired to travel to Jamaica. She first read the script
ile at a party with Kirk Douglas, and later recalled that those
esent felt the film would turn out to be laughably bad. As with
ny of the Bond women who followed, Andress' voice was
bbed.

As Dr. No, Broadway actor Joseph Wiseman's performance was
thing less than brilliant. He portrayed No with a unique mechanical
ovement that was almost robotic. His monotone delivery of such
es as "I never fail, Mr. Bond", helped to lend a horrifying eeriness to
villainy. He reluctantly respects Bond's abilities, yet announces his
rsonal superiority to 007 by referring to him as "a stupid
liceman". Wiseman's devotion to the role resulted in his spending
veral days in a hospital for prosthesis patients, to become
customed to using the metallic hands he would wear in the film.

Other key contributors to the film include Jack Lord as the first of
e Felix Leiters, and one of the best to date; Anthony Dawson as the
ur and evil Professor Dent; John Kitzmiller as Quarrel, the native
maican who does not fear Dr. No as much as the legendary dragon
troling No's island fortress of Crab Key; and Eunice Gayson, the
ching damsel who earns the honor of being Bond's first onscreen
dmate. Bernard Lee and Lois Maxwell demonstrated a unique
emistry with Connery that would lead to career-long associations
th the series.

On the technical side, set designer Ken Adam created phenomenal
t pieces on a relatively meager budget. His magnificent laboratory
etched across an 18,000 foot soundstage at Pinewood Studios and
as so complex and hazardous in its operation that a special corps of

trained laboratory technicians supervised many of the sequences.
Director Terence Young warrants considerable praise for his insight
into the Bond persona, and the creation of a dynamically paced
thriller that would help revolutionize the action adventure genre of
the 1960s. High marks also go to Peter Hunt, whose lightning-fast
editing was both innovative and trend-setting. Although a collaborative
affair, Richard Maibaum must take the lion's share of the credit for a
screenplay filled with eye-popping action sequences and razor-sharp
wit.

Nevertheless, there was little confidence in *Dr. No*'s ability to
generate box-office revenue. United Artists virtually buried the film
with an inauspicious debut in second run theaters and American
drive-ins. Despite this, James Bond caught on with audiences
immediatley and became a major box-office success.

Critical opinion was divided, however. Some reviewers praised
Dr. No for its presentation of a spy thriller that transcended all others in
pace and style, while others condemned the film on the basis that
Bond's acts of violence were as shocking and unjustified as those of
the villains. One particularly malicious review termed Fleming's stories
to be "the most sadistic writing of our day" and warned audiences
that Bond was really "a very nasty, cruel and depraved upper-class
thug". Even the Vatican issued a statement expressing its disapproval
of agent 007. The *New York Times*, more attuned to the joke, called
the film "lively and amusing and nifty to the end", while *Variety*
perceptively noted: "As a screen hero, James Bond is here to stay.
He will win no Oscars, but a heck of a lot of enthusiastic followers".
Indeed.

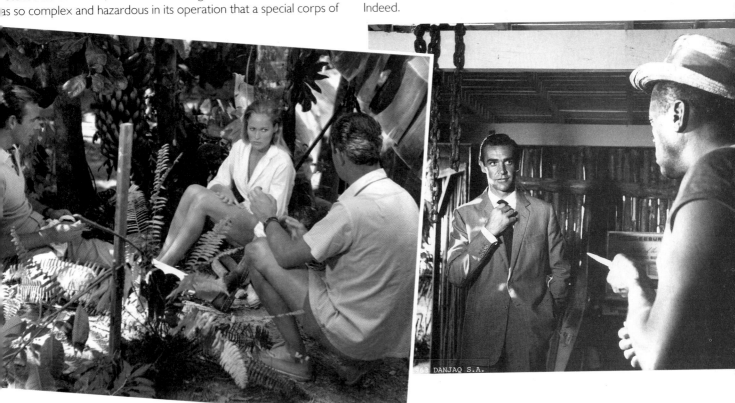

FROM RUSSIA WITH LOVE

The ultimate success of any film series rests squarely on the quality of the second film in the proposed cycle, as it *must* possess at least an equivalent entertainment value to its predecessor. Cubby Broccoli and Harry Saltzman had long envisioned the cinematic popularity of Agent 007. However, they were quite unprepared for Bond being launched as a cultural phenomenon. With *Dr. No*'s blockbuster success, they faced a dilemma concerning the future of Mr. Bond: should they rush through a quickie 007 thriller to capitalize on the hot word of mouth, or risk a sizable investment on a more spectacular epic in hopes of fostering an enduring screen hero. Fortunately for movie lovers, Cubby and Harry opted to "go for broke" with a screen adaptation of one of Ian Fleming's best 007 adventures, *From Russia With Love*.

United Artists, which had one year from the première of *Dr. No* to decide if they would distribute the next Bond film, were far more enthused about an encore appearance by Mr. Bond than they had been for his debut. The studio granted a budget of $1.9 million (which was eventually exceeded) to insure that *Russia* would be a truly globe-sweeping epic.

There are sociological and political origins for the decision to film *FRWL* as the next screen mission for 007. In the early 1960s, the world was enchanted by John F. Kennedy's personal charisma and charm. The brash young American president influenced everything from international style to the arts, during those short-lived days when it seemed JFK's "Camelot" would last forever.

In an issue of *Life* magazine, Kennedy listed his ten favorite boo of all time. Rubbing shoulders with the likes of Winston Churchill w the unlikely name of Ian Fleming, whose *From Russia With Love* wa JFK favorite. High brow critics were shocked that Fleming's tale of s and violence would be so honored, but the public emulated Kenne and boosted Bond into a household name. JFK was the ultimate pub relations man for agent 007! In return, Fleming sent him autograph copies of 007 novels.

Despite the advance publicity, the Bond team – spearheaded ag by director Terence Young – found that bringing *FRWL* to the scre would not be without its challenges. The first obstacle was to c politicize Fleming's novel. The producers were far ahead of their tir in predicting the emergence of glasnost and did not want prematurely outdate the films by centering on Soviet-Weste tensions. However, future Bond films would not be subject to su concerns.

The screenwriters came up with a compromise: both the Brit and the Soviets would be the unwilling pawns of the *real* embodime of evil – SPECTRE. An elaborate plot is hatched wherein Bond duped into stealing an all-important Soviet decoding machine, t Lektor, with the help of a gorgeous Russian agent who thinks she taking her orders from the Kremlin. SPECTRE then intends intercept Bond, recover the machine and sell it back to the Soviets. the process, Bond is to die "a particularly humiliating death" revenge for his rather ungraciously causing Dr. No to fall into

A collection of (mainly) mean 'n' mood Jameses for the French market.

Far right: 007 checks for bugs in his hotel – but not the kind found in bed.

Right (inset): To Connery's left, Terence Young "doubles" for the terminally ill Pedro Armendariz.

CREDITS	
OF RELEASE	1963
	Sean Connery
	Daniela Bianchi
	Pedro Armendariz
	Lotte Lenya
	Robert Shaw
	Bernard Lee
	Lois Maxwell
	Desmond Llewelyn
	Eunice Gayson
	Walter Gotell
	Vladek Sheybal
CTOR	Terence Young
DUCERS	Albert R. Broccoli
	Harry Saltzman
ENPLAY	Richard Maibaum
	adapted by Johanna Harwood
OR	Peter Hunt
DIRECTOR	Syd Cain
C	John Barry
SONG	Lionel Bart
	performed by Matt Munro

Original Japanese poster, and a collector's item for the fans.

lear reactor. The film introduces us to Ernst Stavro Blofeld, the
CTRE chieftain, whose face would remain a mystery until the fifth
d film.

he next challenge was to find a suitable cast to embody some of
ning's most intriguing characters. Foremost, of course, was the
lyst for all the danger, suspense and sex – Bond himself. The
ducers had wisely signed Sean Connery to a multi-picture deal,
Connery had already shown signs of being a maverick.
mmented Terence Young: "Sean could be the biggest star in
vies since Gable, but he won't be. He doesn't give a damn for the
illary assets of being a star. It's not that he's ungrateful, it's just that
too concerned with personal integrity. A hell of a lot of people
't like Sean because of this." Yet, Connery was just getting used to

> ## " I can kill any s.o.b. in the world and
> ## get away with it. "

ng a genuine movie star, and still had enthusiasm for the role. He
mmented: "For now, I'm reasonably content with what I'm doing.
er all I can kill any s.o.b. in the world and get away with it. I've got
power of the greatest governments in the world behind me. I eat
d drink nothing but the very best, and I also get the loveliest ladies
he world. What could be better?" (Plenty, according to Connery a
v years later.)

FRWL boasts what is probably the most impressive cast of any
nd epic to date, with even the lesser roles benefiting from
peccable acting. For Tania, the naive Soviet agent who initially
ceives Bond only to fall in love with him, the producers cast a
tual unknown – Daniela Bianchi. Ms. Bianchi, a runner-up in the
60 Miss Universe contest, was an Italian actress with limited
perience. Her innocence and occasional awkwardness in the love
enes enhances her performance. Bianchi makes a strong love
erest for Connery, despite the fact her voice was dubbed.

Bond's other key ally is somewhat less glamorous, but even more
emorable: Kerim Bey, the head of Secret Service operations in
rkey. Played with wry wit by Pedro Armendariz in a larger than
performance, Kerim is a classic character in the Bond canon. The
enes between Armendariz and Connery are what screen chemistry
all about. Sadly, Armendariz was agonized by terminal cancer, and
health was deteriorating daily. Terence Young arranged the
hedule so Armendariz's most demanding scenes would be shot
st. Toward the end of filming, the actor was so weak that Young
d to double for him in distant shots. Tragically, Armendariz
mmited suicide shortly after the film "wrapped". He leaves a legacy
one of the most beloved Bond characters.

FRWL also presents two of the series' most inspired villains: Rosa
ebb, the shrewish SPECTRE murderess, and her soldier, Red
ant, a psychotic muscleman with a penchant for strangling

Above: Bond's battle with the evil Rosa Klebb.

Top: Connery and Bianchi on the set in Istanbul.

adversaries with a nylon cord hidden in his wristwatch. For Klebb, the producers were fortunate to obtain the services of noted actress Lotte Lenya. A gentle, cultured woman in real life, Lenya's onscreen persona is a totally ruthless manipulator with Machiavellian methods for eliminating the enemy. The script only hints at the overt lesbianism Klebb displays in the novel, but when she places a hand on

> **❝ Klebb, a totally ruthless manipulator with Machiavellian methods for eliminating the enemy. ❞**

Tania's knee in a non-too-discreet attempt at seduction, the audience shares the young girl's repulsion. Lenya found it amusing that her triumphs onstage in *Cabaret* and *The Threepenny Opera* would always be secondary in the minds of the public, compared to her portrayal of a killer who keeps a poison-tipped knife in the toe of her shoe.

The real scene stealer in *FRWL*, however, is Robert Shaw's Grant. Shaw was better known at the time as a playwright, and had only recently begun to dabble in acting. For this role, he went on a crash dy-building course and took lessons in Greco-Turkish wrestling. ant's existence pervades the film with an omnipresent sense of ead, beginning with the jarringly effective pre-credits sequence. re, he stalks a Bond impersonator in a moonlit garden, and ortlessly strangles the man as part of a SPECTRE training exercise. ant has one purpose: to act a killing machine, and he has been hand osen by Klebb to murder Bond via the most torturous method ssible.

Grant says nothing onscreen until he successfully poses as Bond's ntact aboard the Orient Express. Although 007 takes an immediate like to Grant, he is duped, thus causing him to be at the mercy of absolute madman with whom it is impossible to reason. Shaw es a brilliant performance which enabled him to launch a successful reer as a leading man in such screen epics as *Jaws*.

Stalwarts Bernard Lee and Lois Maxwell return in good form and ere is an amusing scene with a red-faced "M" and an intrigued oneypenny listening to a tape of 007 reminiscing about an counter he and "M" shared with some Oriental women in Tokyo. is unlikely occurrence is all the more amusing as we are left to agine the details.

Of significance is Desmond Llewelyn's first screen appearance as ." Llewelyn had yet to develop the good-natured animosity with

Bond that would characterize later efforts, possibly because 007 had yet to establish a habit of destroying "Q"'s creations while "in the field". Here, "Q" presents Bond with the first of his trademark gadgets: an ordinary attaché case that conceals a variety of weapons, and triggers a tear gas canister if mishandled.

While extensive filming took place at Pinewood Studios in England, *FRWL* manages to capitalize on its large budget with considerable location work, mostly in Turkey. Filming in Istanbul was problematic due to the inexperience of many of the locals in dealing with a film of this caliber, and key sequences involving the Orient Express had to be reshot several times at great expense.

A nightmarish scene to shoot depicted Bond, Tania, and Kerim besieged by an army of rats while escaping through the sewers of Istanbul. The rodents proved to be temperamental actors, and were filmed from behind glass to minimize danger to the crew. However, in true Bondian fashion, they engineered an escape, causing everyone to double-check before they sat down. The sequence lasts only seconds onscreen, but it is quite harrowing.

Unquestionably the highlight of the film is the famous gut-wrenching fight to the death between Bond and Grant aboard the Orient Express. The suspense is riveting as Bond is completely helpless and seconds away from death. However, he lures Grant

left: Bond and Kerim arrive at the sy camp.

t: Bond takes aim during the exciting osy camp battle.

ht: Eavesdropping on a tape of 007's norous adventures: "M" and oneypenny.

into opening "Q"'s attaché case, and the tear gas mechanism explodes in his face. What follows is probably the most exciting fight sequence ever filmed. Using three cameras, director Young and stunt co-ordinator Peter Perkins staged a wild free-for-all within the dimly lit train compartment in which Bond and Grant punch, kick and karate-chop each other with brutal intensity. Bond gets in his "licks", but must rely on a hidden knife from the attaché case to disable Grant, who is ironically strangled with his own wristwatch device. Due praise must also go to editor Peter Hunt, whose work on this sequence is nothing less than brilliant, and enthused one critic to cite the scene as the most exciting two minutes of cinema imaginable.

Although many argue that this scene is the actual climax of the f[ilm], FRWL still has plenty more thrills in store for the audience. I[n] sequence reminiscent of the crop dusting scene in Alfred Hitchco[ck's] North By Northwest, Bond must flee on foot from a SPECT[RE] helicopter, which he destroys in spectacular fashion. Filmed in the [hills] of Scotland, the scene placed Connery in real jeopardy, when [the] helicopter came dangerously close to hitting him. Nevertheless, s[uch] close calls help to make the sequence even more thrilling.

The most difficult aspect of filming FRWL centered on the clima[ctic] pursuit of Bond and Tania's speedboat by a fleet of SPECTRE cra[ft.] Bond disposes of the evil armada by dropping barrels of gasoline i[nto]

Right: This Italian poster illustrates the classic battle between Bond and Red Grant.

Far right: 007 meets his literary creator: Connery and Ian Fleming on the set.

> ❝ *The look of panic on the faces of the SPECTRE agents is more than just good acting!* ❞

RY SALTZMAN e ALBERT R. BROCCOLI presentano

DALLA RUSSIA CON AMORE„

Dal romanzo omonimo di IAN FLEMING

ONNERY nella parte di JAMES BOND

RO ARMENDARIZ · LOTTE LENYA · ROBERT SHAW · BERNARD LEE nella parte di "M..

DANIELA BIANCHI per la prima volta sullo schermo

RICHARD MAIBAUM · Adattamento di JOHANNA HARWOOD

e„ è di LIONEL BART · Commento musicale composto e diretto da JOHN BARRY

SALTZMAN e ALBERT R. BROCCOLI · Regia di TERENCE YOUNG

TECHNICOLOR (R)

the water and igniting them with a shot from a flare gun. The result is a huge inferno that nearly got out of control, and the look of panic on the faces of the SPECTRE agents is more than just good acting!

The actors were not the only ones in danger. While scouting the area, Terence Young's helicopter developed engine trouble and plummeted into the sea. Narrowly escaping from under ten feet of water, with a nonchalance worthy of 007 himself, the director was back on the set in less than an hour! Originally filming was to have taken place off the coast of Greece; however, when mechanical problems with the boats and weather conditions proved disruptive, the crew moved to Scotland.

The results from all these efforts is a Bond film that is a classic in every respect. It's difficult to find a   t of *FRWL* that does not approach perfection. The performances, script and direction are all top-notch, as is John Barry's marvelo   score. Even the notoriously shy Fleming made visits to the set, and backtracked on his earlier criticisms of Sean Connery as Bond, claiming: "It was a great piece of casting. He certainly looks like Bond and I don't know who could have done it better."

Critics agreed enthusiastically, with the *New York Times* gushing: "Don't miss it! ... deliciously fantastic and delightfully well played"; and *Time* magazine exclaiming: "An intentional heehaw at whodunnits, an uproarious parody that may become a classic of caricature." Only Stanley Kauffman of *The New Republic* failed to get infected by the Bond bug, astonishingly claiming that Sean Connery "is not very good" at portraying James Bond. With prophecies like that, Mr. Kauffman probably also favored making "Heaven's Gate II" and "Return to Ishtar"! Audiences for *FRWL* surpassed those of *Dr. No*, and James Bond became an international celebrity.

GOLDFINGER

If cinema historians were to label one James Bond film the prototype of all others to follow, it would undeniably be *Goldfinger*, the movie that influenced the action film genre in much the same way that *Sgt. Pepper* revolutionized the world of rock music. This third 007 entry established a formula so perfect that it still works today. Critic Roger Ebert once elaborated on this recipe, cataloging elements indispensable to any James Bond film. The authors have embellished Ebert's list to arrive at these essential trademark sequences inherent to most 007 films:

- A spectacular pre-credits sequence often unrelated to main plot. It generally depicts Bond escaping certain death incredible stuntwork and derring-do. Often, the sequence ei begins with Bond being interrupted in a romantic interlude culminates in his rewarding himself with one.
- A main titles sequence featuring erotic nudes seductiv writhing, dancing, gyrating, etc. to the sounds of a memorable song performed by a well known recording artist.
- Scenes establishing the villain's grandiose scheme.
- Bond's arrival at the office, his flirtation with Miss Moneyper the pre-requisite deadly "giftware" courtesy of "Q"; his receiv orders from a stern-faced "M", and an intense and often hig technical briefing on the latest mission, which, more often than r is "the big one!"
- 007's involvement with a woman of dubious loyalty.
- A civilized duel of sorts between Bond and the main vill usually in the form of a game of some sort. Invariably, Bo aggravates his opponent by winning handily.
- The villain assigns a hulking henchman to kill Bond. Howev a friend or confidant of 007's inevitably ends up taking the hit the mandatory sacrificial lamb.
- Bond gains entrance to his opponent's stronghold, is captur and promised certain death, but not before his host wines a dines him while matching wits with 007.
- An elaborate, high speed chase, generally through congest areas, with the resulting significant wreckage. (New York City not usually utilised, as traffic has not moved above 10 m.p.h. decades!)
- 007 has only minutes to foil the villain's plans for glob disaster. He must first dispose of the henchman, and then his ma opponent, often through some inventive method.
- A last minute deathtrap is set for Bond in the epilogue. 00 emerges victorious, and the film climaxes with 007 romancing t leading lady, often near a body of water.

Connery on the set for the pre-credits sequence.

Above: Deluxe laser disc jacket.

CREDITS	
OF RELEASE	1964
	Sean Connery
	Honor Blackman
	Gert Frobe
	Shirley Eaton
	Tania Mallet
	Harold Sakata
	Bernard Lee
	Martin Benson
	Cec Linder
	Desmond Llewelyn
	Lois Maxwell
CTOR	Guy Hamilton
DUCERS	Albert R. Broccoli
	Harry Saltzman
ENPLAY	Richard Maibaum
	Paul Dehn
DUCTION DESIGNER	Ken Adam
OR	Peter Hunt
C	John Barry
SONG LYRICS	Leslie Bricusse
	Anthony Newley
	performed by Shirley Bassey

Pussy demonstrates her (temporary) immunity to 007's charms.

Bond: "Do you expect me to talk?"
Goldfinger: "No, Mr. Bond. I expect you to die!"

Gert Frobe as Goldfinger, the man with the Midas touch.

Goldfinger captured many of the Bond trademarks, and represented the high-water mark of the series. Jam-packed with action and cliff-hanging suspense, it contained enough hi-tech gadgetry to fill Ft. Knox, which is also featured in the film. *Goldfinger* has enough hairbreadth escapes to rival any work by Hitchcock. The producers followed the old adage: "Leave the messages to Western Union", and instead concentrated on a rollercoaster ride of thrilling adventure.

Though *Goldfinger* is larger-than-life fantasy, the filmmakers maintained Ian Fleming's original philosophy: "Bond may go wildly beyond the probable, but not beyond the possible". As in the novels, the mythical world of James Bond onscreen was characterized by nightmarish danger and unexpected death. Guy Hamilton, directing his first Bond film, later recalled: "My problem with *Goldfinger* was a matter of creating an atmosphere of belief in surroundings of utter improbability." To his credit, Hamilton handled the assignment successfully. Only a skilled director could compel an audience to believe a situation in which a British agent, portrayed by a Scottish actor, is handcuffed to an atomic bomb inside Ft. Knox, while a mute Korean muscle-man menaces him with a razor-brimmed derby!

❝ Bond may go wildly beyond the probable, but not beyond the possible. ❞

Goldfinger also benefits from its deliberate and abrupt transition of atmosphere. Bond's use of the Aston Martin gadgetry to destroy pursuing villains is quite amusing. Seconds later, however, it turns to tragedy as his companion Tilly falls victim to Oddjob's lethal derby. Future Bond films were to make the "sacrificial lambs" quite apparent early on, but here the gimmick was still in its infancy – despite the deaths of Quarrel and Kerim Bey in the previous films – and it contributed a vital element of suspense to a film that often emphasizes humor.

While keeping the spirit of Fleming's novel, the screenwriters made Goldfinger's scheme to rob Ft. Knox somewhat more spectacular by employing laser beams and a nuclear bomb to destroy the gold supply, thereby multiplying the value of Goldfinger's personal bullion. Ken Adam created a classic set for Ft. Knox, that is monumental in scope. Denied access to the actual treasury, Adam let his imagination go wild and created a magnificent design which undoubtedly puts the real depository to shame.

Goldfinger's cast is letter-perfect in almost every aspect. Gert Frobe is impeccable as Goldfinger, the madman with the Midas touch, whose civility and charm conceal the festering evil within. As the classic title song informs us, "He loves only gold". This is quite evident in the film's most gripping scene: Bond is strapped to a table, threatened with dissection by laser beam. Goldfinger engages in friendly, idle conversation while staring at the golden beam as though it were a beautiful woman. As the laser closes to within inches of emasculating Bond, a cringing 007 asks Goldfinger if he expects him to talk. In one of the screen's classic lines, an amused Goldfinger replies, "No, Mr. Bond – I expect you to die!"

Equally memorable is Harold Sakata as Oddjob, the mute b bloodthirsty Korean muscle-man whose duties range from being golf caddy to insuring a Lincoln Continental is crushed to the size o breadbox – with its occupant inside. (No wonder they say go domestic help is hard to find!) Sakata was discovered when G Hamilton saw his appearance in a wrestling match under the nar Tosh Togo. A gentle and generous man offscreen, on celluloid he w the personification of evil. His famous battle with 007 in the vaults Ft. Knox is a classic sequence rivaled only by the train fight in *Fro Russia With Love.*

" *Bond discovers Jill Masterson's iridescen corpse lying on his bed.* "

Bond's love interest this time around is Goldfinger's personal pil with the memorable name of Pussy Galore. As played by Hon Blackman (former co-star of *The Avengers*), her lesbian tendenci described in Fleming's novel are minimized, though she does infor Bond she is "immune" to his charm. Blackman does retain a cert tomboyish quality, and is almost a match for Bond in the physic confrontation department. Naturally, she eventually relents to rtures and insures that Goldfinger's scheme is ultimately foiled. d attributes her new allegiance to his having appealed to her ternal instincts".

onnery also receives support from Cec Linder as the series' ond actor to portray Felix Leiter. A friend of Guy Hamilton's, er was originally earmarked to play the hapless victim of dfinger's card cheating scam in the Miami sequence. Linder, like y of the Leiters to follow, is not given much to do, and there is chemistry between his character and Bond.

he most memorable scene in the film however, belongs to Shirley n, as Bond's ill-fated lover Jill Masterson. It is poor Jill who is ninated by Goldfinger in that unforgettable sequence wherein d discovers her iridescent corpse lying on his bed. Abhorrently

Far left: Bond explains to Bonita that his Walther PPK is merely a cure for his "slight inferiority complex".

Below: A classic image from a classic film: Bond with "Golden Girl" Shirley Eaton.

Left: If Tania Mallet is complaining of a headache, it's with good reason: she's just been struck by Oddjob's Derby!

Pussy "escorts" 007 to his cell at Goldfinger's Kentucky Estate.

. . . and the battle begins!

vered in gold paint, Eaton is displayed as a blood-chilling warning to one who would incur Goldfinger's wrath.

The procedure to "coat" Miss Eaton was potentially very ngerous. During the two-hour session in which the paint was olied, her blood pressure and body temperature had to be ntinually monitored to insure she did not suffer the skin suffocation m which her onscreen alter-ego expired. (An unpainted patch s left on her midriff to allow her skin to "breathe".) As a reward this rather messy, though visually erotic assignment, Miss Eaton's d-clad body was immortalized on the cover of *Life* gazine.

The most impressive element of this most impressive film is the rformance of Sean Connery as Bond, perfectly capturing the aracter's confidence and ultra-suave style. For probably the last e in the role, Connery appears to be genuinely enjoying himself. even commented to the press that he did not resent 007, but vied him. Connery did not radically alter the character of Bond m his first two outings; rather, he modified it from a cold-blooded, ait-laced persona to a demeanor that was stylishly cool. He delivers re one-liners this time with all of them landing on target thanks to excellent screenplay by Richard Maibaum and Paul Dehn. erence Young originally collaborated on the screenplay, but bowed t when he couldn't agree with the producers on terms of his ntract.)

It should be noted that with *Goldfinger*, technology and gadgetry would become a permanent staple of 007's world. It features the first important appearance by "Q", and Desmond Llewelyn works wonders converting what could have been a bland role into one of the screen's more memorable and likable characters. Grim-faced and fussy, he explains the workings of the gadget-laden Aston Martin DB5 to an incredulous 007, who asks rhetorically whether "Q" is joking about the inclusion of a passenger ejector seat. Insulted, "Q" looks sternly at Bond and deadpans, "I never joke about my work, 007!"; a line which brings the inevitable big laugh from the audience.

Goldfinger was both an enormous box-office hit and a pop culture phenomenon. Anyone who had not seen the film by the end of 1964 ran the risk of being socially ostracized. It launched in earnest the James Bond phenomenon which continues to this day. More importantly, it was the main catalyst for the spy craze which dominated the international media throughout the mid-1960s. Its influence inspired other pop culture hits such as *The Man from U.N.C.L.E.*, *I Spy*, and *Our Man Flint*.

Broccoli and Saltzman became major forces in Hollywood, and the very studios that rejected their idea to bring James Bond to the screen a scant three years before, now scrambled to capitalize on the franchise through 007 imitations. While *Goldfinger* mesmerized moviegoers, it became common knowledge that the men with the *real* Midas touch were named Cubby and Harry.

THUNDERBALL

"LOOK UP! LOOK DOWN! LOOK OUT! Here comes the biggest Bond of ALL!"** screamed the immodest, but accurate, advertising campaign for James Bond epic number four. While *Goldfinger* was still raking in box-office bullion around the globe, production began on the $5.5 million 007 adventure whose sheer spectacle would dwarf any of its predecessors: this one would immortalize James Bond as *the* fictional icon of the 1960s. The international 007 phenomenon would escalate into an absolute mania thanks to *Thunderball*.

The story behind attempts to bring *Thunderball* to the screen seemed as challenging as Bond's cinematic mission to prevent SPECTRE from plunging the world into a nuclear nightmare. In the late 1950s, Ian Fleming began anxiously searching for a cinematic outlet for his literary creation. Entering a collaboration with yo filmmaker Kevin McClory and an old friend Ivar Bryce, they per an original screenplay for the first in a proposed series of 007 t which McClory hoped to direct and produce. Titled at various sta "James Bond of the Secret Service", "James Bond – Secret Age and "Longitude 78 West", the trio produced many revisions of screenplay; and later they were to be joined by writer Whittingham. However, gradually, the relationship between Flem Bryce and McClory somewhat cooled, and their project never fruition.

The entire affair might have been dismissed by all parties as exercise in futility, had Fleming not adapted much of the screenpla the basis for his 1961 novel *Thunderball*, prompting McClory to f

Claudine Auger (below, left) and Luciana Paluzzi (below, right) and the two leading contenders for their roles: Maria Grazia Buccella (above, left) and Gisela Hahn (above, right).

CREDITS	
OF RELEASE	1965
	Sean Connery
	Claudine Auger
	Adolfo Celi
	Luciana Paluzzi
	Rik Van Nutter
	Martine Beswick
	Bernard Lee
	Lois Maxwell
	Desmond Llewelyn
NTED BY	Albert R. Broccoli
	Harry Saltzman
DUCER	Kevin McClory
CTOR	Terence Young
ENPLAY	Richard Maibaum
	John Hopkins
CTOR	Ted Moore
OR	Peter Hunt
N TITLES	Maurice Binder
DUCTION DESIGNER	Ken Adam
IC	John Barry
E SONG LYRICS	Don Black
	performed by Tom Jones

ht: "It's a dirty job, but somebody's
to do it".– Connery assists Auger on
set.

ow: Bond and Leiter deal with
go's "little fish", the henchman Quist.

plagiarism suit. The resulting trial in late 1963 caused Broccoli and Saltzman (who had subsequently purchased the screen rights from Fleming) to replace *Thunderball* with *Dr. No* as the vehicle for 007's screen debut.

By the time the trial began, James Bond had established himself as a literary and cinematic smash, thus prompting a swarm of paparazzi to descend upon the normally reclusive Fleming, who despised being the center of this scandalous case. A settlement was eventually reached wherein Fleming would retain all rights to his novel in return for monetary damages *and* granting of film rights to *Thunderball* to McClory. An additional stipulation insured McClory and Whittingham would be credited, in all future editions of the novel, as the co-writers of the screenplay upon which *Thunderball* was based. The trial took a terrible toll on Fleming, who was already in poor health, and the author passed away less than a year later.

Bond and Largo match wits under
nervous eye of Domino.

: A familiar face in a familiar
ng: Connery as Bond in 007 epic
er 4.

Connery and wife Diane Cilento
y the spectacle of the Junkanoo
de.

With the Bond franchise approaching its peak, Broccoli and
zman feared McClory's competing film might besmirch the image
y had so painstakingly perfected for Agent 007. An agreement
s negotiated allowing McClory to co-produce *Thunderball*, thereby
uring that Eon Productions retained creative control of Mr. Bond's
ematic exploits. McClory, an avid underwater sportsman, contri-
ed many aquatic suggestions acquired from the years of research
had spent preparing his own Bond film. With the legalities out of
way, the filmakers could now concentrate on bringing this
mmoth production to theater screens.

The filming of *Thunderball* was an arduous affair. The Bond films
d become so enormous in scope, virtually every creative element
s decided by committee. Screenwriter Richard Maibaum, director
rence Young, editor Peter Hunt, and production designer Ken
am would meet with Broccoli, Saltzman, and McClory, and lock

themselves into combative strategy sessions with each man defending
his own proposals with the ruthlessness of SPECTRE itself! When the
smoke cleared, these creative geniuses emerged with the framework
for yet another classic 007 adventure.

In *Thunderball*, SPECTRE has hijacked two NATO atomic bombs
and threatens to destroy a major city unless paid a fortune in ransom.
With the sand in the hourglass draining rapidly, it falls upon James
Bond to somehow defeat this evil scheme orchestrated by SPECTRE's
Emilio Largo, a charming but ruthless megalomaniac.

Filming began in March, 1965 with an 18-week production
schedule ranging from Pinewood, to location work in France and
extensively in the Bahamas. *Thunderball* would cost a fortune, but
every penny spent would be reflected onscreen. The script called for
spectacular locales, exotic women and enough hi-tech gadgetry to
equip a small army.

The center of the action, of course, would again by Sean Conne
who by now was becoming increasingly frustrated by the pub
blurring of actor and character. Connery gave the obligat
interviews to the world press, but was blunt about fears of be
typecast. The pressures of playing Bond had driven a wedge betw
Connery and his wife Diane Cilento. When Ms. Cilento arrived
the set, in an attempted reconciliation, the press had a field
speculating about the Connery's sex lives, causing Sean to beco
more irritable.

However, on a technical level, even Connery admired the state-
the-art gadgetry and special effects. A full $500,000 was invested
the DISCO VOLANTE, Largo's private yacht, capable of shedding
"cocoon" and transforming into a speeding hydrofoil. A full-sc
mock-up of a Nato fighter plane was also built at enormous cost, a
the gadgetry employed by both Bond and SPECTRE star
impressive even by today's standards. These deadly instrume
included the Bell Jet Pack – allowing Bond to literally fly away fro
pursuers – and Largo's fleet of underwater "sleds", used to transpo
the atomic bombs and provide armament during the climactic s
battle between SPECTRE and U.S. Aquapara forces. That sequen
was so complicated, it had to be rehearsed extensively in a Baham
parking lot! To maximize the impact of *Thunderball*'s extravagan
this became the first Bond film to be shot in the widescre
Panavision process.

Many complicated sequences were fraught with danger. O
scene called for a Largo henchman to be tossed into a pool of shar
Volunteers were, understandably, scarce for this dubious hono
before stuntman Bill Cummings reluctantly performed the deed (
the basis of a $450 bonus.) Later, Connery himself was persuaded
enter a shark pool to battle a SPECTRE agent to the death. Desp

Far left: "Shall we dance?" – Bond
enjoys the charms of Largo's "kept
woman" Domino.

Left: Connery enjoys a massage *au
naturel* as reward for punishment
sustained in onscreen battles.

Right: A SPECTRE thug finds it's
dangerous to interrupt 007's phone
calls!

Domino pleads with Bond to avenge her brother's murder by destroying Largo.

assurances that the sharks were drugged, Connery was less th enthused about the task. Actually, the shark which almost nips him he exits the pool was a recently deceased specimen pulled via cable!

Another scene called for the destruction of SPECTRE agent Cou Lippe's car by a rocket-firing motor cycle. Master stuntman and Bo alumnus Bob Simmons narrowly escaped death when the stunt we awry, causing him to jump out of the car, his sleeve aflame. Direct Terence Young and the crew thought Simmons had perished in tl fire, but the latter emerged from the bushes asking "How was tha Terence? Alright?" It took years for Young to forgive Simmons for tl anguish he felt at having caused his "death".

Young had his share of frustrations dealing with other logistic matters. In a spectacular and suspenseful scene, Bond evades h pursuers in a Bahamian parade known as the Junkanoo – a local Mar Gras. Young had the entire event restaged for this sequenc employing literally hundreds of extras in a spectacle that extende two miles. With only one opportunity to capture a final take, tl camera crew shot the parade from every conceivable angle. Tl results are remarkably exciting, thanks in no small part to Pete Hunt's masterful editing and John Barry's exhilarating score.

" Thunderball *boasts two memorable additions to humanity's "Hall of Shame".* "

Thunderball also succeeds on the acting level as well, thanks to sterling cast. Connery, of course, is the epitome of style and wi although the 007 character is overshadowed by his arsenal. As usua the more fascinating roles are those of the villains, and *Thunderba* boasts two memorable additions to humanity's "Hall of Shame Adolfo Celi is an excellent Emilio Largo, rendering a chilling portray of a man possessing Bondian wit and seductive charm, masking hi obsession for the subjugation of mankind.

His evil counterpart, Fiona Volpe, also possesses those attribute using her ravishing looks and raw sexuality to lead her enemies t their doom. As portrayed by Luciana Paluzzi, Fiona smolder onscreen, and her playful yet deadly encounters with Bond are bot amusing and erotic, notwithstanding today's liberal standards. M Paluzzi is wonderful in the role, and gained a reputation as *the* femm fatale for 1960s spy films – Robert Vaughn had to escape he charming menace twice, in *To Trap a Spy* and *The Venetian Affair*.

Naturally, Bond is not without allies, and in *Thunderball* most c them happen to be buxom bombshells. Foremost is Claudine Auge a former Miss France, in the pivotal role of Domino, Largo's reluctar mistress who falls in love with 007 and risks death to help him. Lik

Celi, Ms. Auger was dubbed (quite effectively), but this cannot totally explain her less than commanding screen presence. While her performance is certainly satisfactory, it is clearly Paluzzi's Fiona who provides most of the sexual sparks.

Martine Beswick appears as Paula, Bond's "helper" in the Bahamas, and the film's mandatory sacrificial lamb. Beswick had been associated with the Bond films previously, having danced in the title credits for *Dr. No* and appeared as one of the warring gypsy girls in *From Russia With Love*.

Rounding out Bond's paramours is Molly Peters, the gorgeous blonde spa nurse who beds 007 during his recuperation at the Shrublands health resort. Peters possesses a rare combination of comedic skills and an erotic persona. The steamroom sequence with Connery also provides the series with its first ever-so-modest touch of nudity; unless one counts the racy main titles.

Back home the MI6 office team is very much in evidence, with both Lois Maxwell's Moneypenny and Bernard Lee's "M" particularly amusing. The scene when the death-defying Bond boldly enters Moneypenny's office only to be reduced to the status of an embarrassed schoolboy, by one disapproving look from "M", is priceless in its understatement. In an equally memorable scene, "Q" is sent to the Bahamas to equip Bond with new hardware.

nd socks Jacques Boivert in the pre-dits sequence.

rare production still of Bond's battle ith Largo aboard the DISCO VOLANTE.

Bond is also aided and abetted by Felix Leiter, in the shape of Rik Van Nutter, a prematurely gray-haired actor with boyish good looks. Van Nutter was envisioned to portray Leiter in future Bond films, but it was not to be and the character of Leiter would not reappear until *Diamonds Are Forever* (1971). Mr. Van Nutter does a good job, and displays a camaraderie with Connery that is far more convincing than Cec Linder's Leiter in *Goldfinger*.

The highlight of *Thunderball* is clearly its action sequences, beginning with the infamous pre-credits scene where Bond battles a female impersonator alternately played by actress Rose Alba and stuntman Bob Simmons – Alba is the one with the great legs! The fight is ferociously staged, and well choreographed and edited; likewise, the battle to the death between Bond, Largo and the crew of the DISCO VOLANTE, while the hydrofoil speeds out of control, is thrilling.

> **Bond battles a female impersonator alternately played by actress Rose Alba and stuntman Bob Simmons.**

The spectacular underwater battle is yet another testament director Terence Young's skill at co-ordinating massive actio sequences.

Curiously, Young has always expressed a dissatisfaction with th

Facing page: Connery in deep conversation with Harry Saltzman.

In the finished sequence, Bond punches the living daylights out of SPECTRE'S number 2 man.

n, claiming that the extensive underwater sequences slowed the ce. This is true of some of the earlier scenes, such as the capture of e warheads and camouflaging of the Vulcan. However, the free-for- climax is stunningly effective, even if Young himself is not prepared admit it!

Thunderball was released at Christmas, 1965 and within months, ded on *Variety*'s chart of the top ten grossing films of all time. heaters couldn't accommodate the crowds even with 24-hour reenings. Some critics complained, somewhat accurately, that the ovie was basically a cinematic version of *Popular Mechanics*, with the -tech gadgetry reducing the actors to button-pushing robots. While e film over-emphasizes the mechanical aspects of Bond's world, nunderball remains an extremely entertaining film worthy of ranking ith the three previous "gilt-edged Bonds". Less stuffy critics agreed

and the normally staid *New York Times* uncharacteristically named the movie among the year's ten best.

Ironically, the legal battles that affected the original screen version of *Thunderball* reared their heads again when Kevin McClory tried to produce an independent remake of the film. The legal arguments raged for years, but eventually the film was made in 1983 as *Never Say Never Again* starring Sean Connery but minus the Eon banner.

In 1990 the James Bond Fan Club rented the National Film Theater in London to celebrate a 25th anniversary screening of the 1965 epic, only to discover that virtually every good theatrical print of the film had been destroyed. A new print was created, utilising footage from 56 reels of precious celluloid. The reward was a gala event, attended by Terence Young and many others associated with the film – yes, *Thunderball* was still a winner!

YOU ONLY LIVE TWICE

Inspiration for the title of the fifth Bond screen adventure came from an unlikely source: the seventeenth-century Japanese poet Bassho, who wrote:

> You only live twice;
> Once when you're born,
> And once when you look death in the face.

Fleming, impressed by this simple, but thought-provoking line, titled his twelfth novel *You Only Live Twice*, inspiring the book's eventual secondary life as a film. By 1967, James Bond had been immortalized and joined the legion of legendary screen heroes. The Bond franchise was lucrative enough for Broccoli and Saltzman to get *carte blanche* from United Artists for ever-increasing budgets. There seemed to be only three certainties in life: death, taxes, and the success of the next James Bond film.

Yet, Bond faced an obstacle more threatening than anything SPECTRE could devise. With the entertainment industry awash in spy-mania, 007 risked falling victim to the very craze he inspired. The producers felt compelled to keep topping the previous effort's spectacle to insure Bond remained unique in a sea of imitators.

Twice was allocated the then astronomical budget of $9.5 million, a sum which nearly equalled the combined budgets of the first four films! When veteran Bond screenwriter Richard Maibaum proved unavailable, well known novelist Roald Dahl signed on to pen the script, despite his aversion to screenplays. Dahl produced a first draft script in only six weeks, discarding almost every aspect of the source

CREDITS	
YEAR OF RELEASE	1967
CAST	Sean Connery
	Akiko Wakabayashi
	Tetsuro Tamba
	Mie Hama
	Teru Shimada
	Karin Dor
	Donald Pleasence
	Bernard Lee
	Lois Maxwell
	Desmond Llewelyn
	Charles Gray
DIRECTOR	Lewis Gilbert
PRODUCERS	Albert R. Broccoli
	Harry Saltzman
SCREENPLAY	Roald Dahl
PRODUCTION DESIGNER	Ken Adam
EDITOR	Thelma Connell
MUSIC	John Barry
TITLE SONG LYRICS	Leslie Bricusse
	performed by Nancy Sinatra

Studio contact sheet of Connery as Commander James Bond, CMG RNVR.

Right: Bond is lead into the "inner sanctum" of Blofeld.

Left: Bond avenges Henderson's assassin.

Right: Connery on the set with Akiko Wakabayashi.

Below: Bond makes short work of a would-be assassin on the Kobe docks.

novel. Gone was Fleming's moody story of an amnesia-ridden Bond stalking the reclusive Blofeld at his Japanese castle. In its place was a space-age adventure which propelled audiences literally out of this world. *Twice* boasted the most thrilling spectacle and special effects of any 007 epic to date.

Filming Dahl's expansive screenplay proved costly and challenging. Principal photography required more than seven months, and spanned nine major Japanese locations, each besieged by fanatical Bond fans. One entrepreneur even arranged bus tours for those eager to witness location filming.

Additionally, a second unit headed by former Bond editor Peter Hunt toiled full-time on sequences in Hong Kong, the Bahamas, Gibraltar, and in the skies over Spain for a stunning aerial battle.

Twice impresses by its lightning fast pace and highly polished look. Thanks to director Lewis Gilbert, the film not only offers constant action, but also a stunning panorama of Japanese scenery superbly

...tographed by cameraman Freddie Young. The real star of the ..., however, is production designer Ken Adam whose volcano ...dquarters for SPECTRE were appropriately described by one ...ic as "worthy of exhibit at a World's Fair". Adam was allocated $1 ...lion for this single set, and his creation surpassed all expectations.

...The giant crater contains a working monorail, a moveable ...licopter platform, a launch pad, and a full-scale spaceship capable of ...ng 50 feet in the air! The set required the services of 400 ...orkmen, and was so vast that it had to be built outdoors on the ...newood lot. The volcano is the centerpiece for the spectacular ...nactic battle.

...Christmas week of 1966 was a noisy time for the neighborhood ...rrounding Pinewood as flying helicopters, roaring engines and ...rth-shaking explosions became the norm. As Roger Moore would ...er reflect on this production aspect of the Bond films: a fortune ...ould be spent building sets only to have another fortune spent ...owing them up.

The film fully exploited its Japanese locations, and did not allow the technology to overshadow interesting glimpses of Far Eastern culture and traditions. Refreshingly, the culture is treated with respect, and Bond is the odd man out instead of a know-it-all who manipulates his Oriental counterparts.

> ## " A fortune would be spent building sets only to have another fortune spent blowing them up. "

Some critics called *Twice* a glorified travelogue, but what a travelogue it is. We are treated to authentic Sumo wrestling matches, gorgeous views of the Japanese coastlines and mountains, and a visit

Left: Bond and Kissy's "honeymoon" interrupted upon their discovery of SPECTRE volcano.

Facing page
Top left: Donald Pleasence as Ernst Stavros Blofeld.

Top right: The ultimate triumph: Bond and Kissy watch Blofeld's volcano self destruct.

Below: Bond furiously tries to avert World War III by detonating the SPECTRE spacecraft.

to an ancient castle serving as the headquarters for Bond's Ninja allies. Filming was temporarily halted when it was discovered that the weaponry utilized in these scenes was damaging the stonework. Eon had to assure Japanese authorities that no further damage would occur.

There is a memorable sequence filmed at Mt. Nachi, a symbolic shrine, where 007 "becomes" Japanese and "weds" his beautiful female contact Kissy. Actually, Connery posing as a Japanese in Beatles' fright wig is about as convincing as John Wayne's infamous portrayal of Genghis Khan in *The Conqueror*.

The logistics involved in bringing *Twice* to the screen were enormous: more than 3,000 miles were travelled to capture the authentic settings.

For all of its positive aspects, however, *Twice*'s screenplay presented one of the least involving plots to date. Logic was often sacrificed for action, and credibility became occasionally strained beyond even Bondian standards. Consider: the villainess Helga lures Bond onto a sabotaged plane, then parachutes out, rather than simply shooting him earlier when she held him captive. With logic like this, SPECTRE would soon be crushed by the sheer weight of their operatives' expense accounts.

Yet *Twice* is perhaps the inevitable result of the hi-tech elements that audiences craved at the time. This is still an enormously entertaining film, featuring a never-ending array of sensual girls, larger than life villains, and above all, action and gadgetry.

Memorable elements abound, including two likable Oriental lo for Bond: Akiko Wakabayashi's ill-fated Aki, and Mie Hama as Bo "bride" Kissy (whose name, incidentally, is never spoken in the f Originally the actresses' roles had been reversed, due to Ha difficulties with the English language, and it looked as though she to be dropped from the cast. However, the producers relen when they were told that Mie was suffering from acute depress she was worried that being replaced in the film would bring disho to her family.

Twice also offers the first look at Ernst Blofeld, until this mom never referred to by name, and seen only in the shadows, as delegated his schemes for the subjugation of mankind to underl. As portrayed by Donald Pleasence, he looks eerie but l conviction when compared to the character conceived by Fleming fairness to Pleasence, he was a last-minute replacement for Cz actor Jan Werich, who was unwell.) While Pleasence doesn't po physical threat to Bond, the character remains intriguing, with monotone threats reminiscent of Joseph Wiseman's Dr. No.

Other main cast members include Tetsuro Tamba who is an a and capable ally of Bond, even if he is far too young to be "equivalent in the Japanese Secret Service. Karin Dor is the rav haired German beauty who seduces, then tries to eliminate Bo Her characterization is not unlike Luciana Paluzzi's Fiona in *Thunder* although admittedly her performance is not nearly as memorable.

Teru Shimada appears as Mr. Osato, a Japanese industrialist wh

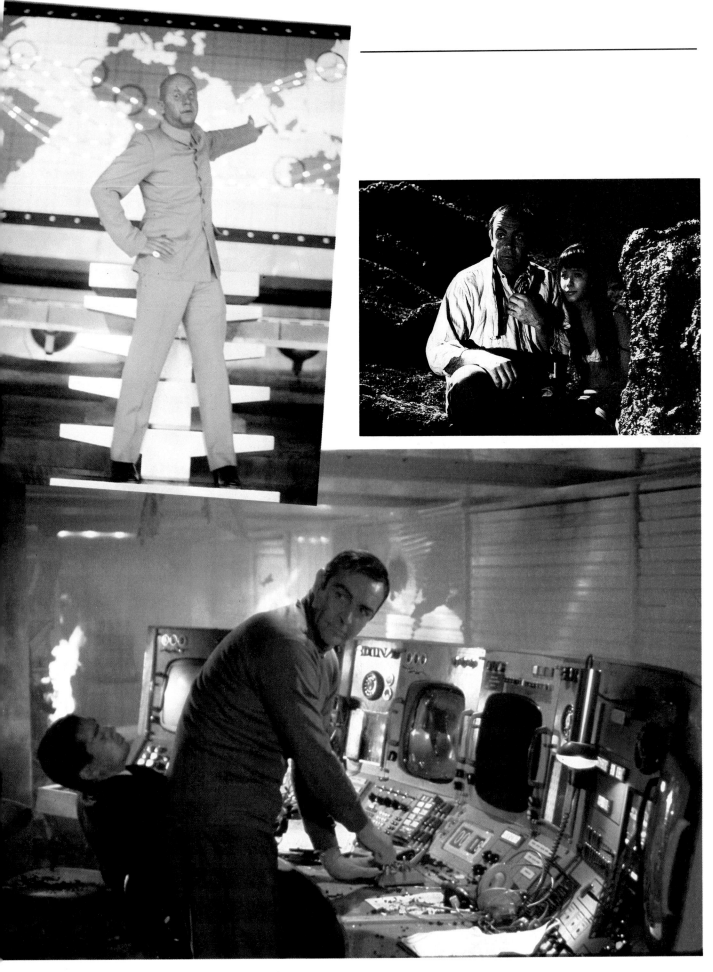

empire is a key element in SPECTRE's plans to initiate yet another World War by sabotaging both American and Soviet space flights. Interestingly, during a visit to Paramount Studios Broccoli noticed Shimada and cast him for the role. The actor was working temporarily as a janitor, despite having previously acted in some high profile films including an appearance in the "Man From U.N.C.L.E." film *One Spy Too Many*.

Unsurprisingly, *Twice* packed 'em in at the box-office despite competition from Columbia's $12 million slapstick version of *Casino Royale*. Cynics predicted that bad word-of-mouth on the latter would inevitably hurt the "real" Bond film. Audiences were not fooled, however. Despite a good initial showing, *Casino*'s bad reviews, thanks mainly to an incoherent plot, kept audiences away, while *Twice* played profitably throughout the entire summer of 1967.

> ## 66 *Sean Connery's tolerance for making the 007 epics had long ago worn thin.* 99

Yet, there was trouble in paradise. Sean Connery's tolerance for making the 007 epics had long ago worn thin. He disliked the increasing emphasis on technology and gadgetry, complaining these elements overshadowed Bond's character. Critics called his perform-ance in *Twice* his least inspired.

Add to this the actor's well-publicized disputes with the producers, plus his outspoken fears of being typecast as Bond and you have a shaky relationship.

Between 1964-67, he appeared in several major films includir underrated thriller *Woman of Straw*, Hitchcock's lukewarm *M* and the screwball comedy *A Fine Madness*. Undoubtedly, illustrated his versatility as an actor, yet failed at the box-office. frustrating of all was the fate of *The Hill*, a masterful drama for v Connery was widely touted as an Oscar contender. Despite glc reviews, it was not a hit and had faded from the Academy's me by year end.

Connery's irritability was further tested by the increasing leng time necessary to complete a Bond film. He complained that took six months to shoot, during which time his privacy was existent.

While in Japan, he exploded in anger on one occasion v Oriental paparazzi followed him even into the men's room, in h of prolonging an interview.

At the conclusion of filming, Connery announced what Bond had feared was an inevitability: he was resigning from the lucrative role ever possessed by an actor. Sean Connery determined to see if his screen career – like Bond – could live tw

Bond and Hans in the climactic fight Blofeld's lair.

A tense introduction to a friend: Bond meets Henderson.

ON HER MAJESTY'S SECRET SERVICE

CREDITS	
YEAR OF RELEASE	1969
CAST	George Lazenby
	Diana Rigg
	Telly Savalas
	Gabriele Ferzetti
	Ilse Steppat
	Bernard Lee
	Angela Scoular
	Lois Maxwell
	Catherine von Schell
	George Baker
	Desmond Llewellyn
DIRECTOR	Peter Hunt
PRODUCERS	Albert R. Broccoli
	Harry Saltzman
SCREENPLAY	Richard Maibaum
PRODUCTION DESIGNER	Syd Cain
EDITOR	John Glen
MUSIC	John Barry
SONG	"We Have All the Time in the World"
LYRICS	Hal David performed by Louis Armstrong

Let's now do justice to one of the most underrated films in movie history by stating unequivocally that *On Her Majesty's Secret Service* is a triumph. Sadly, however, upon its initial release, most of the attention lavished on this sixth James Bond epic focused anxiously behind-the-scenes. For years, the movie was largely dismissed by general audiences, as Eon began to concentrate on promoting the Sean Connery and Roger Moore Bond adventures. For some of those involved with the production, bringing Ian Fleming's novel to the screen was about as pleasant as a dip in Blofeld's piranha pool.

Originally planned to follow *Goldfinger*, and later *Thunderball*, the producers feared audiences might perceive similarities between the emphasis on underwater sequences in the latter film and those set on ski slopes in *OHMSS*. Also, the unfavorable weather conditions in Switzerland – the main locale – had made the project unfeasible.

Although *OHMSS* would have allowed Sean Connery his high-water mark performance as 007, the afore-mentioned factors convinced the producers to choose *You Only Live Twice* as the next 007 adventure. And so Connery said *Au Revoir* to Mr. Kiss-Kiss-Bang-Bang and tried to shed the 007 image via the western *Shalako*.

The most publicized talent hunt since the search for Scarlett O'Hara was undertaken to find the man who could fill Bond's shoulder holster. At this time, a 28-year-old Australian named George Lazenby was working in London as a part-time model and car salesman. Determined to break into acting, he took the advice of his agent and made plans to take on virtually every other actor in England for the coveted role of James Bond.

Lazenby's gimmick was to embody the very personification of Se Connery's James Bond. He spent the last of his money acquiring tailor-made suit from Connery's own clothiers; he also purchased Rolex watch. Shortly afterwards, while having a Connery-ty

> ## " George Lazenby made plans to take on virtually every other actor in England for the coveted role of James Bond. "

haircut, Lazenby was surprised to find Cubby Broccoli in the sar salon. The image Lazenby projected clicked with Cubby who made mental note that the young Australian possessed many of the qualiti inherent in the Bond persona.

After meeting with Harry Saltzman, when Lazenby brazen pretended to be a nonchalant playboy with acting experience, he w introduced to Peter Hunt, the former Bond editor now directing first 007 spectacular. Lazenby's gamble continued to pay off. Hu confided that he was "sold" on George as the next Bond, and shot series of screen tests to convince the studio and producers.

For four months, literally hundreds of actors were put through t nerve-wracking process of vying for one of the most sought-aft screen roles of all time. Frustratingly for all of them, bar one, all futu contact with the world of Bond would be via the box-office at the

Left: Italian photo busta showing Lazenby in action.

Above: The new 007, George Lazenby, enjoys a few fringe benefits of the role.

est cinema. Lazenby emerged on the short list of candidates, and
n he performed superbly in the rehearsal of a brutal fight scene,
rge was rewarded with the news that he was now the screen's
James Bond.

ut, what could have been one of the great Horatio Alger stories
reen history turned into a woeful tale of poor judgement and
ed opportunity, with Lazenby haunted by the reputation of a
who snatched defeat from the jaws of victory.

uccess went to Lazenby's head even before the cameras began to
He proved to be a publicity man's nightmare, insinuating to *Life*
azine that his primary interest in the film was due to the inevitable

materialistic rewards it would provide. He cynically stated: "I'm looking forward to being Bond for the broads and bread ... I wouldn't even care if they didn't put my name up on the marquee." He would later boast: "I've even done things Bond never did – things you couldn't print." Needless to say, the producers and studio were

Bond leads the assault on Blofeld's lair at Piz Gloria.

" The essence of Bond is that of a young man who has an inherent sexual assurance. "

not enthused by their new employee's less-than-diplomatic approach to courting the press. Nevertheless, Peter Hunt optimistically exhorted: "I am more convinced than ever that the choice of George Lazenby was right. With Lazenby, we revert to the concept of the Bond implicit in Ian Fleming's books. The essence of Bond is that of a young man who has an inherent sexual assurance, something which was predominant in my mind during the search for the new 007."

A tense atmosphere prevailed as filming began at spectacular locations in Portugal and Switzerland. Hunt had boldly convinced Broccoli and Saltzman to reject the successful hi-tech elements of the series. Screenwriter Richard Maibaum's script closely followed Fleming's novel – undoubtedly the most romantic and realistic of the series. As Hunt stated at the time: "OHMSS happens to be the Bond story everyone acclaimed as the best Ian Fleming wrote. Apart from providing everything – and more – which we expect from Bond, it is also a love story. We see him as a man with genuine emotion; as a man really in love."

Although there was no need for inventive gadgets from Q Branch this time around, the filmmakers were faced with a challenge in finding the proper locale for Blofeld's Alpine headquarters. As described in the novel, the evil one's lair was a large fortress situated high atop a mountain accessible only by helicopter and cable car. Obviously, there was not a wealth of such locales, but Eon chanced upon a restaurant that had been under construction since 1961, and greatly resembled the conceived Blofeld fortress. A spectacular circular building, the edifice was located atop the 10,000-foot peak of the Schilthorn mountain, which towered above the sleepy hamlet of Murren. The owners were delighted to permit filming, in return for Eon furnishing the interior and constructing a helicopter landing pad costing $125,000. The producers secured what is, arguably, the most majestic of all Bond locales; while the restaurant so benefited from the publicity, that it retains its onscreen name of Piz Gloria to this day.

Transporting equipment and personnel to the Piz Gloria setting was expensive and time-consuming, as – true to the novel – the site was accessible only by helicopter and cable car. The altitude made it

difficult for the cast and crew to breathe normally, particularly during the extensive action sequences. For the spectacular ski chases, insurance regulations precluded the principal actors from engaging in any actual skiing. Stuntmen had to be employed for every shot, thereby mandating that the sequences had to be accurately matched to rear screen projected images of the actors.

The breathtaking overhead shots of the ski chases were the result of brave teamwork between cameramen Johnny Jordan and Willy Bogner, Jr. Jordan was a fearless professional, despite having lost a leg in a mid-air collision while filming *You Only Live Twice*. He devised a harness allowing him to be suspended eighteen feet below a helicopter, thus making it possible for him to film in a complete circle without any interference. Bognor, a brilliant skier, displayed similar courage by filming with a hand-held camera while skiing backwards! The efforts of these men paid off handsomely, as the camerawork in *OHMSS* is stunning. (Tragically, Jordan died the following year while filming *Catch-22*.)

OHMSS literally brims with edge-of-the-seat excitement. Witne the thrilling stock car race in the village of Lauterbrunner, whe Bond's car escapes his pursuers by becoming a reluctant participant the wild race on the ice. Later, a spectacular avalanche plays a ke element in the script, and was a challenge to film.

Likewise, the most impressive action sequence – the prolonge battle between Bond and Blofeld on the bob-run – was a dangerou and exasperating assignment for the filmmakers. Stuntmen Heinz Le and Robert Zimmerman literally cheated death on several occasior to insure the scene would be as realistic and thrilling as possible. Wil Bogner captured some seemingly impossible camera angles by tyir himself to the speeding bob-sleds via a tow-line! After each take, th stuntmen and crew had to be transported by helicopter back to th top of the bob-run – a laborious process repeated up to eightee times a day! The results, however, speak for themselves.

But, there were other problems to contend with as well. Th onscreen tension between Bond and Blofeld was harmoniou

pared to Lazenby's rapidly deteriorating relationship with the
ducers. And the press ran wild with exaggerated stories about
hatred between the new 007 and his leading lady, Diana Rigg,
would have the distinction of becoming Bond's doomed bride
cy. Although Brigitte Bardot and Catherine Deneuve were
sidered for the role, Ms. Rigg landed the part largely because of
performance as the ultra-liberated Emma Peel on television's
ular show *The Avengers.*

> ## " *To the amazement of the industry,*
> *Lazenby resigned from all future*
> *assignments as Bond.* "

Tabloid gossip reached absurd proportions when Rigg was accused
eating garlic to "turn off" George during the love scenes.
deniably, however, the offscreen relationship between Mr. and
. Bond more resembled that of George and Martha in *Who's*
aid of Virginia Woolf?

Rare candid moment with
nby, Savalas and Ferzetti enjoying a
h on the set.

right: "Q" demonstrates his latest
ntion – radioactive lint – to an
npressed "M".

ht: No, that's not studio brass
sting George's arm to sign a multi-
ture contract!

Lazenby began to listen to the radical views of friends who convinced him he was being exploited by the producers, but this advice overlooked the fact that he didn't have a track record at the box-office. To the amazement of the industry, he resigned from all future assignments as Bond, certain he could establish a successful screen career on his own. While obviously disappointed, the

> ## " *The movie's final image of a heart-broken Bond is both haunting and memorable.* "

producers tried to shrug off Lazenby's departure with Cubby Broccoli noting flippantly: "There were fourteen Tarzans!". Lazenby later admitted: "Cubby Broccoli said some things to me, and they were true. They didn't need me. I was a dead loss after all the money they'd spend grooming me. They'd told me I'd end up making spaghetti westerns, instead I ended up making kung-fu movies in Hong Kong." Cubby himself would later reflect; "He could have been a success, except he lost his head in the middle of the picture. He couldn't handle it, but he's a nice guy, George."

Credit for the impressive visual impact of *OHMSS* must be shared all round, but special mention must go to John Glen who did the editing and second unit work. Glen's distinctive lightning-fast editing is a marvel to behold. For example, look closely at how many individual shots comprise the spectacular fist fight between Bond and a muscle-bound thug in Tracy's hotel room. The mind boggles at the editing

Top left: Lazenby samples some alpine pleasures between scenes.

Above: New Bond, old frustrations for the long-suffering Miss Moneypenny.

Top right: 007 weds Tracy, to the satisfaction of her father, Marc Ange Draco.

s which created so much excitement for only sixty seconds of ʒen time. The film also boasts what is probably John Barry's ɪtest score for a Bond film. Accolades too for Maurice Binder who ʒniously incorporated glimpses from previous Bond escapades ʒ the main credits.

ʒhe supporting cast in *OHMSS* is excellent. While it has become ʒionable to denounce Telly Savalas's Blofeld as being too uncouth ɪ "American" for the role, the authors respectfully disagree. ʒough Telly is a bit rough around the edges in exuding an air of ʒopean sophistication, he poses a formidable physical menace to ʒd.

ʒalian actor Gabriele Ferzetti is distinguished and amusing as ʒcy's crimelord father, and Ilse Steppat is jarringly effective as ʒeld's Rosa Klebb-type henchwoman Irma Bunt. The loyal office ʒw – Bernard Lee, Desmond Llewelyn and Lois Maxwell – are a

welcome presence, but seen only too briefly. Maxwell works wonders as the heart-broken Moneypenny at Bond's wedding. When 007 gives an embarrassed grin and tosses her his hat, as he prepares to drive off on his honeymoon, her sobbing acceptance of the situation is enormously moving.

Many have said the film works well despite the presence of George Lazenby. This is neither accurate nor fair. Whatever problems Lazenby made for himself and others on the set are irrelevant to a performance which deserves a good deal of praise. Although a bit wooden at times, he succeeds in showing both the compassionate and ruthless side of Bond. He rivals Connery in the action sequences, and does a credible job in the romance department. He is particularly effective in the film's tragic ending, as a shock-stricken 007 grieves over the body of his murdered wife. The movie's final image of a heart-broken Bond realizing that his world has collapsed around him, is both haunting and memorable thanks in no small part to Lazenby's thesping.

As for George Lazenby, the man, his wise business investments have made him very wealthy. He has continued to find work as an actor, patiently awaiting another shot at "the big break". Ironically, he has not totally shed the Bondian image. In 1990, still displaying his youthful good looks, he hosted a U.S. television showing of the Ian Fleming biography *Goldeneye*. He has also appeared in a cameo role of a Bondian-type agent in the delightful 1983 TV movie *Return of the Man from U.N.C.L.E.*

OHMSS was released during the Christmas season of 1969. It was not a blockbuster by Bondian standards, but rumors that the film was a financial disaster are complete fabrications. In fact, *OHMSS* was enough of a moneymaker to encourage Broccoli and Saltzman to immediately begin work on planning the next 007 epic.

DIAMONDS ARE FOREVER

With George Lazenby's hasty departure as 007, the entire Bond franchise landed in jeopardy. The main obstacle: to find an actor who could establish an *immediate* rapport with the Bond role and endear himself to audiences the way Sean Connery did. The obvious answer was to lure Connery back. However, this prospect seemed unlikely for various reasons. Foremost, Connery was desperate to find success in a non-Bond film. His recent films won critical praise, but little in the way of popular enthusiasm. His return to "Bondage" might be cynically viewed as an act of desperation.

Connery's disputes with the producers had reached legendary proportions in recent years. Could such intense differences be overlooked by all parties? Well, Broccoli and Saltzman were determined to find out. They formally approached Connery who promptly rebuked them, with a colleague noting: "Sean would rather play golf." Other actors considered included Roger Moore and Timothy Dalton. The former was contractually obliged to develop the television series *The Persuaders*, while Dalton felt he was too young and intimidated to step into Connery's shoes. Ultimately, American actor John Gavin was signed for the role. Gavin proved to be an unexpected choice, not only because of his nationality, but also because he had little in the way of box-office appeal – his most notable role was as the heroic boyfriend in Hitchcock's *Psycho*.

United Artist's President, David Picker, was less than enthused with the choice and decided to get Connery – at any cost. The price UA paid to achieve this was steep enough to have Sean lauded in the Guinness Book of World Records. Connery received a large sala percentage of the gross rentals and a commitment from U.A finance two non-Bond films of his choice. Today it's not unusua superstars like Connery to routinely exceed these terms, but in I the deal was the talk of the industry. Unexpectedly, the gene Mr. Connery donated his entire salary to the Scottish Internat Trust, a charity he formed to help the underprivileged in his n land.

The next challenge was to find the right leading lady to celeb Connery's return to the Bond role. Raquel Welch craved the ro *femme fatale* Tiffany Case and was briefly considered. However producers rejected her as being "too much animal". Other actre considered were Jane Fonda and Faye Dunaway. Attorney Sid Korschak, a friend of Cubby Broccoli, had asked him to consider J John for the supporting role of Plenty O'Toole. Instead, St. J ended up playing Tiffany, after director Guy Hamilton had dete her potential for the female lead.

Production went rather smoothly in Las Vegas, and the studic not have to pay Connery the lucrative overtime payments contract required in the event of going beyond schedule. S actually seemed to enjoy this romp as Bond, and occupied his time the set by indulging in his passion for golf with other members of crew.

The script for *Diamonds* sought to return Bond as the larger t life fantasy figure of the pre-*OHMSS* era. Gone was the more hur emotional and vulnerable 007 enacted by George Lazenby. In

Bond confronts Blofeld in the penthouse home of Willard Whyte.

CREDITS	
R OF RELEASE	1971
T	Sean Connery
	Jill St. John
	Charles Gray
	Lana Wood
	Jimmy Dean
	Bruce Cabot
	Bernard Lee
	Desmond Llewelyn
	Putter Smith
	Bruce Glover
	Lois Maxwell
ECTOR	Guy Hamilton
DUCERS	Albert R. Broccoli
	Harry Saltzman
EENPLAY	Richard Maibaum
	Tom Mankiewicz
DUCTION DESIGNER	Ken Adam
ORS	Bert Bates
	John W. Holmes
SIC	John Barry
LE SONG LYRICS	Don Black
	performed by Shirley Bassey

ck in "Bondage": Connery returns as
7 after a four-year absense in this
ian photo busta.

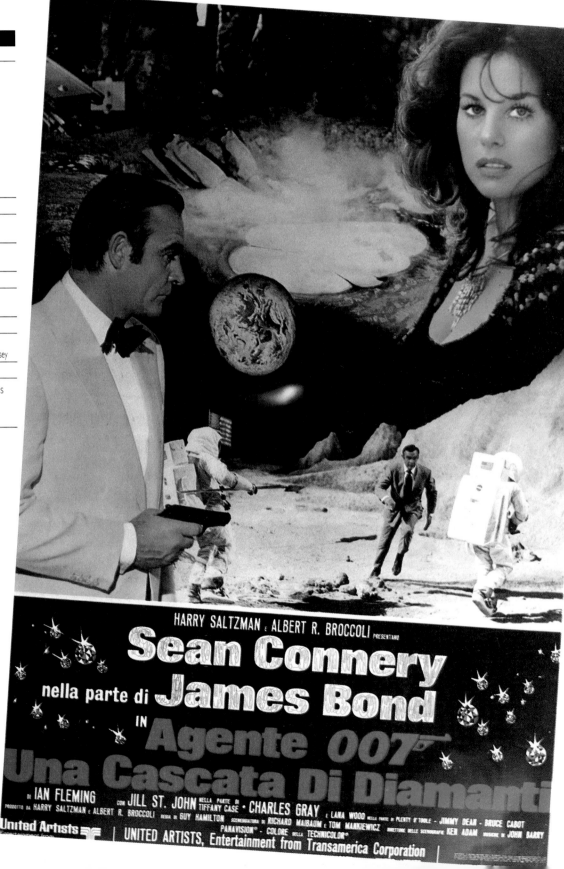

place was the superhero who charmed audiences with tongue-in-cheek witticisms while cavorting in an exaggerated, yet stylish adventure.

This time, Bond is assigned to investigate the disappearance of a large cache of the world's diamonds. He later learns that the gems are being hoarded by his old nemesis Blofeld, who plans to construct a diamond-powered satellite death star capable of emitting a deadly laser force. Naturally, Blofeld wants to hold the world to ransom, though it is rather puzzling just what ransom could appease a man who possesses enough diamonds to cover an entire satellite. The plot is sometimes rather confusing, and not as interesting as previous efforts.

If *Goldfinger* was the blueprint for the Bond films of the 1960s, then *Diamonds* was surely the inspiration for the 007 adventures of the 1970s. Film critic Leonard Maltin noted that *Diamonds* marked a departure for the James Bond series from the serious, often violent depiction of spy intrigue to a more light-hearted approach. This film marks the emergence of the zany humor later to characterize the Roger Moore films. Not everyone was pleased with this innovation, with some fans complaining that the series lost the careful balance between humor and suspense.

« *Diamonds displays an abundance of witty dialogue.* »

Addressing the new style Bond film, Guy Hamilton said: "There had been so many [007] imitators that we had to play for something fresh and outrageous. 007 has to be greater than anything else; any movie hero and even life itself." Granted, but one wishes that Connery was as ruthless throughout the film as he is in the excellent pre-credits sequence in which he journeys on an obsessive world-wide manhunt for Blofeld, presumably to avenge the death of Tracy in *OHMSS*.

Interestingly, Peter Hunt, the director of *OHMSS*, informed the authors that Tracy's death was to have occurred in the pre-credits scene of *Diamonds*. However, with Lazenby's departure, it was decided the film should "wrap up the loose ends". In retrospect, the downbeat ending of *OHMSS* was a significant factor in making the film the Bondian classic it is.

Diamonds is a very mixed bag, given that it represents Connery's last Eon sponsored appearance as Bond. The casting is weak in key areas: Charles Gray portrays Blofeld as a *bon vivant* with a great deal of avuncular charm. Yet, he would appear more comfortable pottering about his garden than seeking world domination. Gray is a fine actor, but does not exude the least bit of menace. He is also hampered by being the third actor to play Blofeld is as many films, and resembles his predecessors as much as he does Ursula Andress – not a very convincing villain.

"Hi, I'm Plenty" "But of course you are!"

Connery and his femme fatale: Plenty O'Toole, played by Lana Wood.

Connery and director Guy Hamilton rehearse the pre-credits fight with Blofeld.

Right: 007 admires Tiffany – the loveliest link in the diamond-smuggl pipeline.

Two prominent symbols of capitalism collide: 007 in Las Vegas.

ll St. John's Tiffany Case is first seen as a brash, tough opportunist
ose moody disposition rivals 007's machismo. Unfortunately, as
script progresses, Tiffany evolves into a bimbo whose bra size is
ificantly larger than her IQ. Consequently, St. John's scenes with
nnery onscreen are somewhat less steamy than the sparks they
layed offscreen.

Diamonds *was surely the inspiration for the 007 adventures of the 1970s.* 99

Norman Burton is miscast as Felix Leiter, playing the part in a
er bumbling manner that makes it difficult to imagine that he and
d shared life-threatening adventures. Putter Smith and Bruce
over as the homosexual "hit men" Wint and Kidd are amusing, but

again pose more laughs than menace even though their demise at the
film's climax is imaginatively done. Jimmy Dean, the country singer, is
creatively cast as reclusive billionaire Willard Whyte.

Memorable sequences in *Diamonds* include a spectacular car chase
throughout the gaudy streets of Las Vegas, a scene which delights
even by today's standards. There is also an amusing encounter with
two of Willard Whyte's "butch" female bodyguards; a tense
sequence in which Bond is almost cremated; and a claustrophobic
fight in a glass-paneled elevator, between Bond and a diamond
smuggler, which is superbly directed and edited.

Diamonds also displays an abundance of witty dialogue. Examine a
scene loaded with in-jokes alluding to Sean's absence – and return –
as J.B.: Bond converses with "M" (who seems to have a particular
disdain for 007 this outing), and Sir Donald, head of the diamonds
syndicate. "You've been on holiday, I understand – relaxing I hope,"
says Sir Donald, in obvious reference to Connery's absence from the

Bond smells a rat, as Mr. Wint's "rather potent" aftershave is about to betray him.

The crew helps Connery steal Willard Whyte's moon buggy.

previous film. Connery replies, "Oh, hardly relaxing, but most satisfying," possibly an oblique reference to his having made four non-Bond films since his retirement as 007 in 1967. The MI6 establishment gets the last laugh when "M" counters, "We do function in your absence, Commander!"

Another great line comes when Bond first meets the well-endowed Plenty O'Toole. "Hi, I'm Plenty," she coos. Bond examines her assets, and replies, "But of course you are". "Plenty O'Toole." "Named after your father perhaps!"

Unfortunately, *Diamonds* sags where it should be the liveliest, most notably in the assault on Blofeld's oil-rig headquarters. This uninspiring battle scene also fails to capitalize on John Barry's stimulating score. However, Ken Adam's sets are fantastic, the locations are lush, and the return of Connery was a cause for celebration by Bond fans throughout the world.

Critics generally praised this Bond epic, with the *Village Voice* noting that: "*Diamonds* deserves to make a billion dollars", and the *New York Times* stating with unusual sentiment "It is great absurd fun [and Connery's return] is enough to make one weep with gratitude".

The film was a success for all involved. Connery became the highest paid actor in history while Broccoli and Saltzman proved they still had the Midas touch. *Variety* summed up the glee at United Artists with a story about the film's incredible grosses headlined appropriately "Diamonds are for U.A. Now!"

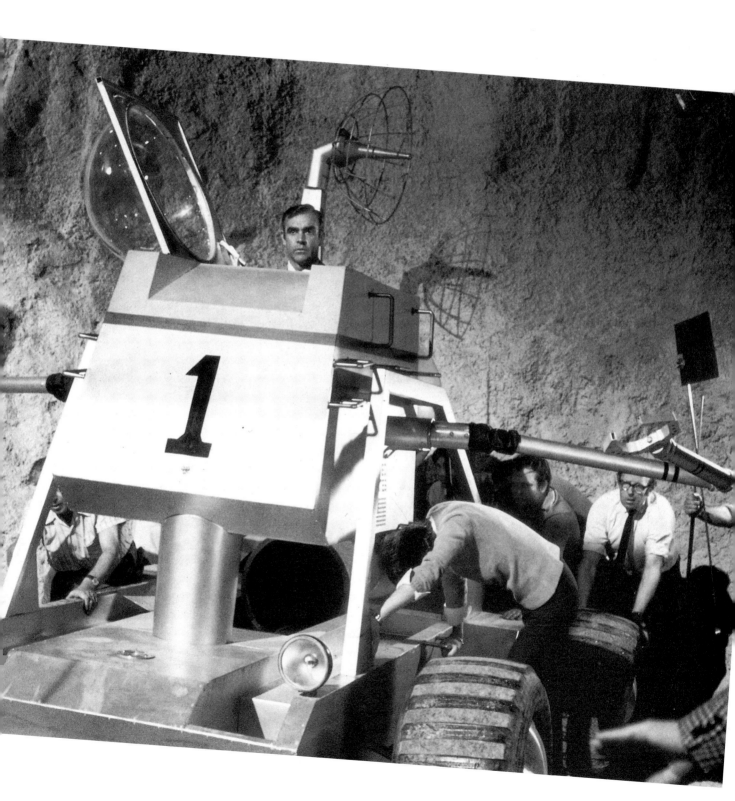

LIVE AND LET DIE

Despite the enormous success of *Diamonds Are Forever*, Sean Connery repeated his oft-stated intention never to return to the role of 007. United Artists made various attempts to lure Connery back into Bondage again, while a screenplay was already being penned to allow filming to commence on schedule in October, 1972. As the casting of Bond was uncertain, the script alluded to a generic concept of Bond that would not be tailored to a particular actor or style. When it became obvious that Connery would not return, the producers decided to employ the services of another bona fide star rather than a novice, à la George Lazenby.

United Artists wanted an American superstar, while the producers insisted that 007 be played by an Englishman. Cubby Broccoli resurrected the name of Roger Moore, but this time, it was Harry Saltzman who was not overly enthused about the choice. As the studio applied pressure to pursue names like Burt Reynolds, Paul Newman and Robert Redford, Saltzman began to relent. Cubby advised Moore to lose some weight and have his long hair cut and shaped into a Bondian style.

Ironically, Moore should not have been available for the role. He and Tony Curtis were signed to do the big budget TV adventure series *The Persuaders* for Sir Lew Grade. Although the series was a hit in Europe, it never caught on in the all-important U.S. market and the show was canceled despite predictions of a long run. Thus, unexpectedly, Roger Moore was available.

The producers were determined to try a new image for 007 to keep him in step with the 1970s. This necessitated updating Fleming's novel, which had a patronizing "Step-'n'-Fetch-it" attitude toward blacks, most of whom are presented as villains. This was a rather bold premise by the 1970s, when it was fashionable to show blacks as heroes in such films as *Shaft* and *Superfly*.

The producers argued that true equality meant allowing minor to play a wide variety of roles – including villains. The script care insures that even the most evil black characters are presented intelligent and capable. In fact, it is Bond who seems foolish when naïvely tries to blend in with the crowd in a Harlem bar. This lead predictable trouble and a reprimand from a black CIA agent cynically berates Bond's "clever disguise."

> ## " *Cubby advised Roger Moore to lose som weight and have his long hair cut.* "

The film was shot in Jamaica, New Orleans, New York City, and course Pinewood Studios in England. *Live* boasts an impressive c including Jane Seymour as Solitaire, Bond's primary love inter Broccoli had seen her in the BBC television series *The Onedin Line* immediately felt she would be perfect for the part. Cubby's instin proved to be sound, as Seymour has become one of the m successful of the Bond women.

For Bond's nemesis – Dr. Kananga – Yaphet Kotto was the mu choice. A versatile actor, Kotto was very much in the midst involvement with social reform movements. This lead to a f problems on the set. For example, Kotto used a publicity photo sho to demonstrate the Black Power salute. Cautioned by the fil publicity director that political statements were inappropriate or Bond set, Kotto proved awkward, and feelings ran high for a while most of the black stuntmen followed his example.

Live and Let Die had its fair share of production problems. Shor after filming commenced, Roger Moore collapsed and was rushed hospital, suffering from a painful kidney stone attack. Later, filming

Italian photo busta.

Bond with friend and foes: (*left to right*) Solitaire, Tee-Hee, Baron Samedi, Whisper and Kananga.

CREDITS	
YEAR OF RELEASE	1973
CAST	Roger Moore
	Jane Seymour
	Yaphet Kotto
	Julius W. Harris
	Clifton James
	Geoffrey Holder
	Gloria Hendry
	David Hedison
	Bernard Lee
	Lois Maxwell
DIRECTOR	Guy Hamilton
PRODUCERS	Albert. R. Broccoli
	Harry Saltzman
SCREENPLAY	Tom Mankiewicz
ART DIRECTOR	Syd Cain
MUSIC	George Martin
TITLE SONG	Paul and Linda McCartney performed by Paul McCartney and Wings

speedboat chase, he was involved in a potentially serious accident, but escaped with some minor injuries. The climate in the Louisiana swamps was intolerably hot and humid, and the cast and crew were plagued by snakes and omnipresent mosquitoes. Through it all, however, Roger Moore maintained an amiable spirit which boosted morale on the set. The new Bond had a great sense of humor, and enjoyed the opportunity to co-star with long-time friend David Hedison, cast as Felix Leiter. Harry Saltzman also tried his best to keep the mood light, and once flew in a favorite chef from Harry's Bar in Venice just to prepare meals for the cast.

Live and Let Die abounds with amazing stuntwork including a spectacular feat when a speed boat soars over a car, and lands back in the water. This stunt was engineered by fitting a jet-propulsion de to the boat, and placing ramps in its path, setting a world record of 110 feet. In another exciting sequence, a London bus dr doubled for Moore and managed to swing a double-decker bus complete circle — a stunt not quite as dangerous as driving a through London at rush hour!

Stuntwork aside, the real question is: does *Live and Let Die* succ in launching a new James Bond era? The answer is yes: quite well, with some reservations. Those reservations have to do with development of cartoonish humor, initiated with *Diamonds Forever* and becoming even broader in Tom Mankiewicz's screenp This is exemplified by the presence of Clifton James's Sheriff J

The final confrontation between
[a]nd Kananga.

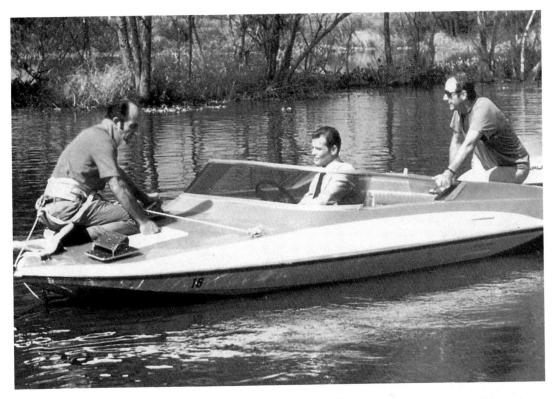

[dire]ctor Guy Hamilton (*right*) helps
[prep]are Moore for the monumental
chase.

[Belo]w *right*: Moore gets some
[arm]aments advice from a Louisiana
[State] Trooper.

[Troo]per. The character is straight out of a comic book, and though his
[rac]ist diatribes about "a swamp full of black Russians" are undeniably
[amu]sing, they are totally out of place in a 007 movie.

[T]he central action piece is the prolonged boat chase on the bayous
[whi]ch dominates much of the film. It is a hodgepodge of incidents:
[som]e don't succeed, but others are an absolute wow, particularly the
[on]e where several boats sail across a highway directly in front of
[spe]eding police cars. Here, unlike in future outings, Moore does many
[of] his own stunts. One small criticism is that George Martin's sparse
[sco]re does not support the excitement, and the scene cries out for a
[Joh]n Barry-type tempo to improve the pace.

[T]he script is limited, and *Live and Let Die* is not the epic its
[pre]decessors were. Bond is simply assigned to resolve a series of
[mu]rders, linked to Kananga's plot to cultivate a bumper crop of
[her]oin and distribute it free through his confederate Mr Big, a Harlem
[dr]ug dealer. This will force competitive drug distributors out of
[bu]siness while increasing the number of addicts. Kananga will then use
[his] monopoly of the heroin market to excessively raise prices. The
[plo]t seems hardly larger than life, but it is refreshing in that it allows
[Bo]nd to tackle an assignment with roots in a real social problem.

[A]s a villain, Kotto is not of the Goldfinger caliber. However, his
[sce]nes ring with conviction and he poses a formidable physical
[me]nace to Bond, as exemplified in the well-staged knife fight. What is
[no]t convincing is a sequence where Kotto strips off a phony looking
[gr]ey wig and a ghastly shade of makeup, to reveal that Mr Big is his

Bond and Solitaire enjoy a rare moment of quiet.

Far right: Pick a card – any card, offers 007. But be warned – it may mean death!

Right: Moore and Seymour enjoy the Jamaican climate.

-ego – (apparently everyone *but* Bond can grasp this at once). [wit]h his droopy eyes accentuated and his skin a milky tone, Kotto [rese]mbles a cross between Robert Mitchum and Casper the Friendly [Gho]st.

" *Seymour is not only beautiful, but also is skilled enough to reflect a genuine sense of innocence.* "

[M]ore satisfactory is Julius W. Harris as Kananga's gleeful giant [hen]chman Tee Hee, who uses a hook for a hand, with often deadly [res]ults. In a memorable scene he has Bond locked into a chair and [thre]atens to snip off 007's fingers. When he fumbles a bit, Moore gets [o]ne of his better wisecracks by muttering "butterhook".

Other positive elements include Jane Seymour's portrayal of Solitaire, Kananga's personal psychic. But her powers will only last as long as her virginity. With our James on the scene, it isn't long before both are a thing of the past. Seymour is not only beautiful, but also is skilled enough to reflect a genuine sense of innocence. Less impressive is Gloria Hendry, a black beauty queen whose sexual interlude with Bond breaks a racial barrier of sorts. Hendry plays a bumbling CIA agent in league with Kananga; but Bond should realize a lot sooner than he does that the only way Hendry could work for the CIA would be if a Jerry Lewis character took control of the agency. Later, when 007 threatens to kill her for deceiving him *after* the customary love-making session, Hendry asks if he could be capable of harming her after what they have just done. "I certainly wouldn't have killed you *before*," replies Moore with a twinkle in his eye.

A notable scene-stealer is the international choreographer Geoffrey Holder as Baron Samedi, a mystical henchman of Kananga, revered and feared for his alleged voodoo powers over the populace of the

Publicity pose or deleted scene? Bond captured by thugs.

Roger Moore slips on 007's holster the first of seven cinematic missions

Below: Bond's closet obviously contains *everything* a playboy needs.

Haiti-like island of San Monique. The script wisely restricts Samedi's appearances, thus keeping him shrouded in an air of mystery.

Moore's 007 could have benefited from a harder edge. Yet, Moore should get credit for not imitating Connery, thereby successfully establishing his own persona in the Bond role, although it would not be until *The Spy Who Loved Me* that Moore would find his niche.

There are a few reservations to mention. The most conspicuous is the unforgivable absence of Desmond Llewelyn's "Q". Also, the movie has a "confined" feeling to it despite its extensive location scenery – no Panavision photography this time. On the plus side, Bernard Lee and Lois Maxwell are welcome sights and help ease the transition for the new Bond (Mr. Lee was ill prior to shooting and his role was almost assumed by Kenneth More). David Hedison proved to be an inspired choice for Felix Leiter (a role he would reprise in *Licence to Kill*), and Paul McCartney's title song is a Bond classic.

Critics were indifferent to Moore's Bond, although the film grosses were quite impressive. Audiences would eventually embrace Roger Moore as much as they had Sean Connery. The only difference was that this James Bond truly seemed to enjoy going along for the ride.

THE MAN WITH THE GOLDEN GUN

Following the release of *Live and Let Die*, Broccoli and Saltzman paused just long enough to insure audiences had indeed accepted Roger Moore as the new Bond, before beginning preparations for this, the ninth 007 epic. The idea was to move quickly while the image of the new 007 was still fresh in the mind of the audience. For the first time since *Thunderball*, a Bond film would be released in consecutive calendar years.

Screenwriter Tom Mankiewicz envisioned a storyline similar to the classic western *Shane*. In place of the duel between Alan Ladd and Jack Palance, Roger Moore would battle it out in a contemporary setting against Christopher Lee's arch-villain Scaramanga, the "anti-Bond" incarnate. (Earlier plans to have Palance play the "heavy" fell through.) On this occasion Lee would exchange his Dracula fangs for an even more peculiar anatomical abnormality – a third nipple. But even this can't milk any suspense out of a lethargic screenplay. The

contest would pit Bond's Walther against Scaramanga's tradema[rk] the golden gun which he employs to deadly effect as the world's efficient assassin. The unique 24-carat weapon in question co[ntains] but a single round of ammo, which leads Bond to scoff: "Six bulle[ts to] your one!" Unperturbed, Scaramanga counters with characte[ristic] ego, "I only need one!"

If only the remainder of the film maintained the same level o[f...] *Golden Gun* is perhaps the weakest of all the Bond films to date. [The] hero is entangled in a convoluted plot in which he must track do[wn a] "solex agitator" capable of converting energy from the sun [to] electricity for industrial purposes. *Gun* was shot during the en[ergy] crisis of the mid 1970s, but on this one occasion the accent [on a] contemporary problem has dated a Bond film.

While on assignment, Bond is relieved of his duties when [M] discovers 007 has been targeted by Scaramanga, an assassin who [works]

> ## " The contest would pit Bond's Walthe[r]
> ## against Scaramanga's trademark –
> ## the golden gun. "

for a one-million-dollar fee. Bond wonders aloud who would pay [that] kind of money to have him murdered. In the film's wittiest line, [M] replies: ". . . jealous husbands, outraged chefs, humiliated tailor[s –] the list is endless!"

The two plot lines are awkwardly merged, allowing Bon[d to] conveniently track the missing solex device to Scaramanga's islan[d,] where the antagonists indulge in a duel to the death, and B[ond] deposits Scaramanga "flat on his *coup de grâce*".

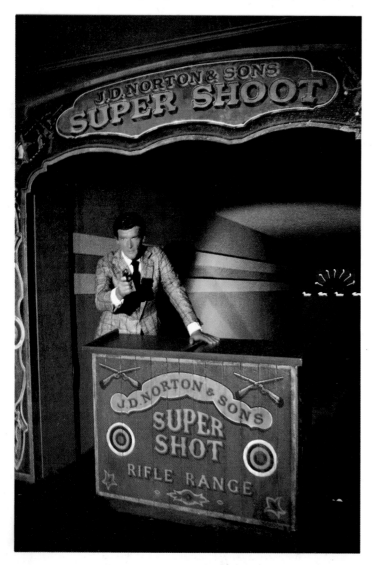

Left: A publicity shot of Bond in Scaramanga's deadly funhouse.

Right: Some guys have all the luck. Roger Moore in a publicity shot with Britt Ekland and future *Octopussy* star Maud Adams.

CREDITS	
YEAR OF RELEASE	1974
CAST	Roger Moore
	Christopher Lee
	Britt Ekland
	Maud Adams
	Herve Villechaize
	Clifton James
	Soon Taik Oh
	Bernard Lee
	Desmond Llewelyn
	Lois Maxwell
DIRECTOR	Guy Hamilton
PRODUCERS	Albert R. Broccoli
	Harry Saltzman
SCREENPLAY	Richard Maibaum
	Tom Mankiewicz
PRODUCTION DESIGNER	Peter Murton
EDITOR	Ray Poulton
MUSIC	John Barry
TITLE SONG LYRICS	Don Black
	performed by Lulu

Bond is forced to test his martial arts skills while held captive at the kung fu academy.

attempt to retrieve a vital clue
seductive belly dancer has
ous consequences.

capture the prized solex, Bond must first disarm a solar
ered ultra-weapon his nemesis has created. The problem is that
of this is overly engrossing and certainly isn't Bondian in scope.
ll of its considerable budget, *Golden Gun* has a hurried look to it
for once does not reflect the extent of the lavish production
es.
he film does benefit from a strong protagonist. As portrayed by
stopher Lee, Scaramanga is a far more interesting character than
)07 we see this time around. One wishes the script could have

> **❝ Never throughout Moore's tenure as Bond is he actually seen ordering a 'Martini – shaken not stirred'. ❞**

ided a good deal more insight into Scaramanga's past. Yet, he is
o Bondian standards for villains, in that he demonstrated
iderable charm and wit. Lee presents a cheerful and colorful
ona masking the cold and ruthless professional whom he later
ribes as "the dark side of Bond".
his analogy manifests itself in the film, but it is rather unconvincing
oore's Bond is so amiable it is impossible to imagine him having a
side. Perhaps if Connery had played Bond, the reference would
been more appropriate. Interestingly, Lee's involvement with

the film has unusual origins. He is actually Ian Fleming's first cousin,
and it was at the author's suggestion, some years before, that he
consider playing Dr. No.

Director Guy Hamilton insisted that Lee "play it light" in order to
adopt a persona contrasting the Dracula he had immortalized in the
Hammer Studios horror films. Lee recalls playing Scaramanga was
"one of the happiest experiences I ever had making a film".
Particularly enjoyable were the constant jokes he shared with Roger
Moore on the set.

Another positive modification of *Golden Gun* was the return of
some traditional Bond elements eliminated from *Live and Let Die* so
Moore could establish his own Bond identity, and not have Connery's
shadow looming over him. Here, Bond would return to his
customary formal attire as well as receive standard briefings at the
offices of British Intelligence. He also returns to the gambling tables,
and displays his knowledge of fine wines. Never throughout Moore's
tenure as Bond is he actually seen ordering a "Martini – shaken not
stirred". It was also "welcome back" to Desmond Llewelyn's "Q",
whose absence in *Live and Let Die* was conspicuous and unforgivable
to Bond fans.

Yet, *Golden Gun* lacks the "larger-than-life" feel of its predecessors,
as it fails to boast the mammoth set pieces that have become
standard elements of the Bond films. Though Peter Murton
contributes two somewhat memorable sets, these are never fully
exploited. The first is Scaramanga's funhouse – an elaborate
recreation of an old fashioned amusement park attraction; and the

Scaramanga (*left*), the world's grea
assassin takes aim at . . .

James Bond (*right*), the world's gre
secret agent.

second, a solar power plant on Scaramanga's island. The latter
two months to build and featured in nine days of filming. W
looks impressive, it does not have the impact of Ken Adam's se
Goldfinger's Ft. Knox or the volcano in *You Only Live Twice*.

Filming took place primarily in Thailand and required long da
shooting in scorching heat; modern conveniences were also lir
Scaramanga's island hideaway was actually an abandoned fragme
volcanic rock located six hundred miles from Bangkok on the isla
Phuket – don't ask how to pronounce that one! An amusing ane
Roger Moore recounts concerns an occasion on Phuket in v
Moore and Lee enter a cave, only to encounter a large numb
flying bats. In a spoof of his Dracula image, Lee threw up his arm
shouted: "Back Stanislaw! Not now!".

Lee's wit is not exercised in the screenplay, which is the
satisfactory of the entire series. There is an abundance of ju
humor, highlighted by the return of Clifton James's Sheriff
Pepper from the previous film, and some too-obvious product
like, Pepper shopping for an American Motors car – whil
vacation in Thailand!

The casting of Herve Villechaize as a pint-sized killer is a
mistake. Somehow the threat posed by an irate midget doe
bring to mind the menace exuded by Red Grant. This is
apparent in the "sting in the tail" epilogue fight as Bond is humil
by Nick Nack's kick to his rump. As one critic inquired: "Is it pos
to show a midget onscreen without the accompaniment of 'am
bassoon or flute music?"

Having said all this, one might think there is very little to
ommend in *Golden Gun*, when, in fact, many elements are quite
oyable. Despite the emphasis on humor, Moore does get a chance
exhibit a tougher side. In one scene he violently smacks Maud
ams to get information (remember Sean Connery's handling of
niela Bianchi in *From Russia With Love*"?)

Moore seems a bit more relaxed and confident, as though he is no
ger consciously avoiding comparison with Connery. He is also
oressive in a well-choreographed fight scene in the dressing-room
a belly dancer – this is undoubtedly the best action sequence in the
ovie.

Impressive, too, is an amazing stunt in which Bond's car "jumps"
oss a river, completing a 360-degree spiraling rotation to land
right on a bridge. The logistics of the scene were calculated by
mputer, and six cameras were positioned to film a stunt taking only
few very terrifying seconds to accomplish. The action is slowed
wn on screen so that audiences carefully appreciate and absorb
e skills and risks involved.

eft: Duel of the Titans – 007 versus
aramanga.

Guy Hamilton directs Roger Moore in a sequence set in "M"'s office.

It would be remiss not to mention the film's leading lady, but the less said about Britt Ekland's role the better. It isn't fair to blame the actress, as the screenplay presents her as a cross between Gracie Allen and Lucille Ball – a natural impediment to 007. At the risk of being totally sexist, she does look impressive in a bikini. Ekland had long desired to become a Bond girl, declaring: "When I saw Ursula Andress walk out of the water, that was the epitome of womanhood, movie star and glamour – and that's what I wanted." She had originally auditioned for the role of Scaramanga's mistress, but was rewarded

❝ Gun *was the first Bond film to be screened at the Kremlin.* ❞

with the lead. Maud Adams is far more convincing in the former role, exuding sensuality, fear and passion as the sexual slave of Bond's adversary.

Critically, *Golden Gun* met with mediocre reviews. Audiences also seemed uninterested for once. An uninspired advertising campaign, that too closely resembled the one for *Live and Let Die*, also hindered interest. However, *Gun* was the first Bond film to be screened at the Kremlin. There was some grumbling when it is disclosed that Scaramanga was trained by the KGB. When the houselights came up, one Soviet official commented to Broccoli that the KGB did not do a very impressive job, much to everyone's amusement.

Significantly, *Golden Gun* represented the last joint effort for

Broccoli and Saltzman. As business and creative differences continue to plague the partnership, the duo alternated the lion's share of producer's duties on the Moore Bonds: Cubby oversaw product of *Gun* while Harry did likewise for *Live and Let Die*. When Ha Saltzman decided to abandon the future of 007 to Cubby, Uni Artists bought out his share of interest in the films. Industry insid and Bond fans alike wondered about the future of James Bond.

Bond enjoys a light moment with Mary Goodnight.

Director Guy Hamilton discusses the beach duel with Roger Moore and Christopher Lee.

Would the lukewarm reception of *Golden Gun* accomplish what ramanga had failed to do: kill off Bond? Would the Bond franchise ve under Broccoli's sole care, or would the production of the es prove too much for a single individual? Bond fans had little to . Though it would be two-and-a-half years until the release of the t Bond film, Broccoli would prove that he had used his time ductively: Bond would be back in 1977 — with a vengeance!

THE SPY WHO LOVED ME

Following the relatively disappointing public reception to *The Man With the Golden Gun*, Cubby Broccoli became a man obsessed with a mission: to prove James Bond was still a viable property. Freed from an often tense relationship with Harry Saltzman, he could now concentrate on giving 007 a much-needed shot in the arm, by making his first solo Bond production the most spectacular to date.

Broccoli could not have chosen a more challenging effort than attempting to film *The Spy Who Loved Me*. Ian Fleming had been displeased with the source novel, and specified in his contract for the film rights that only the title could be used. *Spy* would thus represent the first Bond film not to have a foundation in a Fleming story. An army of writers was enlisted to submit a screenplay, and among the "rejected" contributors were such big names as Stirling Silliphant, Anthony Burgess and John Landis. Early drafts resurrected the venerable Blofeld and his SPECTRE legions, but *Thunderball* producer Kevin McClory – in the midst of preparing a soon-to-be-aborted rival 007 epic titled *Warhead*, ironically co-scripted by Sean Connery – threatened legal action, contending he had exclusive use of the SPECTRE concept.

Facing page: Italian photo busta illustrates the excitement of Bond epic number nine.

Cubby Broccoli with Roger Moore and Barbara Bach on the "007 stage" which now bears his name.

CREDITS	
YEAR OF RELEASE	1977
CAST	Roger Moore
	Barbara Bach
	Curt Jurgens
	Richard Kiel
	Caroline Munro
	Walter Gotell
	Geoffrey Keen
	Bernard Lee
	Desmond Llewelyn
	Lois Maxwell
DIRECTOR	Lewis Gilbert
PRODUCER	Albert R. Broccoli
SCREENPLAY	Christopher Wood
	Richard Maibaum
EDITOR	John Glen
MUSIC	Marvin Hamlisch
TITLE SONG LYRICS	Carole Bayer Sager
	"Nobody does it Better"
	performed by Carly Simon

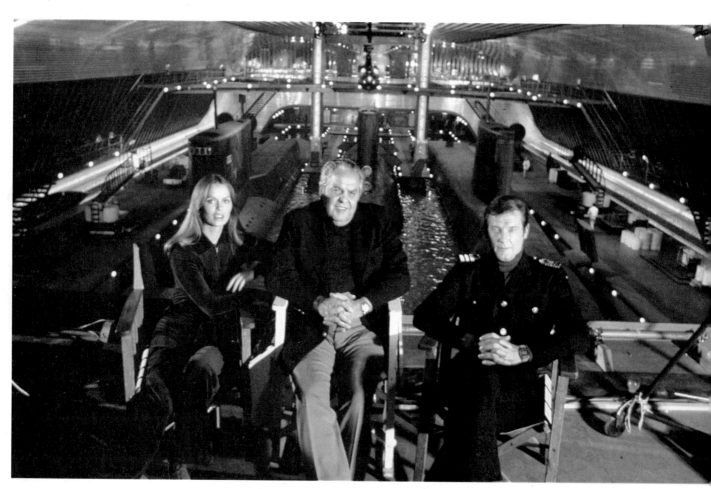

THE SPY WHO LOVED ME

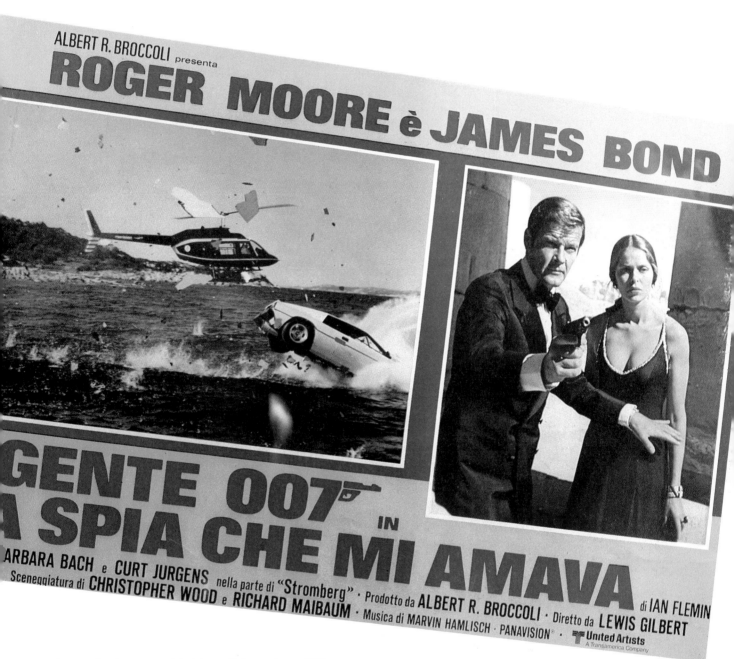

protracted court battle was avoided by enlisting veteran 007
[wri]ter Richard Maibaum, whose revision of the screenplay replaced
[SPE]CTRE with a ruthless terrorist organization planning to wreak
[worl]d-wide havoc. Broccoli insisted on a rewrite, claiming the story
[was] too political for a 007 film. Writer Christopher Wood was
[brou]ght on board to collaborate with Maibaum and expand upon
[Broc]coli's personal concept for the film: Bond's involvement with a
[beau]tiful Soviet agent who was every bit 007's equal. Wood came
[reco]mmended by old friend Lewis Gilbert (*You Only Live Twice*), who
[was] signed to direct *Spy* after Guy Hamilton departed to helm
[Super]*man*.

**❝ Spy *would represent the first Bond film*
not to have a foundation in a
Fleming story. ❞**

"How does that grab you?" Asks 007
he uses an industrial magnet to give t
steel-toothed Jaws a lift.

The finished shooting script is not unlike that of *You Only Live Twice*, though criticism that *Spy* is a virtual remake is unjustified. The story centered on Stromberg, an evil shipping magnate who utilizes the world's largest tanker to literally "swallow" Soviet and U.S. nuclear submarines with the intention of precipitating World War III. His goal: rid the world of its vices and create a new society under the sea. In the spirit of *détente*, James Bond teams with the beautiful Soviet KGB agent Anya Amasova on a world-wide race to prevent a nuclear holocaust.

The film's action set pieces defied any existing studio dimensions. For a climactic battle scene within the confines of Stromberg's supertanker the LIPARUS, the set had to accommodate the warring armies plus two full-size submarines. Production designer Ken Adam

told Cubby the gloomy news that no studio in existence was la enough to furnish such accommodations. Broccoli mulled problem over for a few seconds, and replied with character bluntness: "Then build it!"

To fulfill this vision of the most spectacular 007 epic to date, entire soundstage was erected on the grounds of Pinewood Stud The dimensions were staggering: 374 feet long; an exterior t measured an additional 38 feet; 160 feet wide and 53 feet hig dwarfing the soundstages for *Cleopatra* and *Ben Hur*. Christened "007 Stage" (final cost: $1 million), the grand opening featured a st studded guest list topped by British Prime Minister Harold Wils The stage proved to be a wise investment, as it has been leased other production companies over the years.

As the scope of the film expanded, so did its budget, but Broccoli
...ured the then staggering sum of $13.5 million from United Artists.
..., problems developed. Britain – in the midst of a drought –
...ldn't meet the enormous aquatic demands of the film. Miraculously,
...as discovered that the stage had been constructed over a large
..., thus allowing the filmmakers access to the vast amounts of water
...uired by the script.

> **_Stuntman Rick Sylvester carried out
> what is arguably the most daring stunt
> in film history._**

Filming took five months, with locations in Sardinia, Egypt, the
...amas, Scotland, and other exotic points around the globe. For the
...w classic pre-credits sequence, the crew flew to Baffin Island in
...nada for filming atop the Asgard mountain. Here, stuntman Rick
...vester carried out what is arguably the most daring stunt in film
...tory. Doubling as Bond, Sylvester eludes his pursuers by skiing off
... mountain and freefalling for what seems like an eternity before
...gaging a parachute to land safely. Several camera crews were
...ployed, as only one take was possible. The main shots were to be
...en by helicopter, complemented by cameramen on the mountain
...pes covering other angles. In an occurrence reminiscent of the old

...o right: Not "The Addams Family",
...close. Stromberg with his
...chmen, Sandor (left) and Jaws.

...ne-up-manship" spy-style. Bond and
...ya compare notes on their
...owledge of each other's dossier.

"But James, I need you!" "So does England!"

"ready when you are, C.B." gag, the helicopter crew was unable to capture the stunt! Fortunately, a cameraman on the mountain was able to provide excellent footage of the remarkable event, for which Sylvester was paid $30,000.

All of the grueling effort poured into *The Spy Who Loved Me* proved to be worthwhile, as the film stands as Roger Moore's finest 007 epic. Gargantuan in scope, it is fondly remindful of the "gilt-edged Bonds" of the 1960s, with Moore finally in command of the role. He confidently assumes his own characterization of 007: accentuating his talent for playing romantic light comedy, while displaying Bond's more ruthless persona in dramatic highlights enacted with measured seriousness. With *Spy*, Roger Moore's James Bond had definitely arrived.

Moore was aided considerably by his co-stars. As Anya, Barbara Bach displays a natural beauty that is nothing less than stunning; a former model, she was discovered by Lewis Gilbert and *Spy* would be the vehicle to launch her to stardom. (Several years later she would also hit the headlines by becoming Mrs. Ringo Starr.)

Ms. Bach's acting abilities are considerably less impressive than her stunning figure, but when Anya enters a Cairo night spot wearing a black evening gown, or when she prepares for bed wearing the sexiest nightgown imaginable, her shortcomings as a thespian are immediately forgotten. If KGB agents *don't* look like Barbara Bach, well they should.

Spy also introduces a memorable villain in the form of Richard Kiel as Jaws, a giant, mute psychopath whose steel teeth are not only strong enough to devour human jugular veins, but wood and metal ones as well! These metallic "munchers" were so painful that Kiel could only wear them for five minutes at a time. Jaws, the insanely loyal henchman of Stromberg, is quite unique. Kiel is perfect in the role, having portrayed an identical character in *Silver Streak* (1976). His fight scenes with Moore are creatively staged and directed. However, one wishes that the cartoonish lampooning of his seemingly indestructible abilities were toned down, as they detract from any severe menace. Some of the gags admittedly work well, as in the final showdown when Bond uses a gigantic magnet to clamp Jaws by the teeth and deposit him into the shark tank below, where the ultimate "man-eating-shark" joke occurs.

Veteran German actor Curt Jurgens brings an air of sophistication to the character of Stromberg. He is the typical Bond megalomaniac – you can't help being charmed by him, even as he dumps his secretary into yet another conveniently located shark tank. In between plotting the destruction of western civilization, Stromberg is not above taking a break for some old fashioned heterosexual dalliances. His ritualistic preparations for sampling the captive Anya's charms caused that usually sour critic John Simon to slobber: "When Jurgens has Miss Bach tied to his couch and prepared for a fate . . . considerably less bad than death, how dare that officious PG rating come between every man and his vicarious desires?"

On the macho-front Jurgens poses no serious physical menace to Bond other than pressing some rather deadly buttons with his

Jaws drops in on 007's train compartment for a quick bite.

Bond, Anya, KGB-chief Gogol and "M" observe a demonstration of the latest technology in "Q" branch's pyramid based headquarters.

bbed fingers, and he is disposed of rather casually when 007 cold-
odedly shoots him in the groin. (Moore was to quip "Ballseye,
nfinger!" but the line was deleted.)
The office team of Bernard Lee, Lois Maxwell and Desmond
welyn are as amusing and charming as ever. Caroline Munro is a
ow-stopper as Stromberg's "personal assistant" Naomi, who
rally goes to pieces over Bond when 007 destroys her helicopter
h a missile from his Lotus Esprit.
Yet, the pièce de résistance is the colossal battle waged within the
ARUS, pitting Bond and his allies against Stromberg's army. It's a
nax worthy of the best of the Bond films, and is stunningly directed
Lewis Gilbert.
The brilliance of Ken Adam's sets are evident with Atlantis, the
ean-based headquarters of Stromberg which rises tarantula-like
m the sea; and the locale for "Q" Branch discreetly tucked away
de a pyramid – how did the Secret Service get permission for *that*

one! As usual, Adam's creations are marvels of futuristic design, and
contain more steel and chrome than a dozen roadside diners and
Jaws' mouth combined.
   Marvin Hamlisch's score did not please the purists but the themes
are serviceable and the title song "Nobody Does It Better" remains a
standard today. All other aspects of *Spy* are top-notch, and these
factors combined to make this the most satisfying Bond romp since
OHMSS. Praise for the film, and particularly Moore's performance,
was unstinting.
   Lewis Gilbert stated: "It's the most ambitious Bond film ever made
. . . we pulled out all the stops. We are proving that not only is Bond
alive and kicking in the 1970s, but is ready to continue successfully
into the 1980s". Little could Gilbert know that, thanks to *Spy*'s
achievement in renewing interest in 007, the franchise would be alive
and well in the 1990s. Cubby Broccoli's gamble had paid off
handsomely.

MOONRAKER

CREDITS	
YEAR OF RELEASE	1979
CAST	Roger Moore
	Lois Chiles
	Michael Lonsdale
	Richard Kiel
	Corinne Clery
	Emily Bolton
	Desmond Llewelyn
	Bernard Lee
	Lois Maxwell
DIRECTOR	Lewis Gilbert
PRODUCER	Albert R. Broccoli
SCREENPLAY	Christopher Wood
PRODUCTION DESIGNER	Ken Adam
EDITOR	John Glen
MUSIC	John Barry
TITLE SONG LYRICS	Hal David
	performed by Shirley Bass

Right: Roger Moore with latest Bond girl Holly Goodhead (Lois Chiles).

Left: The beautiful Corinne escorts bond to a meeting with Drax.

The selection of *Moonraker* as the eleventh James Bond epic came as a surprise to 007 fans who were informed by the end credits of *The Spy Who Loved Me* that *For Your Eyes Only* would be the next Bond film. Producer Cubby Broccoli, inspired by the phenomenal success of *Star Wars*, felt the time was appropriate to send Bond to his one remaining unexplored frontier: outer space. As the trailer would later boast, "Other films promise you the moon. *Moonraker* delivers!"

Meticulous care was taken to insure that *Moonraker* had its technical aspects rooted not in "science fiction, but science fact." NASA provided technicians and advisers to work with the filmmakers in order to maximize accuracy, while still allowing for the customary artistic licence. For example, during the climactic battle in space, one hears a crescendo of bombs and laser blasts, when, in reality, sound is undiscernible in space.

The plot concerned Bond's attempts to investigate the circumstances surrounding the mysterious disappearance of a U.S. space shuttle on loan to the British. The trail leads to billionaire Hugo Drax, a megalomaniac who plans to use the shuttle to transport his confederates to a city he has built in space. Here, he hopes to rule over a master race, while unleashing satellites to destroy the earth by means of a deadly nerve gas. Notably, Drax is an Equal Opportunity Dictator, as the "master race" includes beautiful, and corrupt, individuals from all races.

To say that this production is large in scope is an understatement akin to describing Jaws as a man with a slight dental problem. To launch the filming, Cubby Broccoli wined and dined his cast and cr in an elaborate party aboard the ISLE DE FRANCE. This was a symb gesture, as the film was shot primarily in France due to prohibit British tax laws in place at the time.

Moonraker's scope was such that the film tied up three of biggest studios in France, leaving only special effects functions to filmed at Bond's traditional base at Pinewood. A budget of $30 mill was allotted, a sum so staggering it caused director Lewis Gilbert observe that he could make several films for the cost of *Moonrak* phone bill.

> ❝ **Moonraker** *had its technical aspects rooted not in 'science fiction, but science fact'.* ❞

The production spanned exotic international locales including canals of Venice, the jungles of Brazil, the carnivals of Rio and the v limits of outer space. *Moonraker* would be Roger Moore's *Thunderb* rivaling the latter as "the biggest Bond of all." Every penny is up the on the screen as reflected in eye-popping special effects a gorgeous locales. Yet, *Moonraker* rivals *The Man With the Golden G* as the least satisfying entry in the series.

Bond attempts to escape an ambulance driven by Drax's henchmen.

A rehearsal shot for the pre-credits fight aboard the jet.

...se moment in the bell-tower ... with Chang.

What went wrong? The answer is humor, or rather, an overflow ... slapstick. To Bond fans, there never was a danger of the series ...ting stale. Therefore the decision to "lighten up" the Bond character ...he 1970s was seen by many as an unnecessary change. *Moonraker* ...rificed thrills for juvenile laughs at every turn. The pity is the film

> ## " *Take care of Mr. Bond – see that some harm comes to him.* "

...rowly misses being a satisfying effort. It is not poorly made or ...pelessly flawed. With tighter editing this could be a very exciting ...nd film. As it is, the sum of *Moonraker* totals less than its parts. As ...ger Moore biographer Roy Moseley pointed out, *Moonraker*'s ...ion sequences tend to rely on in-jokes and sight gags "instead of ...uations where Bond is fighting for his life."

The return of the Jaws character, used properly in *The Spy Who Loved Me*, is also a step in the wrong direction. Here, he is a Herman Munster-clone, who poses no formidable threat to anyone. By the way, just when will Bond learn that punching Jaws in his metallic teeth only causes damage to his own hand? The low point of Jaws's involvement with the series occurs when he falls in love with a buxom lass named Dolly. The two of these characters do more damage to the Bond image than anything Drax could ever dream up.

It is not fair, however, to dwell on the shortcomings found in *Moonraker*. In fact, the film contains many positive aspects and it never commits the cardinal sin of being dull. Just when one becomes disappointed at a less than satisfactory sequence, another more effective scene is already on the screen. Indeed, the first half hour or so is quite good, particularly during the early encounters between Bond and Drax, who is certainly the drollest of the Bond villains. As played by Michael Lonsdale in the role originally offered to James

Mason, Drax speaks in a monotonous tone that barely conceals a treacherous air of malevolence. He is also a man of dry wit, earning the biggest laugh in the film when he advises his henchman to, "Take care of Mr. Bond – see that some harm comes to him."

There are many other memorable scenes in *Moonraker*. One of the best occurs when Bond is duped into testing a centrifuge, which is used to acclimatize astronauts for the gravitational forces they will encounter during their mission. Bond is strapped into the unit, unaware that Drax has ordered his henchman, Chang, to engage the centrifuge to full speed, thereby causing 007's death. Experiencing ever-increasing gravitational forces, Bond realizes he is doomed. For the first time since Bond's encounter on the sabotaged exercise table in *Thunderball*, he is helpless to the point of near panic. Although he utilizes a device from "Q" to escape, the impact of the scene is considerable, because it is not compromised by any "Moore-ism". Bond suffers after this encounter in much the same way as he did when the tarantula crawled up his body in *Dr. No*. Roger Moore plays it straight this time, allowing Bond's human emotions to surface and the results are impressive.

While Moore does not break any new ground, the film does provide him with some good scenes. A particularly witty encounter with Drax remains one of Roger's best moments as 007. This occurs when Drax insists that Bond try his hand at pheasant shooting, thus making him a prime target for an assassin lurking in a nearby tree. Bond's shot misses the pheasant, causing Drax to scoff, "You missed, Mr. Bond". "Have I?", responds Bond as the sniper falls from the tree, the victim of Bond's "bad aim". The sequence is superbly played by both actors, with Moore delivering his line in an uncharacteristically understated fashion.

Bond's love interest is Dr. Holly Goodhead, played by Lois Chiles. Goodhead, a CIA agent planted in Drax Industries, reluctantly sides with Bond to track the missing shuttle. Chiles was considered for the role of Anya in *The Spy Who Loved Me*, but she informed Eon that she had temporarily retired. Years later she happened to be on an airplane seated next to Lewis Gilbert, who suggested she play the role of Goodhead, and this time a deal came to fruition. Chiles performance is pleasing, and her character represents the quint-essential Bond woman for the 1980s – beautiful, intelligent and self-reliant.

Another prominent love interest is Corinne, portrayed by French actress Corinne Clery. When we first meet her she is a humble employee in the Drax empire. She builds an affection for Bond that results in a night of lovemaking, but with tragic consequences. In a very eerie sequence, Drax confronts her with her betrayal, which leads to her gruesome demise courtesy of Drax's bloodthirsty Dobermans.

There is a spectacular climax in space in which Bond destroys Drax's space city with the aid of U.S. armed forces as well as Jaws, who has a last minute change of allegiance. While the effects are impressive, the laser battle between the space-suit clad armies lacks excitement, primarily because the actors must maneuver in slow

motion to simulate the lack of gravity. More effective are the sc[e] of destruction inside Drax's headquarters. Here Bond manage[s] dispose of Drax by utilizing a deadly dart gun and tossing the v[illain] into space with the witticism: "Take a giant step for mankind."

While it is undeniable that *Moonraker* confronts the audience [with] a mega-buck spectacle, it is difficult to relate to this James Bon[d as] the same character from earlier films. Yet, *Moonraker* receive[d a] generous share of positive reviews, largely from critics who did[n't] compare it to previous entries, but merely reveled in its gig[antic]

007 and Holly make zero-gravity love during the "climax" of *Moonraker*.

A moment of danger for 007 and Manuela at the carnival.

ope and humor. The film soared to the top of the summer box-
ffice hits, becoming the highest grossing Bond film to date.

The filmmakers could have pursued this lucrative path and ignored
e protests of Bond enthusiasts who demanded a return to more
elievable thrillers. However, despite the world-wide financial
ccess of *Moonraker*, Eon admitted that its slapstick content was
tistically wrong. In *For Your Eyes Only*, Bond would be brought "back
earth" in one of the best films of the Roger Moore era.

FOR YOUR EYES ONLY

Moonraker had elevated Bond-mania to its highest level since the mid-1960s, thus providing an eager audience for the return of the basic 007 in *For Your Eyes Only*. The formula chosen was not ground-breaking, but refreshing: it was decided that James Bond should return to his origins – in a suspenseful espionage thriller emphasizing mysterious characters and *earthly* adventures. To recapture 007's basics, the screenwriters combined elements of the two Ian Fleming novelettes: *Risico* and *For Your Eyes Only*, and added a liberal dose of original material. Eon believed the ultimate Bond spectacle had been achieved with *Moonraker*, and would not try to top its sheer visual spectacle.

A screenplay emerged emphasizing Bond as a cloak and dagger detective experiencing danger and anguish rather than a wise-cracking pundit who merely pushes buttons to escape life-threatening situations. The decision to send Bond on this path of gritty realism was not entirely without risk, as there still remained a huge audience embracing a hi-tech 007. Would audiences still embrace a human 007? Only once since *From Russia With Love* had such a realistic formula been attempted: recall *OHMSS* – the least successful 007 film at the box-office.

As with all Bond productions, numerous obstacles had to be overcome before the cameras could roll. Foremost, Roger Moore announced his retirement from the series, stating: "I don't want to take another six months out of my life to play James Bond again." When Moore refused all offers from Eon, Cubby Broccoli let it be known that the Bond films would continue – with or without Roger's

presence. Replacement actors underwent screen testing whil[e] script was being tailored for a new 007. Indeed, *FYEO*'s pre-cre[dits] sequence, set at the grave of Bond's deceased wife, was wri[tten] specifically to enable a new Bond to immediately establish a link w[ith] previous films.

> **❝ The filmmakers were burdened by the shortest pre-production period they had ever encountered. ❞**

Eventually, the personal intervention of Cubby Broccoli and United Artists' brass secured a deal allowing Moore to retur[n as] Bond. Because of these delays, the filmmakers were burdened by [the] shortest pre-production period they had ever encountered. [A] maddening pace was set in motion to insure a tight shooting sche[dule] at a number of globe-spanning locations including Greece, It[aly,] England, and the Bahamas.

Although Bond fans eagerly awaited the much publicized retur[n to] realism, skepticism arose during the pre-credits sequence. Thi[ngs] start promisingly, as we witness Bond solemnly visiting Tra[cy's] grave (shot on location at the historic Stoke Poges Church[yard]

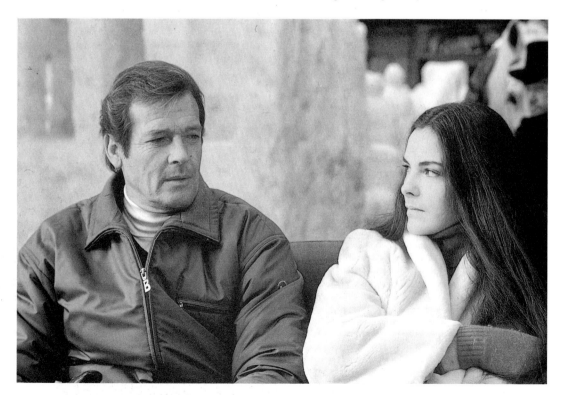

Bond and Melina get to know each other during a carriage ride.

kinghamshire). Roger Moore exhibiting a somber, introspective
ment is decidedly refreshing and one is grateful this sequence was
deleted upon Moore's re-signing.

hen it's business as usual, when Bond is summoned to head-
rters via helicopter. Within moments, his pilot is electrocuted
007 finds his chopper controlled by a bald-headed, wheelchair
nd villain (John Hollis, who although only seen from behind,
piciously resembles good old Blofeld) utilizing a cumbersome
tronic device that looks less complicated than a VCR remote
trol.

begins the perilous climb to
atos' mountain-top lair.

CREDITS	
OF RELEASE	1981
	Roger Moore
	Carole Bouquet
	Julian Glover
	Topol
	Lynn Holly-Johnson
	Cassandra Harris
	Jill Bennett
	Michael Gothard
	Jack Hedley
	Walter Gotell
	Lois Maxwell
	Desmond Llewelyn
TOR	John Glen
UCER	Albert R. Broccoli
UTIVE PRODUCER	Michael G. Wilson
ENPLAY	Richard Maibaum
	Michael G. Wilson
UCTION DESIGNER	Peter Lamont
	Bill Conti
SONG LYRICS	Michael Leeson
	performed by Sheena Easton

Left: 007 poses with Lotus number two while on location.

Above: Bond and his contact, Ferrara, become personally acquainted with the evil Kristatos.

e dismay of Gogol, Bond opts to
by the ATAC.

a mocking tone, he informs Bond that he has only moments to
Bond, however, simply disconnects a wire to gain control of the
copter, which he uses to scoop up his adversary's wheelchair and
p him into a smokestack. The scene is impressive from a technical
dpoint, as it embodies terrifying stuntwork and marvelous editing.
really do believe that's Roger Moore dangling perilously outside
helicopter, but again the accent on overt humor compromises the
ense.

ond purists may have groaned during these first minutes of Eyes.
vever, fans would discover that the filmmakers kept to their
d, delivering an exciting adventure story. Eyes works not only as a
itional Bond epic, but also as a first rate action thriller. This
ess is apparent during the sequence immediately following the
its. A fishing trawler (actually a British spy ship) housing a top
et device known as the ATAC strikes a mine and sinks within
onds. The ATAC, a device sending encoded signals to submarines
activate their nuclear missiles, remains intact and sets off an
rnational race to possess this powerful tool. For this gripping and
enseful sequence, thanks in part must go to John Grover's adroit
ing. We soon realize the mood of this Bond film will be heavier
anything experienced since OHMSS. In FYEO characters get hurt;
en they fall, they bleed and because of these basic rules, we fear
d himself might face considerable danger.

key player in creating the realistic atmosphere of FYEO was John
n, receiving the directorial reins following his work as editor and
ond unit director on several previous Bonds. According to Glen: "I
ost fell out of my chair when [Broccoli] said he wanted me to take
r the direction."

Glen confessed to experiencing "nervousness" but managed to
acquit himself admirably, bringing to FYEO a unique and refreshing
style.

Returning to the storyline, Bond is assigned to track down the
missing ATAC before enemy forces locate it and use it to launch
British missiles against NATO installations. Unfortunately, two
operatives of the Secret Service, marine biologist Timothy Havelock
and his wife are murdered prior to informing headquarters of the
ATAC's whereabouts. Bond joins forces with the Havelocks'

" As Melina, Carole Bouquet brings empathy, intensity, and depth to her role. "

daughter Melina, a beautiful and self-reliant woman who displays
considerable skill in both fending off Bond's advances and in wielding a
deadly crossbow. Bond wants the ATAC. Melina wants to avenge her
parents' murder. The trail leads to a charming, yet brutal, aristocrat
Kristatos, who plans to sell the ATAC to the KGB.

FYEO impresses on every level, especially with its first-rate cast. As
Melina, Carole Bouquet brings empathy, intensity, and depth to her
role, making her character the most fascinating Bond girl since Tracy
in OHMSS. Julian Glover's Kristatos is a most intriguing character. His
avuncular charm leads us to believe he is an ally of Bond. Later, his
brutal demeanor becomes all too apparent. Glover exhibits a
refreshing energy when compared to some Bond villains whose
physical menace was limited to impolite stares.

The scene-stealing trophy belongs to Topol of *Fiddler on the Roof* fame as Kristatos's arch-enemy Colombo, a lovable rogue who joins forces with Bond. His scenes are inevitably amusing and his character is warmly reminiscent of Kerim Bay in *FRWL*.

John Glen deserves praise for achieving what many thought to be an impossibility – persuading Roger Moore to portray Bond as though he were actually taking the part seriously. *FYEO* is, arguably, his best performance as 007. The witty one-liners still remain, but this time they are not at the expense of realism. Moore initially opposed the de-emphasis on the comedy content, and argued that audiences would not accept him in a sequence where Bond coldly kicks a precariously perched car, containing the assassin Locque, off a cliff. Glen won the argument and the scene is truly a highlight of Moore's contribution to the series.

The screenwriters wisely incorporated some excellent ideas from Fleming's novels that had not as yet been used in the films. They resurrected a sequence from *Live and Let Die* and wrote it into the *FYEO* script. This scene finds Bond and Melina being keelhauled by

Kristatos's motorboat. Menaced by sharks and razor-sharp coral, two appear doomed until 007 utilizes his wit, instead of a conver gadget, to effect an escape. Roger Moore and Carole Bouc performed many aspects of these stunts, ingesting enough sea w to float the DISCO VOLANTE! It is a remarkable scene contai something which is absent from most recent Bond adventu namely legitimate suspense.

> **❝ Roger Moore always looked heroic, whe he really couldn't stand heights. ❞**

FYEO also impresses with an exciting ski-chase (filmed by champ Willy Bogner); an assault by Bond and Colombo's for against an Albanian stronghold; and a hair-raising climax in which good guys try to recover the ATAC from a monastery secured Kristatos. In the latter scene, Colombo, Melina, and a

federates watch as 007 attempts to scale the sheer cliff-face of the
untain fortress, only to be savagely kicked by a villain. He plunges
r one hundred feet, jerking to an abrupt halt – his rope preventing
lummeting to certain death. Bond desperately resumes his climb,
he villain methodically hammers out the pinion bolts securing 007's
e to the cliff-face. The actual fall was accomplished by stuntman
Sylvester, who previously skied off a mountain in *The Spy Who
ed Me*.

Moore was not entirely out of harm's way, however. He later
alled: "I was paralyzed [on the mountain]. . . . I felt like I was going
all to my death, or else I was going to throw myself over the edge.
ok a lot of Valium to get me up there. I always looked heroic,
en I really couldn't stand heights."

Facing page: Bond, Colombo and their forces attack the Albanian stronghold of Kristatos.

Below: 007 takes cover from enemy fire.

Stunts represented only part of the challenge in a production plagued by problems. Most notably, stuntman Paolo Rigon was killed in an accident while filming the ski-bobsled chase. Sadly, veteran actor Bernard Lee, who for twenty years portrayed "M", died of cancer while preparing for *Eyes*. His death was a tragic blow to the entire Eon family. As tribute to Bernard, Cubby Broccoli refused to recast the role for *Eyes*, honoring "the only man who could push James Bond around".

If these calamities weren't enough to cope with, winter scenes at the Italian ski resort of Cortina were jeopardized by an unusually warm winter – snow was a rare commodity. Trucks had to be sent to the mountains to import the white stuff, and no fewer than forty-five trips were made. When the crew began filming in a 600-year-old monastery in Kalambaka, Greece, production was temporarily disrupted by monks of nearby monasteries who frowned on James Bond's reputation and renounced the film. The monks tried to halt filming by hanging protest banners across the landscape, hindering exterior shots. So, all things considered, director Glen faced quite a challenge to maintain any semblance of an organized schedule.

Yet, there was little doubt the patience of the cast and crew would be amply rewarded at the box-office. *Eyes* made theater cash registers jingle from New York to Hong Kong. This time, even the critics seemed inclined to praise a Bond film, primarily because the accent on realism was considered to be invigorating. *Variety* called the film "Top notch Bond" and the best directed 007 film since *OHMSS*. The review pinpointed what the filmmakers had hoped to achieve, stating: "It's a terrific, non-stop romp and only those exclusively into Bondian hardware should be disappointed."

Left: 007's romance with the Contessa will soon end in tragedy.

Below: Living on the edge: Bond and Melina in Cortina, Italy.

OCTOPUSSY

For James Bond, another celebrated plateau was reached with *Octopussy*, the thirteenth globe-hopping feature spanning a glorious 21-year celluloid lifetime. Over 007's landmark history, his filmmakers have delivered a wealth of guns, gadgets, glamour, guffaws and girls. During these turbulent years, the world would witness numerous triumphs and tragedies, as well as many short-lived fads. One of the few pop-era icons to survive and thrive throughout these years was Agent 007. Bond's everlasting popularity was precisely the problem Eon faced in 1983, as they prepared to release *Octopussy*. Ironically, their rival was none other than Sean Connery, who shocked the industry by enlisting for one more assignment as James Bond in an oft-delayed remake of *Thunderball*.

Titled *Never Say Never Again*, Connery's (non-Eon) mission, after a twelve-year hiatus, would be released in direct competition with *Octopussy* – a strategy which could threaten the box-office receipts of both films. The press geared for the "Battle of the Bonds" with 007 facing his greatest challenge – from himself! However, Connery's film was in trouble and the release date was postponed until the Fall. The film scored with audiences, but it was *Octopussy* which easily w the box-office battle, with even Connery praising its fantastic act sequences.

Octopussy blasts off to an unforgettable start with a pre-cre sequence that director John Glen touted as boasting the m incredible stuntwork ever filmed. The scene has Bond using

> **❝ Octopussy *contains more action in the first five minutes than can be found in most feature length films.* ❞**

Acrostar mini-jet to escape a heat-seeking missile, and w destructive consequences for his enemies below. As one critic state *Octopussy* contains more action in the first five minutes than can found in most feature length films.

llegedly initial plans called for the character of Octopussy to be a geful villainess using her knowledge of 007's tragic marriage to st his aid in annihilating SPECTRE. However, legal complications e still unresolved concerning the SPECTRE concept, and a plot "hatched" centering on priceless Fabergé eggs and other jeweled sures smuggled by a mysterious businesswoman who has her n female army of spiritual followers. (Shades of Pussy Galore!) ir simple smuggling operation rapidly evolves into something far re sinister, with thousands of lives and the safety of western ope dangling by a thread. Coupled with the traditional espionage- e intrigue, was a sub-plot centering on a maverick Soviet general o plots to heat up the Cold War via detonating a nuclear device in ope.

Advance word was that *Octopussy* would continue the trend ward realism resurrected with *For Your Eyes Only*. However, the shed product is reminiscent of *Goldfinger*'s embellishment of ndiose fantasy elements, while retaining intriguing aspects of ming's stories, notably *Octopussy* and *Property of a Lady*.

Apart from the occasional lapse into *Moonraker*-esque humor, for ample, 007 uttering a Tarzan yell while swinging on a vine, this nd film would satisfy not only general audiences but die-hard fans well. The result was the record-grossing 007 epic so far.

CREDITS	
YEAR OF RELEASE	1983
CAST	Roger Moore
	Maud Adams
	Louis Jourdan
	Kristina Wayborn
	Kabir Bedi
	Steven Berkoff
	Desmond Llewelyn
	Lois Maxwell
	Robert Brown
	Geoffrey Keen
	Vijay Amritraj
DIRECTOR	John Glen
PRODUCER	Albert R. Broccoli
EXECUTIVE PRODUCER	Michael G. Wilson
SCREENPLAY	George Macdonald Fraser
	Richard Maibaum
	Michael G. Wilson
PRODUCTION DESIGNER	Peter Lamont
EDITOR	John Grover
MUSIC	John Barry
TITLE SONG LYRICS	Tim Rice
	performed by Rita Coolidge

ve right: Bond gets a rude kening from a thug's razor sharp yo- device.

de magazine advertisement nmemorating the first day of filming.

ing page: 007 finds the erotic, but adly, allure of Octopussy too npting to resist.

007 BEGINS SHOOTING TODAY AT CHECKPOINT CHARLIE.

Photography begins this week at Checkpoint Charlie in West Berlin, followed by filming at Pinewood Studios, England and other locations in India, Germany, and the U.K.

ALBERT R. BROCCOLI presents
ROGER MOORE as IAN FLEMING'S
JAMES BOND 007 in

OCTOPUSSY

Produced by ALBERT R. BROCCOLI   Directed by JOHN GLEN
Executive Producer MICHAEL G. WILSON

FOR RELEASE JUNE 1983

MGM/UA ENTERTAINMENT CO

Bond is introduced to Penelope Smallbone, under the watchful eye of Miss Moneypenny.

Prior to filming, the standard stories were heard that Roger Moore would not continue for a sixth mission as Commander James Bond. However, Roger strapped on the Walther for one "last" fling as 007, with some insiders speculating he welcomed a showdown at the box-office with good friend Sean Connery. Cynics complained Moore was too old for the role, with one critic pondering if the credits would shout: "Roger Moore and His Stuntmen as James Bond!" Moore characteristically dismissed these barbs by saying he still performed all

> ## " Maud Adams confessed it took some effort to say the film's title without blushing. "

of his own stunts. He added, with a wink, "I also do all of my own lying!" But the image speaks for itself and Moore still commands a marvelous presence as 007, whether hanging from the wing of a plane, or walking unruffled wearing an immaculately tailored tuxedo through the scorching heat of India. The latter image caused Moore to sarcastically note that while everyone else dresses for the climate "Bond runs around like an idiot in a white dinner jacket!" Yes, Roger, but unlike everyone else, Bond never works up a decent sweat.

Moore had been criticized in the past for being unimpressive in action sequences. Octopussy renders that criticism meaningless. Witness Roger's impeccable timing in his fight with thugs in

Octopussy's palace. For once he seems filled with genuine aggres and we feel he's socking those villains for real. John Glen's direc makes the sequence one of the best in the film.

Equally exciting is the climax (although Octopussy features n climaxes than an X-rated movie!) wherein Bond, disguised as a cl feverishly tries to prevent the detonation of a nuclear devic Octopussy's circus. He is hampered by both officials and the pub he tries furiously to warn of the impending blast. Moore is exce here, conveying his fear and frustration convincingly. Consequen is one of those rare occasions that causes the audience to think worst might actually happen. Director Glen milks every b suspense, with the threat not averted until the bomb has ticked to count of zero. (Why, even Goldfinger allowed Bond seven s seconds!).

Maud Adams is particularly alluring as the title character. W approached for the role, Maud felt there was a mistake as it w long standing policy of Eon not to have actresses appear in m Bond roles more than once. Of course, Adams was Scaramanga fated mistress in The Man with the Golden Gun. Despite rumors either Faye Dunaway or Sybil Danning would land the role, Cu Broccoli personally broke his own golden rule and cast her as mysterious Octopussy. Maud happily accepted the part, confessed it took some effort to say the film's title without blus Her delight in reuniting with Roger Moore sparks a good de sexual chemistry. (Maud later visited Roger on the set of A View Kill, and is rumored to have made an appearance as an extra.)

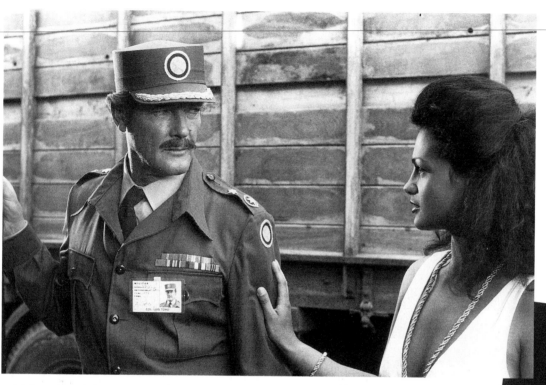

Bond in disguise to sabotage a hi-tech military aircraft.

Louis Jourdan as the devilish Kamal Khan an Afghan prince with evil intentions.

Unfortunately, the background of the Octopussy character is explored only peripherally. It would have been more fascinating to have made her the central villain, instead of a pawn in the grand scheme of Soviet General Orlov and world class smuggler Kamal Khan. However, the script did retain a foundation in Fleming's book, with Octopussy revealing she is the offspring of a rogue former agent of the British Secret Service. Her father, Major Smythe, had absconded with a fortune in gold, and Bond tracked him down and allowed him to commit suicide rather than be disgraced by the scandal.

Octopussy discovers her own talent for smuggling and recruits an organization of young women who are fiercely loyal to her. These ladies include beauty queens from Sweden, Great Britain, and other lands. In fact, the lack of men about the facilities implies that these are women who, shall we say, prefer women. Naturally, such tendencies are put on the "back burner" as soon as 007 arrives.

Octopussy boasts an interesting cast. A standout is Louis Jourdan's portrayal of Kamal Khan, a man who truly exalts in practising evil. Jourdan succeeds in his stated goal of conveying a mood of fun concealing his underlying villainy. In his most memorable scene with Bond, J.B. is – as customary – being wined and dined prior to his execution, with Jourdan describing the tortures 007 can look forward to. It is not the graphic dialogue that repulses as much as the bill of fare served for dinner – stuffed sheep's heads – from which Jourdan enthusiastically plucks and devours an eyeball.

Two distinguished Indian gentlemen are well cast in *Octopussy*. The first is tennis pro Vijay Amritraj, ably assisting Bond in a high-speed taxi chase through an Udaipur market-place. Vijay drives a "compar taxi – a three-wheeled vehicle, built at Pinewood, with a maximu speed of 70 m.p.h. Later, he is amusingly disguised as a snake charm who can be heard playing the James Bond theme on a flute. Amrit is, however, the film's sacrificial lamb and his role is "cut short" by razor bladed yo-yo!.

The second Indian actor cast to excellent effect is Kabir Bedi Gobinda, Khan's Oddjob-like henchman. Bedi and Moore battle it o on top of Khan's jet during the heart-stopping finale. Most of t scene was filmed before principal photography had begun, a insert shots of Moore and Bedi were completed in the last ten days

and his beauties: Roger Moore
Kristina Wayborn *(left)* and Maud
...s.

Octopussy and her loyal bodyguard

Magda investigates a noise, as 007 de
for cover.

ing. The stuntmen participating in this air battle were champion
rachutists whose death-defying proficiency minimized suspense
ording to John Glen. So, to maximize the thrills, he instructed them
lose their footing and slip at key moments. The result is one of the
st action sequences in any Bond film. Another marvelous moment
enjoy is when Khan realizes Bond is on the roof of his airborne jet,
d calmly tells Gobinda to "Go out and get him"; Gobinda swallows
d and the audience chuckles long.

Not without a measure of controversy, is the performance of
ted playwright and director Steven Berkoff as Orlov. Some found
over-the-top acting to be insightful and amusing, while others
nd it to be distracting and totally off the mark. Indeed, even the
hors have argued over this point for years!

However, virtually everyone praised Kristina Wayborn (originally
tted by Barbara Broccoli in a television movie) for her role as
topussy's henchwoman, Madga. Like Maud Adams, Wayborn is a
ive of Sweden, and her extraordinary looks and athletic abilities
used to maximum effect, including some of her own stuntwork.

❝ Octopussy *is majestic in its spectacular entertainment value.* ❞

Also on the supporting front, real life twins David and Tony Meyer
pear as murderous knife-throwers in roles originally written for
onraker. In a haunting sequence, reminiscent of Red Grant's pursuit
Bond's double in *From Russia With Love*, they stalk a doomed
tish agent through the underbrush. The two later engage in a
emorable fight with Bond on top of a speeding train.

Back at British Intelligence HQ, Robert Brown is promoted to the
e of "M", succeeding the late Bernard Lee. Lois Maxwell adds her
ual charm as Moneypenny, but this time she has a rival at the office
the form of her gorgeous assistant, Penelope Smallbone played by
chaela Clavell. What ever happened, Smallbone's typing skills must
ve been less impressive than her physical attributes, and she has yet
reappear in another Bond film. Desmond Llewelyn's "Q", joins
nd in the fray of battle, delivering 007 to the battlefield by way of
t air balloon – complete with Union Jack!

Octopussy is majestic in its spectacular entertainment value.
rticularly impressive are the production values which surpass even
ndian expectations, and where else, but in a Bond film, would India
represented as a paradise? The film's multitude of show-stopping
maxes leave the audience almost breathless. Blending realistic
rigue with traditional Bond fantasy, *Octopussy* was a sure-fire box-
fice smash. Critics also lauded it as outstanding entertainment with
e reviewer aptly noting: "What would summer be … without
nes Bond?"

Roger Moore in his sixth cinematic
mission as 007.

A VIEW TO A KILL

Bond desperately attempts to remove the bomb from Zorin's mine.

Facing page: Tanya Roberts, Grace Jones and Christopher Walken flank Roger Moore in his 007 swan-song.

A *View to a Kill* is not one of the more widely discussed Ja[ ] Bond films, although it closed the Roger Moore era and [ ] entire style of Bond movie produced since 1973. Moo[ ] portrayal of Bond may be eternally debated by 007 aficiona[ ] However, for younger fans, Roger Moore *was* James Bond, as m[ ] as Sean Connery was to the "oldsters".

Prior to filming, Moore announced his retirement from the Bo[ ] role, and on this occasion he appeared adamant. However, des[ ] Cubby Broccoli's determination to test other actors for the 007 r[ ] Roger decided to enlist for one last hitch as Bond. What motiva[ ] Moore's turnaround? It's easier to sweat top secret information ou[ ] Bond than it is to get a straight answer from Moore. Commenting [ ] the press, he explained: "Actually, I'm playing Bond again becaus[ ] feel sorry for Cubby. He'll have a terrible job finding someone e[ ] who works as cheaply as I do". He then added with characteristic s[ ] mockery, "I'm glad people are still misguided enough to employ me[ ]

As usual, contractual challenges were merely the tip of the iceb[ ] in bringing the story to theater screens. Just before production beg[ ] Eon received the shocking news that the 007 Stage at Pinewood h[ ] burned to the ground, jeopardizing the start date for filming. Due [ ] the sheer scope of the film, no other sound stage could accommod[ ] the requirements of the filmmakers. Yet, postponing product[ ] could have been catastrophic, as the cast and crew would be mov[ ] on to other projects. The solution? In an incredible feat worthy [ ] Bond himself, Broccoli insured that the entire stage was rebuil[ ] within four months. To honor Cubby, Pinewood renamed [ ] resurrected work, "The Albert R. Broccoli 007 Stage". The pr[ ]

CREDITS	
YEAR OF RELEASE	1985
CAST	Roger Moore
	Tanya Roberts
	Christopher Walken
	Grace Jones
	Patrick Macnee
	Patrick Bauchau
	David Yip
	Fiona Fullerton
	Alison Doody
	Desmond Llewelyn
	Robert Brown
	Lois Maxwell
	Walter Gotell
DIRECTOR	John Glen
PRODUCERS	Albert R. Broccoli
	Michael G. Wilson
SCREENPLAY	Richard Maibaum
	Michael G. Wilson
PRODUCTION DESIGNER	Peter Lamont
EDITOR	Peter Davies
MUSIC	John Barry
TITLE SONG LYRICS	John Barry and Duran Duran
	performed by Duran Duran

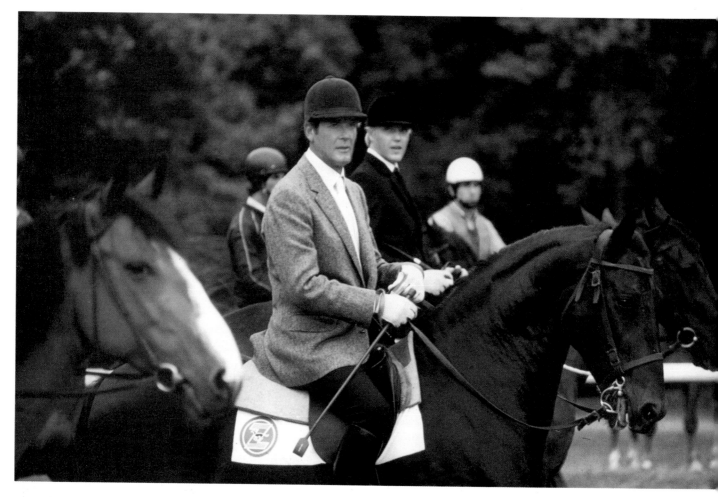

attended the Grand Re-opening Ceremony, hosted by Roger Moore and Tanya Roberts. Roger quipped the huge stage was named for Cubby "... because of the size of his heart – and wallet!"

Roberts, whose performance in *The Beastmaster* impressed Cubby Broccoli, was hand-chosen by the producer to portray leading Bond girl Stacey Sutton. A less than traditional presence was provided by

Bond must escape his pursuers by utilizing skis, snowmobiles, and finally a snow surfboard.

New Wave singer Grace Jones, as villainess May Day. The most inspired piece of casting was Christopher Walken as central heavy, Max Zorin. Snaring Walken was a coup, marking the only time to date that a Bond villain has been played by an Oscar winner ("best supporting actor", *The Deer Hunter*, 1979). Walken was thrilled at

being cast in a Bond film, as he was a self-professed 007 fan who w awed by *From Russia With Love* at age fifteen, and greatly influen by Robert Shaw's portrayal of Red Grant.

Typically, the logistics of bringing a Bond film to the screen prov enormous. Witness the pre-credit sequence, set in Siberia. Bo must escape his pursuers by utilizing skis, snowmobiles, and finall snow surfboard, allowing him to coast atop the frozen tundra. T sequence was filmed at Glacier Lake in Iceland, and Vadrietta Scersen, a locale in the Swiss Alps. The snow-surfing double Roger Moore was a young American named Steve Link, a wo champion in the sport. His task was Herculean, as the caverno openings in the ice were capable of swallowing an unsuspecting skie

Other challenges came in the shape of the Eiffel Tower, Californ Golden Gate Bridge, and downtown San Francisco.

In Paris, city officials were understandably reluctant to gra permission to film Bond's chase of May Day up the Eiffel Tow where the villainess was to parachute off the edifice onto a wait boat on the Seine River. But Broccoli carried enough prestige, a gained permission to film the sequence in the early morning ho the minimum disruption to traffic. In true Bondian fashion, one proved to be all that was necessary.

[Sa]n Francisco city officials delighted Eon by co-operating fully. [Per]mission was granted for City Hall to be set ablaze (under close [cont]rol) and for a spectacular chase in which the police force is [prac]tically demolished while pursuing a fire truck commandeered [by 0]07. For the film's breathtaking climax Bond dangles perilously [from] a tow rope attached to Zorin's blimp as it approaches the [Gol]den Gate Bridge. The stunt was achieved by Moore's double, [wea]ring a harness as he was swept through the sky at 750 feet above [San] Francisco Bay. For camera close-ups of the principals, who [enga]ge in a struggle to the death on top of the bridge, three duplicate [bridg]e sets were built at Pinewood, each of which was fifty feet high.

[Vi]ew's production schedule accelerated at a whirlwind pace, with [up] to six units shooting simultaneously. Extensive time and effort [wer]e required for an "explosive" sequence where Walken double-[cro]sses his men by detonating a series of bombs in a silver mine, [cau]sing the river above to come flooding through – one million gallons [of w]ater stored in a specially constructed reservoir were used.

Facing page: Bond nervously senses that Zorin's steeplechase is far from a standard course.

"Q", Moneypenny, Bond and "M" enjoy a day at the races, but it's all in the line of duty.

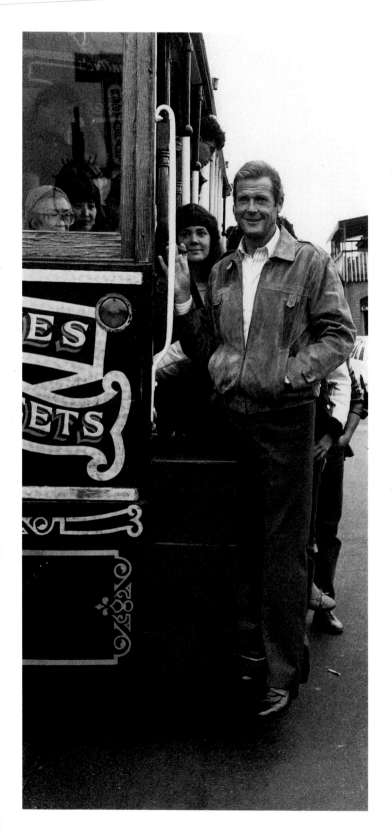

But how does the film fare as entertainment? Well, it ha[s] moments, and that seems to be the problem. The script is not ov[er] involving, so the film is best examined through the effectivenes[s] individual scenes. *View* digresses from the less humorous aspec[ts] Bond we had seen recently, and returns to the slapstick worl[d] *Moonraker*, admittedly with better results. The film's faults [are] exemplified by a comment from screenwriter Richard Maibaum, [who] stated his intent was to capitalize on every chance for the sak[e] humor; unfortunately, much of it is too silly and too frequent.

The pre-credits sequence is undeniably impressive and stunni[ngly] directed. However, it is marred by the inclusion of *California Gir[ls]* an audio joke on the soundtrack as Bond surfs away from [his] enemies. Another scene that impresses from a technical standpoi[nt] the fire truck chase in San Francisco; yet, it exists only as a platf[orm] for some juvenile laughs. In this scene and the taxi chase in P[aris] Bond's driving endangers more of the population than does any [plan] hatched by Zorin. 007 may have a Licence to Kill, but some[one] should revoke his Licence to Drive!

The casting in this film is almost perfect – the key word b[eing] almost. Tanya Roberts' performance inspires unintentional laugh[ter] despite her earlier assurances that Stacey Sutton would not be [just] another dumb blonde. That bravado gains little support when [she] must be warned that Zorin's blimp is "sneaking up" on her. [One] might ask how a blimp the size of a tennis stadium can sneak up [on] anyone; but it seems logical for Roberts' character.

Far more interesting is Grace Jones as May Day. Lean, mean [and] Herculean in strength, she is one of the most fascinating Bond vill[ains] in recent years. Jones feared director John Glen would try to sub[due]

" *View returns to the slapstick world of* Moonraker. "

her bizarre appearance. Instead, he encouraged her to be [as] outrageous as possible. It was a wise decision. Jones is every b[it a] match for Bond both on the battlefield and in the bedroom. Ther[e is] a hilarious scene as Bond attempts to seduce Jones, only to have [the] latter assume a position dominating the world's greatest chauvinist.

As Zorin, Christopher Walken plays the villain in an affable, bo[yish] way. His plan – to gain a monopoly of the world's micro-chip mar[ket] by destroying Silicon Valley – is less an obsessive goal than an amus[ing] time-killer for a filthy rich psychopath. Zorin is the product [of] obscene genetics experiments undertaken by his mentor, a Nazi [war] criminal. Yet, due to Walken's excellent portrayal, there is someth[ing] almost endearing about this lunatic, and his scenes bristle with wit.

On the supporting front, *View* marks the last Bond film bles[sed] with Lois Maxwell's portrayal of Miss Moneypenny. It is touching [to] watch the by-play between Moore and Maxwell, and one is grate[ful] for the wonderful scenes Lois has contributed to the Bond s[aga] Patrick MacNee, a special agent in his own right via *The Avengers*,

rather brief role as Bond's confederate helping to pentrate Zorin's
r. Unfortunately, McNee is strangled by Grace Jones as his Rolls
oyce enters a car wash, no less!

The most impressive sequence in *View* is the fight between Moore
nd Walken high up on the Golden Gate Bridge. The editing and
ecial effects are so good here, it is almost impossible to detect the

> **(As Zorin, Christopher Walken plays the villain in an affable, boyish way.))**

untmen from the actors. Amusing in a strange way is Walken's
eath plunge from the bridge, immediately preceded by his silly little
ckle. It's as though he enjoys the irony of having lost the battle —
en though it has cost him his life. Worthy of special mention is
uran Duran's title song which is one of the most inspired and
xciting of the series.

View clicked at the box-office, particularly in markets outside of the
nited States. Some critics, however, were unfairly harsh in their
eatment of Roger Moore. One cynical scribe noted: "He's not only
long in the tooth — he's got tusks!" Yet undeniably, for twelve years he
accomplished what many felt was impossible – successfully filling Sean
Connery's shoes. He did so by developing his own, unique
interpretation of Bond, and his films were tremendous financial
successes, proving that the public approved his James Bond. The
Moore-Bonds contained some memorable scenes that only Roger
could have played, and 007 fans owe him a huge debt for a job that
was very well done.

As for the continued success of the series, Cubby Broccoli said: "It
seems to work. [The formula] has been going on now for twenty-
four years. Maybe we're doing something right." How is that for an
understatement!

Facing page: Moore enjoys the sights
while on location in San Francisco.

Moore gets an idea of what it's like on
the other side of the lens.

THE LIVING DAYLIGHTS

An important milestone marked the 25th-anniversary of the James Bond films. Prior to 007's fifteenth film adventure, Roger Moore retired with honors from Her Majesty's Secret Service. Hence, an attempt to secure a foundation for Bond in the 1990s was undertaken with the predictable fanfare inherent in finding the right actor to fill 007's shoes. There was no doubt the new Bond had to be a British actor, youthful enough to retain his handsome but deadly look over a number of years, and of course, possessing the acting talent to do justice to a role immortalized by the immensely popular Sean Connery and Roger Moore; but not forgetting George Lazenby who had earned his share of admirers.

❝ *Dalton expressed a desire to recapture the essence of Fleming's novels.* ❞

Some journalists touted the popular and sexy TV actor Pierce Brosnan as the heir apparent; and Brosnan made it clear he wanted to rise to the challenge, and become a major presence on the wide screen. According to Brosnan's wife, Cassandra Harris (a 007 girl in *For Your Eyes Only*), the couple had dined with the Broccolis one evening, and on the way home, Brosnan could not resist practising that immortal line of dialogue: "My name is . . . ." Well, you know the rest. Ironically, when it became known Brosnan was a contender for 007, the producers of his recently cancelled television series *Remington Steele* decided to cash in on the publicity. The show was resurrected for a series of tele-movies, thus jeopardizing any claim Brosnan had to the Bond crown. He grudgingly resumed his television work only to have the show canceled again, a short while later.

Rumors abounded, speculating that everyone from actor Sam Neill to unknown Australian model Finlay Light had received the coveted licence to kill. However, Eon surprised everyone with the announcement that Welsh actor Timothy Dalton was confirmed as the new 007. Hailed by many as the best dramatic actor to assume the role, Dalton had been considered for the part on three previous occasions. This time, Dalton accepted with enthusiasm stating: "It's probably every kid's dream to play James Bond — chasing after gorgeous women and beating up the bad guys. He is the ultimate fantasy figure, and I know I wanted to be 007 when I saw the early Connery films. Now, I am here getting paid to live out a childhood fantasy."

It is significant that Dalton recalled Connery's interpretation of the role, back to the days when Sean's Bond was an agent living on the edge. Timothy Dalton expressed a desire to recapture the essence of

CREDITS	
YEAR OF RELEASE	1987
CAST	Timothy Dalton
	Maryam d'Abo
	Jeroen Krabbe
	Joe Don Baker
	John Rhys-Davies
	Art Malik
	Andreas Wismiewski
	Desmond Llewelyn
	Robert Brown
	Caroline Bliss
	Walter Gotell
DIRECTOR	John Glen
PRODUCERS	Albert R. Broccoli
	Michael G. Wilson
SCREENPLAY	Richard Maibaum
	Michael G. Wilson
PRODUCTION DESIGNER	Peter Lamont
EDITORS	John Grover
	Peter Davies
MUSIC	John Barry
TITLE SONG LYRICS	Pal Waaktaar and John Barry performed by a-ha

007 meets royalty. As Timothy Dalton gives Prince Charles a tour of the set, Cubby Broccoli explains some technicalities to the Princess of Wales.

The new James Bond has an old problem: too many women, not enough time.

eming's novels, stating: "Bond is a man who can get killed at any oment and *that* stress and danger is reflected in the way he lives". alton's desire to take the Bond character seriously was applauded ∙ die-hard 007 fans worldwide, and director John Glen seemed thused about working with the new actor stating "With Timothy, with Sean, he'd just as soon [coldly] kill an adversary". Connery, nself, is on record saying that Dalton was an inspired choice.

Timothy Dalton, promoted as "The Most Dangerous Bond — /ER!" debuted with a mission based on Ian Fleming's novelette, *The ving Daylights*. As the screenplay was already being written while the 07 casting search convened, it was agreed that the dialogue would ve to be modified to match the new Bond's interpretation. When alton assumed the role, re-writes were undertaken to remove the morous references of Roger Moore's Bond, and the emphasis was ifted toward the darker side of agent 007.

The first screen close-up of James Bond number four, Timothy Dalton.

Right: Bond "murders" Pushkin in an elaborate ruse.

We see an example of the new, grittier Bond in the pre-credits sequence. It was decided that Dalton possessed such an impressive, natural screen presence, there was no need for an elaborate build-up to establish his arrival. We meet 007 and some fellow agents carrying out a dangerous training mission on the Rock of Gibraltar. A double agent sabotages the mission and murders Bond's colleagues; 007 gives chase and engages the villain in a superbly directed sequence which finds the men locked in a death struggle within a fiery Land Rover that ultimately plunges over a lofty cliff. Bond complete with parachute conveniently lands safely on a yacht, surprising an inquisitive young lady who asks the name of her unexpected, but welcome intruder. Dalton, unlike his predecessors, initially refuses to succumb to temptation. He gruffly and unemotionally identifies himself with a hurried, "Bond. James Bond", and becomes engrossed in reporting his position to HQ. Dalton's Bond definitely places business before pleasure, although it takes less than thirty seconds before he relents to the bikini-clad beauty.

Daylights returns Bond to the environment from whence he came – the intriguing espionage thriller. It is a topical adventure, with 007 in a complex plot involving political defections, double agents, romance with a beauteous KGB agent, the Soviet occupation of Afghanistan, and a battle to the death with a ruthless arms merchant. The script allows Dalton to bring a welcome intensity to the Bond character, and 007 is as Fleming depicted him: ruthless and deadly, yet capable of tenderness and affection. What Dalton brings to Bond is a human touch akin to George Lazenby's interpretation of the role.

Dalton has many memorable scenes. He means business – he is determined yet unpredictable, and this "wild card" factor helps keep the audience on edge. On the romantic side, Dalton and leading lady Maryam d'Abo exude some genuine chemistry. This is especially evident in the sequences in Vienna as they tour the city in a horse-drawn carriage, and when they cuddle on the famed Wiener Prater's ferris wheel which Bond conveniently arranges to halt as they reach the top.

Maryam d'Abo secured the role of Kara (a naïve Czech cellist persuaded to pose as a KGB assassin) when she was selected to perform screen tests with Pierce Brosnan. In a twist of irony, it was she who ultimately, and unexpectedly, landed a key role in the film.

Facing page: Maryam d'Abo, Timothy Dalton and director John Glen.

Above: Bond and Kara in the film's romantic climax.

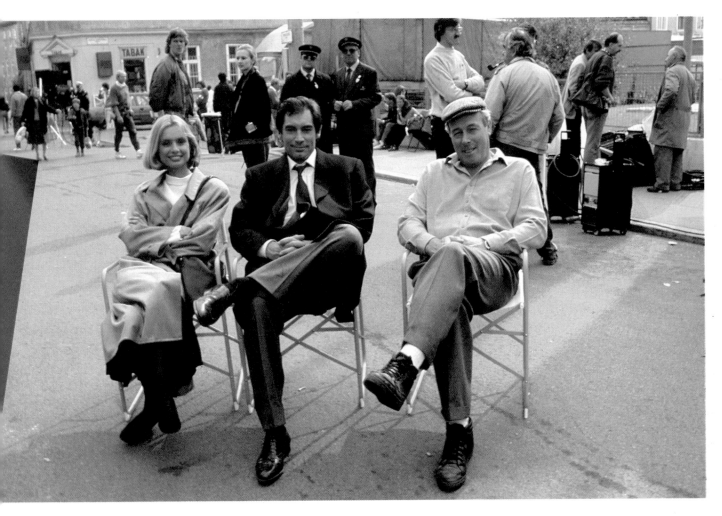

haring Dalton's enthusiasm for realism, d'Abo underwent extensive
ractice with the cello; and like Dalton, she performed many of her
wn stunts.

It is noteworthy that this Bond is an (almost) one woman man.
ome speculated this was to promote the "Safe Sex" environment of
day. But, more probably, the script called for a return to Fleming's
oncept of J.B. involved with but a single love interest in each story.
Vhich also legitimizes the lead female character beyond the level of
1 impersonal sexual plaything for 007. Ms. d'Abo is not the
atuesque, busty type Bond girl traditionally starring in the earlier
ms. As she admitted: "Kara is very intelligent and natural – not a sex
mbol or I wouldn't have been chosen!"

While it is undeniable the lead characters have been somewhat
tered from previous films, the overall Bond recipe of extraordinary
tion and spectacular adventure has not been tampered with.
aylights continues to provide audiences with an abundance of fight
equences, marvelously choreographed to imply brutality with the
inimum of bloodshed. The battle between the terrifying Necros

and a British agent is effectively directed and edited, and described
appropriately by one critic as: "The best kitchen fight since *Gremlins*!"
Likewise, Bond's fight with a sadistic jailer recalls the intensity of the
earlier films.

> ## ❝ *This Bond is an (almost) one woman man.* ❞

Undeniably, the most stunning action scene follows the airfield
battle with Bond and his Afghan allies against the Soviet forces. We
witness Bond and Necros dangling precariously from cargo netting
suspended from the exterior of an airborne Hercules transport
plane. As the two cling to life by a thread, they must also fend off
each other's punches. In a touch worthy of Hitchcock, we see their
only lifeline – a single strand of rope – slowly uncoil while a bomb on
board ticks down toward Armageddon.

Bond tangles with the jailer in a Soviet military prison.

Facing page: Disguised as an Afghan, Bond aids in the assault on the Soviet air base.

This incredible sequence was enacted by stuntmen Jake Lomba and B.J. Worth, who previously parachuted from the Eiffel Tower *A View to A Kill*. The stunt was as dangerous as it appears onscree and Worth came close to losing his life. The sequence ends with Bon dispatching Necros, disarming the bomb, and driving a jeep out of t cargo transport with the plane still in flight. (Dalton had troub controlling the jeep, and the scene required numerous takes.) T end result of all this, however, is an action set piece that caused o critic to exclaim: "I had to keep reminding myself those are actua *people* up there [performing the stunts]".

Mr. Bond is also rewarded with a brand new vehicle – the Ast Martin Volante – proving a worthy successor to its classic pare Thanks to the usual modifications by Q Branch, 007 is provided w amusing opportunities to lay waste to the enemy. For example, th

Aston Martin's laser device dissects the undercarriage of a Czech police car, causing the vehicle to skid uncontrollably while its chassis remains behind. 007 utilizes all of the car's options, including the self-destruct mechanism, allowing the noble vehicle to exit with a bang.

Disappointingly, the villains in *Daylights* are not up to the usual

❝ It's as though Dalton always was James Bond. ❞

megalomaniacal standards of previous adversaries. The principal villain, Soviet general Koskov, is subdued and quite charming; making Charles Gray's Blofeld resemble Attila the Hun! Jovially portrayed by Dutch actor Jeroen Krabbe, Koskov is more amusing than menacing. His conspirator is evil arms merchant Brad Whitaker, a frustrated Rambo with an obsession for military history, whose penchant for

recreating famous battles with an army of miniature soldie ironically leads to his Waterloo. Joe Don Baker's portrayal of t lunatic shows promise, but Whitaker is given too little screen time make an impression. More menacing is famed ballet star and ac Andreas Wisniewski portraying Red Grant-type henchman Necr This cold-blooded assassin kills with tenacity, employing a uni murder weapon: the headphones of his Sony Walkman, wh suspiciously plays only one song – The Pretenders' "Where H Every Body Gone".

Caroline Bliss takes over duties as the new Miss Moneypenny, a although casting a younger actress in the role may have be desirable, one wishes stronger scenes could have been written her debut. She is far too beautiful to convince us she has alternative but to stay home, hoping Bond might drop in for nocturnal interlude. Robert Brown and Desmond Llewelyn are ba of course, and are as watchable as ever. John Barry contributes atmospheric score, and the title song from a-ha is memorable.

The Living Daylights made a perfect vehicle to launch Timothy Dalton into the high-gear world of James Bond. To his credit, the transition was a seamless one. It's as though Dalton always was James Bond. His performance seemed to have inspired the filmmakers as well, with Variety correctly commenting: "[Daylights] will be tough to top . . . everyone seemed up for this one, and it shows." Audiences agreed, and Dalton's debut adventure broke box-office records around the world.

Facing page: Dalton takes aim during the carnival sequence in Vienna.

Below: The struggle to the death with Necros aboard the cargo plane.

LICENCE TO KILL

Simply stated, *Licence to Kill* is the best James Bond movie since *The Spy Who Loved Me* and, arguably, since *On Her Majesty's Secret Service*. Aficionados of the early films were thrilled by Timothy Dalton's debut in *The Living Daylights*, which seemed to confirm that the era of slapstick in 007 films had officially ended. However, even die-hard purists doubted they would be able to revel in a Fleming-type thriller again.

The première of *Licence to Kill* proved that not only was Bond still a viable entity for the 1990s, but also there was always danger in underestimating the surprises agent 007 was capable of springing. Most gratifying is the fact that the movie succeeds not only because it emulates the earlier films, but because it also dares to be highly original. Twenty-seven years after his debut in *Dr. No*, James Bond proves there is more life in him than most of the new generation screen heroes put together.

Bringing the basics back to Bond was not an easy choice for producers Cubby Broccoli and Michael Wilson. They could have been content to follow the old adage, "If it ain't broke, don't fix it." Roger Moore's light-hearted approach generated the most successful films of the series, and Dalton's debut – serious in nature, but retaining many of the humorous elements – was also an international hit. Yet Dalton had longed to bring the series back to the spirit of Fleming's original creation where 007 relied mostly on his wits, as opposed to a hi-tech arsenal, to extricate himself from dea[?] situations. As Dalton stated: "We've got the film back in the wo[rld] James Bond should inhabit. We've left the tongue-in-cheek hum[or] and caricature behind".

Dalton and the producers realized that, just as Roger Moore co[uld] not be accepted in an overly serious Bond thriller, Dalton was unlik[ely] to win plaudits for competing with Bob Hope in the area [of] wisecracks. The veteran members of the Eon team had to quic[kly] adjust to switching gears and rise to the challenge of changing [the] James Bond image while not alienating loyal audiences.

Initially, the concept was to film in China, and two screenpl[ays] were drafted dealing with Bond's entanglement with an Oriental d[rug] lord. However, several factors caused this concept to be shelved. F[or] one, *The Last Emperor* was released and succeeded in being the f[irst] film from the West to showcase the grandeur of China. Secondly, t[he] producers quickly learned that logistical and budgetry conce[rns] would make location filming highly impractical. Co-producer a[nd] esteemed veteran Bond writer Richard Maibaum drafted a revis[ed] script retaining the drug-related aspect, but changing the locale to [a] fictional South American country, Isthmus. Unfortunately, befo[re] work on a finalized shooting script could begin, the Writers' Gu[ild] went on strike, forcing Maibaum to withdraw from the producti[on] and walk a picket line.

007 has a violent introduction to Pam Bouvier, who is well equipped to handl[e] bar-room brawlers.

CREDITS	
YEAR OF RELEASE	1989
CAST	Timothy Dalton
	Carey Lowell
	Robert Davi
	Talisa Soto
	Anthony Zerbe
	Frank McRae
	Everett McGill
	Wayne Newton
	Desmond Llewelyn
	David Hedison
	Robert Brown
	Caroline Bliss
DIRECTOR	John Glen
PRODUCERS	Albert R. Broccoli
	Michael G. Wilson
SCREENPLAY	Michael G. Wilson
	Richard Maibaum
EDITOR	John Grover
PRODUCTION DESIGNER	Peter Lamont
MUSIC	Michael Kamen
TITLE SONG	Gladys Knight

Timothy Dalton strikes a debonair pose
in his second 007 adventure.

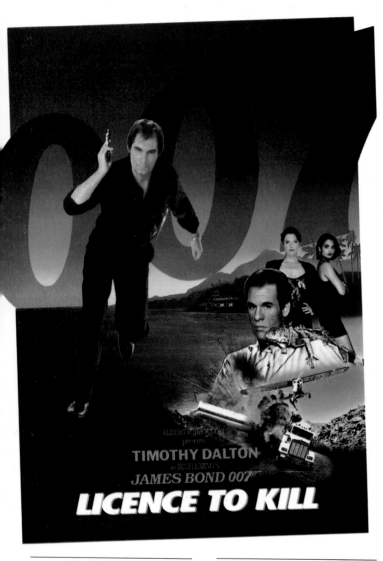

Artwork for the British ad campaign.

Right: Bond goes into action after being discovered aboard the research vessel.

Facing page: Bond gets a jealous glance from Pam when he observes the obvious charms of Lupe.

Michael Wilson wrote the final screenplay and deserves credit, only for producing one of the most engrossing stories in the ser but also for sharing credit with Maibaum as a full co-author. Wils drew from contemporary headlines to create a story involv revenge, drug smuggling, and traditional Bondian spectacle. As other recent Bonds, discarded elements from previously film Fleming novels were incorporated into the screenplay, and there a key characters and scenes inspired by *Live and Let Die* and *Hildebrand Rarity*.

The film begins with a somewhat light-hearted scenario in wh we see 007 and old CIA buddy Felix Leiter *en route* to the latte wedding, where Bond will serve as best man. The men are detour by the opportunity to capture an international drug kingpin nam Sanchez. This is accomplished by Bond lowering himself from helicopter cable to literally tie a noose around Sanchez's plane a hoist it away. Having snared their man, Bond and Leiter jump fr

> ** Sanchez, as portrayed by Robert Davi, is a Bond villain to remember. **

the 'copter and make a spectacular landing in front of the church j in time for the wedding, as the credits begin to roll.

The scene is rather effective and helped by the fact that here, throughout the rest of the film, Timothy Dalton is actually doing m of his stunt work. He is modest in discussing his contribution to t area, stating that knowing too much of how a scene is filmed ruins t impact for the audience. Nevertheless, it's likely that even the fictio 007 would hesitate before dangling out of a plane at 800 feet!

In a suspenseful scene, Sanchez's prison van is hijacked and crashes into the ocean, where scuba divers rescue the drug lord. Sanchez makes immediate, and chilling, plans for revenge. As portrayed by Robert Davi, this is a Bond villain to remember. His Sanchez is a walking paradox – capable of ordering acts of unspeakable cruelty, but somehow maintaining a warped code of honor that is almost admirable. He is also one of those rare adversaries to pose a serious physical threat against 007.

The film takes a nasty turn when Sanchez's men kill Leiter's wife and kidnap Felix. In the grisliest moment ever in a Bond film, Sanchez warns the helpless agent that, "There are worse things than death", and proceeds to feed Leiter to a shark, which devours one of his legs. Bond later discovers the body of Leiter's wife, and the horribly mutilated Felix. In a famed moment from the *Live and Let Die* novel, Bond finds a note on the wounded man that reads: "He disagreed with something that ate him". It is here that Timothy Dalton's acting skills come into full force. His look of rage, combined with the frustration of helplessness, lets the audience know this is a Bond that is unpredictable – and *very* dangerous. It is a superb performance, and one that erases any memory of other Bond actors. With *Licence*, Dalton cements his own persona on 007, and the results are more than impressive.

❝ Bond is now a rogue agent with no official resources to fall back on. ❞

Numerous emotional high points follow, most notably in the scene between Bond and "M" when 007's licence to kill is revoked because of his refusal not to pursue Sanchez to avenge Leiter. The dialogue between Dalton and Robert Brown bristles with a tension not evident since the days of Sean Connery and Bernard Lee. When *Bond* defies his boss and runs off, he is now a wanted man and a rogue agent with no official resources to fall back on.

Pam Bouvier's figure distracts 007 fr[o]
the assignment at hand.

Bond soon comes into contact with two women, Pam Bouvier (Carey Lowell) a freelance pilot with ties to the CIA, and Lupe (Talisa Soto), the reluctant girlfriend of Sanchez. Naturally, the relationships are unfriendly to begin with, but eventually lead to romantic and sexual encounters. Lowell is the perfect Bond girl – gorgeous, self-sufficient, and equally at home in the midst of a bar fight or wearing a stunning evening gown. Oh, yes – she also scores in the acting stakes. Like Lowell, Soto is a well-known fashion model, and *Licence to Kill* was only her second film, and while her emotional range is somewhat limited, she holds her own in some very intimidating company. Her exotic beauty certainly has few equals among her Bondian predecessors.

Licence is perhaps the most meticulously cast of recent 007 epics. Even the smallest roles are expertly filled, and there are no weak links among the actors. Solid support is given by Anthony Zerbe and Everett McGill as the ill-fated confederates of Sanchez. Young Puerto Rican actor Benicio del Toro has a menacing physical presence as the henchman Dario, and even Pedro Armendariz Jr. shows up in a cameo role unrelated to his father's memorable characterization of Kerim Bay in *From Russia with Love*. David Hedison reprises his Felix Leiter role from *Live and Let Die*, the only time that the agent has

been portrayed twice by the same actor. Hedison does well in t[he] role, which for once allows him the opportunity to do some r[eal] acting.

A much needed element of humor in the grim storyline is provid[ed] by the marvelous Desmond Llewelyn as "Q", ironically his largest r[ole] to date in a film which utilizes very few gadgets. His arrival in Isthm[us] to help Bond, "off the record", demonstrates an emotional eleme[nt] between the two men that has not been seen previously. Llewely[n's] timing allows him to drift between genuine sentiment and laug[h] inducing improvision. The scene in which he callously discards a ra[dio] containing a walkie-talkie is a beauty, considering how many tim[es] "Q" has chastised 007 for not treating his gadgets with respect! Mo[re] hilarity is provided by the inspired and off-beat casting of Las Veg[as] legend Wayne Newton as a corrupt evangelist whose empire i[s a] front for Sanchez.

Licence marked only the second time that Pinewood was not us[ed] as the main studio (*Moonraker* being the first occasion). For co[st] considerations, Eon opted to shoot at Churubusco Studios in Mexi[co] City. This saved some money, but added to the frustration as t[he] Mexicans – while very co-operative – did not have the state-of-th[e] art resources to which the Bond team had become accustomed. The polluted atmosphere and oppressive heat added to their worries, and the company doctor had his work cut out for him insuring the cast and crew remained healthy. Notable locations included Key West, Florida, Acupulco, Durango, and Vera Cruz. As virtually everything had to be imported to the Mexican locations, the budget still weighed in at a hefty $36 million.

By far the most grueling aspect of the filming took place at Mexicali, a remote region of desert, where the climactic tanker truck chase between Bond and Sanchez is staged. Eon spent a fortune having the Kenworth company custom-make tankers that could do such demanding stunts as ride through fire on rear wheels. Associate producer Barbara Broccoli earned her pay by overseeing every aspect of this spectacular sequence, which was the brainchild of director Glen.

In total, it took six weeks of work and a lot of blood, sweat and tears to bring the chase to reality. As with all Bond films, every penny is evident onscreen. The sequence provides a thrill-a-second, with some of the most incredible stuntwork imaginable. Again, Dalton's participation in the stuntwork is praiseworthy, and when we see him run from the explosion in which Sanchez is incinerated, it's not hard to believe his statements that he was running for his life.

Praise must go to John Glen for his marvelous direction. As both Dalton and Davi point out, he is woefully underrated, particularly in

nd's reward for a successful
signment.

nd offers a helping hand to the
rrified Lupe in the pre-credits
quence.

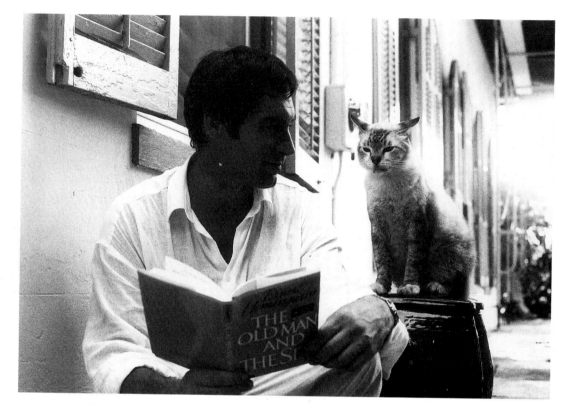

Timothy Dalton takes a a much-needed break to catch up on some appropriate reading while filming at the Hemingway house in Key West.

Right: 007's high-speed pursuit of Sanchez in the film's smashing climax.

Bond cons druglord Sanchez into hiring his deadly services.

rms of his ability to marry the action with the human aspects of the
n. His contributions to the series will long be remembered by Bond
cionados. Full marks also for John Grover's skillful editing. Michael
men's score is serviceable without being remarkable, and one
shes John Barry had been able to participate.

Prior to its release, *Licence to Kill* tested better with preview
diences than any other Bond film. One U.S. poll reported an
nazing 80 per cent of those tested scored the film as "Outstanding".
nfortunately, the film was released at the height of the traditional
S. summer "bloodbath" when the major studios unleash their most
estigious films simultaneously. In a market dominated by *Batman*,
diana Jones and the Last Crusade, and *Lethal Weapon 2*, *Licence*
ver found the audience it deserved. Critics in the U.S. were also
vided. After years of calling the series "too cartoonish," some
viewers now complained that Bond was becoming *too* realistic and
olent. In fact, *Licence* – while gory by 007 standards – is quite tame
mpared to many other action hits of today. Incredibly, British
nsors actually forced the filmmakers to trim several seconds and
en slapped the movie with a rating that excluded anyone under 15
om seeing it. To make matters worse, the studio discarded Eon's
restigious ad campaign, and authorized uninspired print ads that
nore or less hid the fact this *was* a James Bond film. After the first

weekend, the studio cut back on its advertising dollars, and let the film
sink or swim on its own. *Licence* stood up well against the
competition, but it missed its potential to be a blockbuster in the U.S.

Cynics who speculated that perhaps Bond had seen his day were
quickly silenced when the international grosses came in. The film
broke records throughout the world and earned critical praise in
most quarters, proving the 007 movies were indeed a thriving
enterprise.

> ❝ **Licence to Kill** *tested better with*
> *preview audiences than any other*
> *Bond film.* ❞

As of this writing, legal complications have kept Bond off the
screen for far too long. If it's any consolation to the legions of 007
admirers who are thirsting for more Bondian thrills, the delay between
films will only make the next epic more of an event. At the end of
the credits for *Licence to Kill* we read "JAMES BOND WILL RETURN".
Indeed he will, and for two reasons: Cubby Broccoli never breaks a
promise; and Agent 007's adventures – like diamonds – are forever.

JAMES BOND AND THE OSCARS

Since the James Bond films began in 1962, the series has been indisputably popular with audiences throughout the world. Not surprisingly, however, their admiration has often precluded the films from being taken seriously in critical circles. There have certainly been positive notices garnished on the series, yet over the years, less perceptive critics have tended to lump many of 007's adventures together as though they were indistinguishable. This treatment offends Bond fans, who are bemused by anyone who could confuse say, *Moonraker* with *From Russia With Love*.

The theory that popular escapist fare should not be treated to critical accolades had traditionally extended to the Academy of Motion Picture Arts and Sciences, whose annual presentation of the Oscars ignored the Bond films for categories in which they should have been nominated. Among the more glaring omissions: the failure of the Academy to nominate any Bond score or main them composed by John Barry, for example the exhilarating soundtracks *Goldfinger*, *OHMSS*, *Thunderball*, and other memorable scores; t lack of recognition for Peter Hunt's innovative editing on the ea films – a style widely emulated today – who could forget the techni brilliance of *FRWL*'s Orient Express fight or *Thunderball*'s underwat battle; the derisory acknowledgement for art and set decoration, l Ken Adam's spectacular volcano set for *You Only Live Twice*, and legendary Ft. Knox setting for *Goldfinger*.

Nevertheless, justice is not totally blind. To date, Bond films ha been nominated in nine categories, and have won Oscars in two.

The following list contains the nominations for each relevant categor and an asterisk (*****) denotes the winner.

1964 Sound Effects.
Nominees:
Robert L. Bratton *The Lively Set*;
Norman Wanstall *Goldfinger* *****.

1965 Visual Effects.
Nominees:
J. McMillan Johnson *The Greatest Story Ever Told*:
John Stears *Thunderball* *****.

1971 Sound.
Nominees:
Gordon K. McCullum and Gordon Hildyard *Fiddler On The Roof* *****.
Richard Portman and Jack Solomon *Kotch*;
Bob Jones and John Alfred *Mary, Queen Of Scots*;
T. Soderberg and C. Newman *The French Connection*;
G. McCallum, J. Mitchell, and A. Overton *Diamonds Are Forever*.

1973 Song.
Nominees:
"All That Love Went To Waste" (from *A Touch Of Class*)
Music by George Barrie; Lyrics by Sammy Cahn.
"Love" (from *Robin Hood*) Music by George Burns:
Lyrics by Floyd Huddleston.
"Nice To Be Around" (from *Cinderella Liberty*)
Music by John Williams; Lyrics by Paul Williams.
"The Way We Were" (from *The Way We Were*) *****
Music by Marvin Hamlisch; Lyrics by A. and M. Bergman.
"Live and Let Die" (from *Live And Let Die*)
Music and Lyrics by Paul and Linda McCartney.

1977 Song.
Nominees:
"Candle On The Water" (from *Pete's Dragon*)
Music and Lyrics by A. Kasha and J. Hirschorn.
"The Slipper And The Rose Waltz" (from *The Slipper And The Rose*)
Music and Lyrics by R.M. and R.B. Sherman.
"Someone's Waiting For You" (from *The Rescuers*)
Music by S. Fain; Lyrics by C. Connors and A. Robbins.
"You Light Up My Life" (from *You Light Up My Life*) *
Music and Lyrics by Joseph Brooks.
"Nobody Does It Better" (from *The Spy Who Loved Me*)
Music by Marvin Hamlisch; Lyrics by Carole Bayer Sager.

1977 Musical Score
Nominees:
Mohammed: Messenger Of God Maurice Jarre:
Julia Georges DeLerue;
Star Wars John Williams *;
Close Encounters Of The Third Kind John Williams;
The Spy Who Loved Me Marvin Hamlisch.

1977 Art Direction/Set Decoration
Nominees:
The Turning Point Albert Brenner and Marvin March.
Star Wars * J. Barry; N. Reynolds; L. Dilley; R. Christian.
Close Encounters Of The Third Kind Joe Alves; Dan Lomino;
Pil Abramson.
Airport '77 George C. Webb; Mickey S. Michaels.
The Spy Who Loved Me Ken Adam; Peter Lamont; Hugh Scaife.

1979 Visual Effects
Nominees:
The Black Hole P. Ellenshaw; A. Cruickhank; E. Lycette; D. Lee;
H. Ellenshow; J. Hale.
1941 W. A. Fraker; A. D. Flower; G. Jein.
Star Trek: The Motion Picture * D. Trumbull; J. Dykstra; R. Yurichic;
R. Swarthe; D. Stewart; G. McCune.
Alien H. R. Giger; C. Rambaldi; B. Johnson; M. Allder; D. Aling.
Moonraker D. Meddings; P. Wilson; J. Evans.

1981 Song
Nominees:
"The First Time It Happens" (from *The Great Muppet Caper*)
Music and Lyrics by Joe Raposco.
"Endless Love" (from *Endless Love*)
Music and Lyrics by Lionel Richie.
"The Best That You Can Do" (from *Arthur*) *
Music and Lyrics by B. Bacharach; C. B. Sager; P. Allen and C. Cross.
"One More Hour" (from *Ragtime*)
Music and Lyrics by Randy Newman.
"For Your Eyes Only" (from *For Your Eyes Only*)
Music by Bill Conti; Lyrics by Mick Leeson.

---

s perhaps appropriate to mention here that an injustice of sorts s rectified in 1988, when the Academy awarded Sean Connery the scar for Best Supporting Actor – a reward for his superb rformance in *The Untouchables*. For years, Connery was ignored the Academy, despite many performances worthy of nomination: e Hill, *The Offence*, *The Man Who Would Be King*.

His victory was seen not just for his contribution to *The ntouchables*, but also for his many excellent performances, pecially as James Bond.

CUBBY BROCCOLI – THALBERG HONOREE

ey say all things come to those who wait. This proved to be the se for Agent 007 and Cubby Broccoli. After many years, the films, d the man who brought them to life, were given formal recognition the Academy. On March 29, 1982, Cubby was presented with the veted Irving G. Thalberg Award in tribute for his many contributions the motion picture industry. The prize is considered by some to be en more prestigious than the Oscar, as the Thalberg honors the ork of the recipient's entire career.

Although primarily known for the Bond films, Cubby Broccoli was highly successful producer before those epics ever reached the reen. By virtue of receiving the award, Cubby joined a distinguished d honored list which includes Alfred Hitchcock, Walt Disney, muel Goldwyn, and Cecil B. DeMille.

On the big night Bond fans, friends and associates of Cubby's roughout the world, eagerly tuned-in for the much-anticipated esentation. Appropriately, that same evening the title song *For Your es Only* had been nominated, and it received one of the most ectacular stage presentations in Oscar history, featuring Sheena ston, Richard (Jaws) Kiel, and Harold (Oddjob) Sakata. The oduction received an overwhelming, enthusiastic response from e audience.

Then at last, host for the evening, Johnny Carson, introduced ger Moore to make the presentation to Cubby Broccoli.

Left: 1988 – Sean Connery picks up his Oscar for *The Untouchables*.

Above: Cubby Broccoli holds the prestigious Thalberg award, presented to him by Roger Moore at the 1982 Oscar ceremonies.

Moore: "Thank You. The Irving G. Thalberg Award, unlike our friend Oscar, is not given to one film, but rather, is given to a producer for consistent high quality over a number of films. Basically, that means putting every dollar up there on the screen and never cheating the audience. The recipient of the Thalberg Award is a man who has done just that. Of course, I may speak with a little prejudice, but I do speak with first hand knowledge, because he's been paying my rent and contributing to the kids' school fees since 1973. Albert R. Broccoli, who is known from gateman to front office as Cubby, started life as the son of an Italian immigrant farmer who introduced to America the vegetable that bore the family name. That son, Cubby, in turn, introduced a *number* to the screen that none of us will ever forget – 004! I mean, 007! Spies are not perfect!

"Leaving the family farm at an early age, Cubby entered films as a mail boy at 20th Century Fox. From farm to Fox, he became assistant director and after learning his trade, teamed with Irving Allen to produce films like *Paratrooper, Cockleshell Heroes, Fire Down Below* and *The Trials of Oscar Wilde*. He also produced the delightful children's classic *Chitty Chitty Bang Bang*. Twenty-one years ago he formed a partnership with Harry Saltzman to make a picture based on a novel by Ian Fleming, and to star a relatively unknown actor at the time named Sean Connery. That picture, of course, was *Dr. No*, and so began a golden chain of twelve films which have been seen by more than one-and-one-quarter billion moviegoers around the world. And from that first James Bond adventure that drove escapism beyond the larger than life screen entertainment of the past, Cubby Broccoli's vivid imagination has soared constantly higher, producing the longest continual string of successful motion pictures in the history of the art form ... ladies, gentlemen, and counter-spies everywhere, the man who will now expect me to work cheaper, Mr. Albert R. Broccoli – Cubby!"

Broccoli: "Thank you Roger for this marvelous award. It's a tremendous honor to be recognized by the Academy, and I'm grateful to its Board of Governors for selecting me for the Irving G. Thalberg Award. I never dreamed when I came to Hollywood in 1934 that I'd be standing here to receive an award from a man who is the idol of all of us. This is an important moment in my life. I feel a great sense of accomplishment not only for myself, but for all of my colleagues with whom I have worked over the years – the actors, the writers, the directors, those exceptional and dedicated and devoted technicians at Pinewood Studios in Great Britain, and my associates at United Artists.

"In particular, I'd like to acknowledge two men who were my first producing partners. The first was Irving Allen and together we enjoyed making the films that Roger Moore mentioned. The second was my former partner Harry

Saltzman who also envisaged the possible success of James Bond. Together, we received the go ahead from a very dear friend of mine, Arthur Krim. Without Arthur, I would not be standing here tonight at the highest point of my career, and I thank him. And I thank the Academy for allowing a farm boy from Long Island to realize this dream."

Cubby presented with an award from the British Academy of Theatre Arts and Sciences. Timothy Dalton does the honors.

lowing this speech, Broccoli exited the stage. Yet, this marvelous ment lingers in the minds of Bond fans and movie lovers rywhere. As Lee Pfeiffer wrote in a 1989 review of *Licence to Kill*: an age in which critics fall all over themselves praising the tributions of Spielberg and Lucas to the action genre, Broccoli is ally overlooked. It might do well to remind these cynics that had

Cubby not virtually redefined the movie thriller with *Dr. No*, Spielberg and Lucas might be parking cars in the Hollywood Bowl today."

In 1989, Cubby Broccoli received yet another prestigious award, honored by the British Academy of Film and Theatre Arts. The award – in recognition of his lifetime achievement in film – was appropriately presented by Timothy Dalton.

AROUND THE WORLD WITH 007

The international appeal of James Bond has led to some interesting interpretations of the film titles. Here are some examples of how these translations can be as fickle and unpredictable as James Bond's women. Only those titles that differ from the English language version have been used.

Dr. No
Germany: "James Bond Chases Dr. No".
France, Belgium: "James Bond Vs. Dr. No.
Italy: "Licence To Kill".
Spain: "Agent 007 Vs. The Satanic Dr. No".
Japan: "007 Is The Killing Number: Dr. No".
Denmark: "Agent 007: Mission: Kill Dr. No".

From Russia With Love
Germany: "Love Greetings From Moscow".
France: "Hearty Kisses From Russia".
Italy: "To 007, From Russia With Love".
Belgium: "Love And Kisses From Russia".
Sweden: "Agent 007 Sees Red".

Goldfinger
Italy: "Mission Goldfinger".
Spain: "Agent 007 Vs. Goldfinger".

Thunderball
Germany: "Fireball".
France, Italy, Spain, Belgium: "Operation Thunder".
Japan: "Thunderball Fighting".
Denmark: "Agent 007 Into The Fire".

You Only Live Twice
Germany: "A Man Lives Only Twice".
France: "One Doesn't Live More Than Twice".
Japan: "007 Dies Twice".

On Her Majesty's Secret Service
Germany, France, Belgium: "The Secret Service Of Her Majes
Japan: "The Queen's 007".

Diamonds Are Forever
Germany: "Diamond Fever".
France: "The Diamonds Are Forever".
Italy: "A Diamonds Cascade."
Spain: "Diamonds For Eternity".

Live and Let Die
Japan: "The Dead Slave".

Moonraker
Germany: "Moonraker: Top Secret".
Italy: "Moonraker: Operation Space".

For Your Eyes Only
Germany: "A Deadly Mission".
Denmark: "Agent 007: Strict Confidence".
Sweden: "Top Secret".

Octopussy
Italy: "Operation Octopus".

A View To A Kill
Germany: "In The Face of Death".
France: "Dangerously Yours".
Italy: "Moving Target".
Spain: "A Panorama To Kill".
Japan: "The Beautiful Prey".
Belgium: "Dangerous Mission".

The Living Daylights
Germany: "The Skin of A Corpse".
France, Belgium: "Death Is Not A Game".
Italy: "Danger Zone".
Spain: "007: High Tension".

Licence To Kill
Italy: "Private Revenge".
Japan: "The Cancelled Licence".

JAMES BOND ON TELEVISION

XXXXXXDAY on channel 0
see
THE GIRLS, GADGETS & GUYS...

...who create all the excitement in

THE INCREDIBLE WORLD
OF JAMES BOND

a 60-minute
TV special
starring

SEAN CONNERY

0:00 PM

Press-kit advertisement for *Incredible World*.

Television has long been a receptive medium for agent 007. In fact, James Bond's screen adventures began on U.S. television on October 21, 1954 when CBS telecast a one hour live production of *Casino Royale* as part of its "Climax Mystery Theater." Based upon lukewarm reception to the program, few could predict the character of Bond would someday inspire a dynasty of big-budget adventures. The television presentation more resembled a 1950s "kitchen sink" drama than an international thriller.

To Americanize the script, U.S. actor Barry Nelson was cast as Bond, and is referred to periodically as "Card-Sense Jimmy Bond." Nelson portrayed the agent in a style emulating New York cops, and any linkage between his character and Fleming's vision of a sophisticated member of the British Secret Service was purely coincidental. But the teleplay did retain much of the source novel, including some grimly realistic torture sequences. In a slightly more inspired bit of casting, Peter Lorre played the villain Le Chiffre, although the traditional Lorre "mugging" is more amusing than menacing. Linda Christian completed the main trio as the first Bond girl, Valerie Mathis.

The program was ignored by critics and public alike, and the show all but vanished from sight. For years, Bond fans searched in vain for this "ancient" relic. Recently, the program has surfaced on video cassette, and is a must for any Bond video library. But beware: the pre-recorded cassette does not include the climax, where the presumably dead Lorre springs alive, only to be done in once and for all by 007.

Although Bond owes his screen origins to television, 007 has repaid the favor many times by becoming a valuable commodity on the tube. Since the 1960s, periodic TV specials relating to Bond have been favorites with viewers. As testimony to 007's popularity, NBC Television in the US presented two major specials relating to the series. Both shows were intended to take a broad look at the Bond phenomenon, but in reality, were promotions for *Thunderball* and *You Only Live Twice*.

The first 007 special, "The Incredible World of James Bond," premièred in November, 1965. NBC wisely telecast the show in the timeslot traditionally occupied by the enormously successful "The Man From U.N.C.L.E.", thereby insuring the availability of a large audience with similar interests. The one hour program attempted to answer the question "Why do millions of people adore James Bond?" Interspersed with action-packed clips from the previous three films were montages of 007 trademark-bearing merchandise being stocked on store shelves throughout the world. The spotlight also fell on the women and gadgetry and, of course, a generous sampling of the upcoming *Thunderball*.

Produced by television legend David L. Wolper, the show originally planned to feature Sean Connery as host, but ultimately Alexander Scourby handled this responsibility, and his commanding voice lends an air of sophistication to the proceedings, although he does not appear onscreen. The show begins with Scourby intoning a recitation of key Bond villains and their evil schemes. Following the

oll of Dishonor", we are told: "Only one man can stop these
minal masterminds . . . Secret Agent James Bond."

"Incredible World" examines Bond's origins through insights into
e life of Ian Fleming, coupled with rare footage of the author at
ork in his Jamaican retreat, Goldeneye.

Fleming himself would be the subject of two TV movies in the
90s: *Goldeneye* has the author portrayed by Charles Dance, and
sted in U.S. showings by George Lazenby; and *The Secret Life of Ian
ming* with Jason Connery – yes, Sean's son – as the famous
velist.

The speculative links between the real life adventures of Fleming
and his literary creation are touched upon, with Fleming's telling
comment that he emulated Bond in some ways but "lacked the guts
or very lively appetites" of his famed hero.

The highlight of this fascinating hour of television is "behind-the-
scenes" footage from *Thunderball*, including a "line-up" of the stunning
beauties who will appear in the film (Claudine Auger, Luciana Paluzzi,

---

A new generation of heroes: James Bond JR; Tracy Milbanks and Horace "I.Q."
Boothroyd.

James Bond Jr.

Tracy Milbanks

Horace 'I.Q.' Boothroyd

9630 Deereco Road, Timonium, MD 21093
(301) 561-5500 Fax (301) 561-5510

TELEVISION DISTRIBUTION GROUP
10000 W. Washington Blvd., Culver City, CA 90232

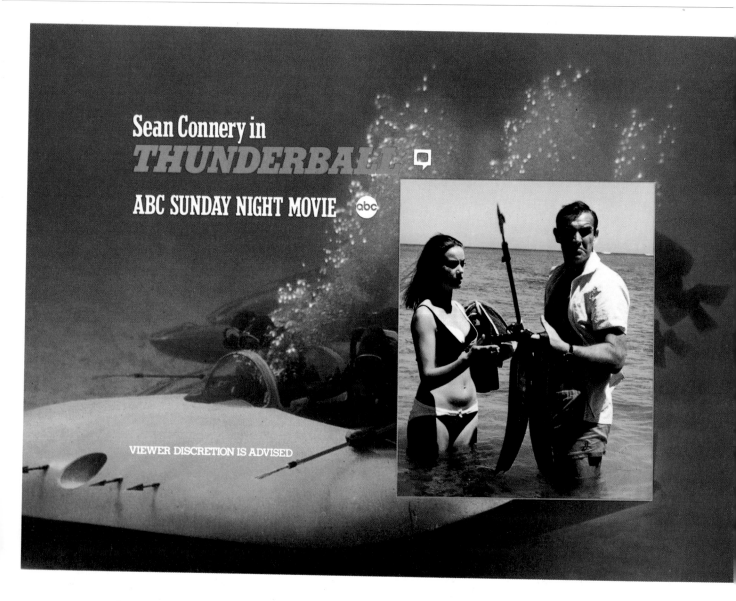

and Martine Beswicke), as they pose in sexy swimwear for the paparazzi. On the action front, we're privy to the rehearsal and filming of the sequence depicting the destruction of Count Lippe's car by Fiona's rocket-firing motorcycle, climaxed by stunt legend Bob Simmon's death-defying leap from the blazing auto. At Pinewood, we take an interesting look at the furious fight aboard the DISCO VOLANTE – a scene taking two full weeks to plan and choreograph.

Viewing the special today, one is most impressed by the wealth of collectibles on view including toys, games, and cases of 007 Vodka. There are also interesting snippets of audiences lining up, throughout the world, to patronize theaters showing the 007 films. The program proved to be a smash, and topped the ratings for the week in the US. The lowest rated program of the week was the appropiately titled "Congress Needs Help" – some things never change.

In June, 1967, NBC Television sponsored "Welcome to Japan, M Bond", designed to publicize the imminent release of You Only Li Twice. Saluting 007's mission to the Orient, the program featured a abundance of film clips stressing the incredible action, gadgetr intrigue, villainy, and eroticism inherent in Bond's world. The show storyline centered on a mysterious, rich young woman (her fac unrevealed, though strongly hinted to be Tracy from the nov OHMSS) who is obsessed with preventing the forthcoming marriag of James Bond. Simultaneously, Lois Maxwell is seen in speciall filmed sequences depicting Moneypenny's jealous speculations abou the identity of the soon-to-be Mrs. 007.

The list of prospective brides includes the traditional Bond leadir ladies coupled with some dubious candidates including Helga Brand Fiona Volpe and – no kidding – Rosa Klebb. Bond must be

Telop slide for ABC's showing of
Thunderball.

t: The 1987 poster
memorating Bond's 25th
versary in the cinema.

suspected necrophiliac as these ladies have something in common apart from their villainy – they are all quite dead. We also take a visit to "Q"'s workshop, where, in addition to consoling Moneypenny, Desmond Llewelyn offers a "sneak peek" at some of the hardware employed by Bond in *Twice*. The amusing, but somewhat corny hour concludes with a glimpse of a Shinto wedding ceremony, where Bond prepares to marry … (Any viewers eager to learn "Mrs. Bond's" identity would have to stand in line at the box-office.)

In 1977, the BBC broadcast a lengthy series of TV specials showing the filming of *The Spy Who Loved Me*. Unfortunately, the program was never seen outside the U.K., and like its NBC predecessors, has never been rebroadcast. These much sought-after shows are as elusive to 007 fans as the Holy Grail is to an archaeologist.

In 1983, British and American television premièred a new 007 special, "James Bond: The First 21 Years". The program was little more than a collection of entertaining film clips, awkwardly linked by a wide range of international celebrities and politicians wishing 007 a "Happy Birthday", in their own inimitable styles. The show gets off to a prestigious start with President Ronald Reagan giving a witty tribute to the star pupil of Her Majesty's Secret Service: "As I see it, 007 is really a 10. He's our modern day version of the great heroes … throughout history. James Bond is a man of honor, a symbol of value to the free world. Of course some critics say that Bond is nothing more than an actor in the movies, but then we all gotta start somewhere".

Others paying homage to James Bond range from the sublime (CIA Director William Colby, Bob Hope, Burt Reynolds, Arnold Schwarzenegger, Frank Sinatra, Alistair Cooke) to the ridiculous (Bjorn Borg, Barbara Woodhouse, Liberace). Little attempt was made to enlist Bond alumni, but Jill St. John is seen briefly, and a film clip with Bond denouncing The Beatles creatively segues to Paul McCartney inquiring as to whether James Bond was a drummer for the now-obscure band Tangerine Dream. The only other Bond veteran to appear is Telly Savalas, who winces after seeing Blofeld's Alpine headquarters destroyed in *OHMSS*. As with the earlier 007 television specials, this one closes with a sneak peek at the next release – *Octopussy*.

In 1987, Roger Moore hosted "Happy Anniversary, 007" commemorating 25 years of 007 adventure epics. Smartly written by film historian Richard Schickel, the one-hour program featured Moore in Bondian garb (Tuxedos, trenchcoats, etc.) guiding viewers on a nostalgic journey through 007 history. Various aspects of Bond's world are edited to reflect specific trademarks of the series: the girls, the gadgets, the fights, etc. Viewers are also treated to their first glimpse of Timothy Dalton, the new Bond, seen at various press conferences and in brief footage from *The Living Daylights*.

Ironically, one of the most intriguing 007 TV specials is among the least seen, and not produced by Eon. Telecast on U.S. cable television in 1983, "Bonds Are Forever" treated viewers to a worldwide tour of 007 locations. The show heavily promotes *Octopussy*, but includes great insight into the series, going beyond the cursory remarks made

U.N.C.L.E. meets Bond: George Lazenby (with original Aston Martin) as a thinly-disguised 007 in *Return of the Man from U.N.C.L.E.* (1983).

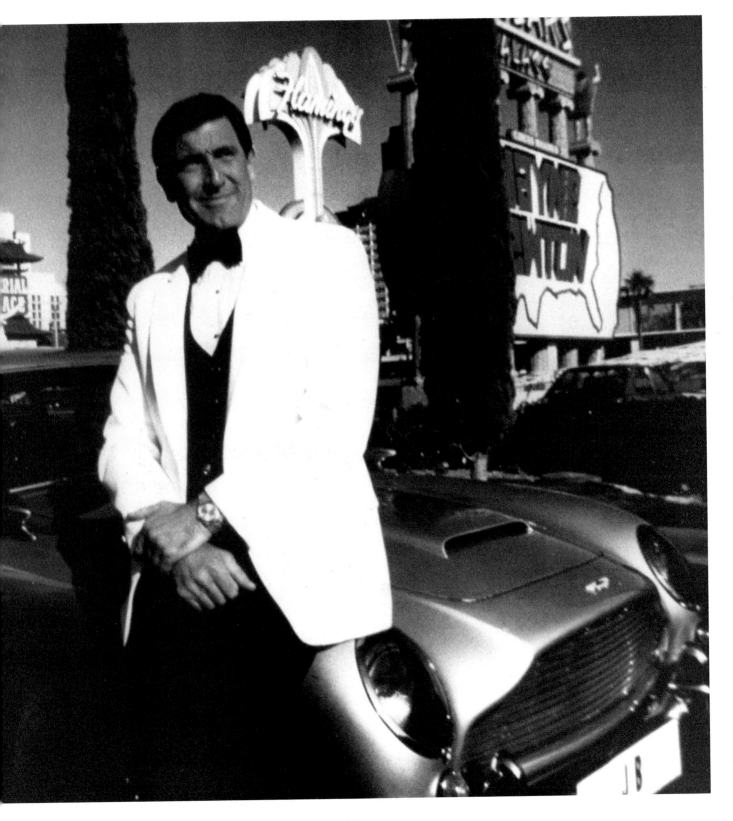

"Telop slide" for ABC T.V.'s U.S. première.

Facing page: Trade Magazine advertisement for *Welcome to Japan.*

in previous specials. Bond alumni are interviewed, including Ursu Andress, Lois Chiles, Desmond Llewelyn, and many others. Geor Lazenby and Cubby Broccoli debate, separately, their recollections OHMSS. Even Sean Connery pops up at a press conference to t about Bond. Copies of this show are difficult to locate, but it's fascinating addition to any 007 video library.

WELCOME TO JAPAN, MR. BOND

featuring

SEAN CONNERY
as
JAMES BOND, Agent 007

All the action, intrigue, sex appeal, exciting spectacle and ingenious invention that made Agent 007 the outstanding cloak-and-dagger adventurer of our time appear in glorious profusion in this new entertainment special. The sum of it all is a unique and colorful hour of exciting Bondiana.

Alluring New Romances! Startling Adventures!

The motivating interest in this entertainment special is the search by a Wealthy Mystery Woman for Bond's rumored bride-to-be. Her hunt serves as springboard for a montage of flashbacks into James Bond's past...with memorable clips from "Dr. No", "From Russia With Love", "Goldfinger" and "Thunderball". Excerpts from the latest James Bond thriller, "You Only Live Twice", show us Bond training with the deadly and dauntless Ninju... and defiantly battling the evil foes from SPECTRE as they prepare to fire world-destructive missiles from a launching pad deep inside a volcano.

The special introduces Bond's latest conquest—the beautiful Nipponese charmer, Kissy Suzuki—"just a plain fishing girl". (Of course, there are many other beautiful girls besides Kissy.)

Of particular interest to the millions of James Bond fans are the new weapons: a cigarette-size rocket launcher...razor-edged whirling discs..."Little Nellie", the portable flying fortress...and explosive eggs! It's the most devilish arsenal ever devised for or against the intrepid Agent 007!

LOCALE	FORMAT
London, Japan and other scenes of James Bond's escapades.	A one-hour special with sponsor identification at the opening, middle and closing and with one minute commercial periods between.

PRODUCTION CREDITS	producer-director DAN DAVIS for HARRY SALTZMAN & ALBERT BROCCOLI

---

mes Bond traditionally receives the Royal treatment in Great ain, where premières of Bond films are major events attended he international jet set, and televised by Thames TV. In addition he stars and major crew members of the latest Bond film, guest list is topped by the Royal Family, seen greeting the makers.

elevision's value in promoting the James Bond films has not been ed to network specials. Like many films, the 007 epics have red 5-10 minute featurettes for promotional use on television.

he featurette for *Dr. No* is likely to inspire more laughter than ls. Hosted by a bespectacled gentleman resembling Wally Cox, low-budget, black and white promo has more value as a "Camp" than a program looking behind the scenes at *Dr. No*.

More successful featurettes were created for the later films. *ffinger*'s black and white promo showcased the background of old (Oddjob) Sakata and showed him demonstrating karate to dren. Also captured is the filming of the "roll in the hay" between Connery and Honor Blackman. *OHMSS* inspired two of the best urettes: *Above it All* and *Swiss Movement*. The former illustrated dangerous filming techniques utilized to shoot the Alpine uences, while the latter centered on George Lazenby as the new

wo years later, a British featurette depicted Guy Hamilton's ction of the elevator fight in *Diamonds Are Forever*. Featurettes re made for most of the later Bond films as well, with recent sions produced in the form of video presskits containing trailers, rviews, and film clips sent to TV stations for promotional plugs. Bond has always had Goldfinger's Midas touch when it came to ngs for broadcasts of the feature films. In 1972, United Artists sold U.S. television rights for the 007 series to ABC Television for the recedented sum of $17 million. *Goldfinger* was first to be broadcast the film promptly zoomed to the top of the ratings, a tradition t continued for most of the premières. Despite the availability of films on cable television and video, Bond still scores big ratings on nmercial TV channels.

While television helps keep the Bond legacy alive, it is shameful w the films have been "edited", apparently with a butcher knife. To dismay of Bond aficionados, entire sequences are routinely cut m the films to allow for more commercials. In the most notorious ance, ABC shockingly "padded" *OHMSS* to allow a two-night wing. The film was completely re-edited, with another actor bing George Lazenby's voice in a lengthy and ludicrous intro-tion, cooly describing most of the film's climactic sequences within first ten minutes. A complaint from Eon insured this tactic was not eated.

n 1991 Turner Broadcasting Systems acquired exclusive U.S. rights the Bond library. The celebration commenced with a seven-night nd festival. The festival remains one of the highest rated weeks in le station history, and the airing of *Diamonds are Forever* set an all-e record for a movie telecast on a cable station. This inspired a r-month Bond festival with 007 films shown once a week. Bond

fans agree: even if they have the films in their own video libraries, it's almost impossible to not tune in to a telecast of a 007 film. Such is the addictive lure of Mr. Kiss-Kiss-Bang-Bang.

In the fall of 1991, the "James Bond Jr." cartoon series premièred internationally. Budgeted at over $300,000 per episode, the series centered on 007's 17-year-old nephew, who resides in Warfield Academy, a school for relatives of individuals in sensitive intelligence positions. James Jr. is aided and abetted in each episode by a bevy of heroic young friends and beauties, including "I.Q." (grandson of "Q"), who provides the teenage adventurer with home-made technological wonders. Gordo Leiter, son of CIA agent Felix Leiter is also a regular. In some episodes Bond Jr. is menaced by his uncle's more infamous acquaintances, including hi tech versions of Dr. No, Jaws, and Oddjob. New menace is provided courtesy of a rogues gallery of villains created for the series. These include Ms. Fortune, Dr. Derange and the SCUM Lord, whose evil organization cheerfully stands for Saboteurs and Criminals United in Mayhem — and you thought the definition of SPECTRE was difficult to memorize!

The cartoon inspired a wave of demand for clever toys and product tie-ins reminiscent of those available in the 1960s. Fathers raised on the Bond films yielded to their sons' pleadings for 007 toys and gadgets, just as *their* dads had done 25 years before. In this bitter-sweet fashion, an old adage was proven true: "The more things change, the more they remain the same." Yes, the James Bond legend is alive and well in the 1990s.

JAMES BOND MERCHANDISE AND COLLECTABLES

LOO7K UP!
007 soars on high via an official Mickgees Kite!

LOO7K DOWN!
A battery operated Lotus Esprit transforms into a submarine!

LOO7K OUT!
A Walther PPK by Crescent Toy sights its target!

JAMES BOND DOES IT EVERYWHERE!

From Melody Alarm clocks that play the James Bond theme, to saw-bladed toy yo-yos; from beach towels and beer cans to wallpaper and walkie-talkies; from Halloween costumes and chess sets, to boxer shorts with the 007 logo – the name James Bond has become synonymous with one of the greatest merchandising booms of the century.

Over the past three decades, all of popular entertainment can arguably be simplified across the arts spectra to the three Bs: Beatles, Batman, and Bond. One reason for 007's staying power was an appeal transcending all age groups. With legions of ultra-fanatics amending their lifestyles to mirror their hero, industries recognized the potential for vast rewards by exploiting 007's popularity. Inevitably, a merchandising blitzkrieg followed tying in consumer goods with a 007 imprimatur. Today Bond items still find their way onto store shelves as succeeding films première. In fact, on the toy and collectables market-place, James Bond mementoes are among the hottest items available.

If any readers can locate the Gilbert battery-operated Aston Martin they played with as a child, they may well possess an item surprisingly valued up to $400. Yes, this is the memorable toy equipped with protruding machine guns, a working bullet-proof shield and an actual ejector seat as its *pièce de résistance*. Or, perhaps one has stashed in a closet the 007 Attaché Case manufactured by

Multiple Products for Christmas, 1965. Pity the poor lad who awo that morning to find he was the only one in the neighborho whom Santa had not rewarded with this superbly styled case inspir by the genuine article in *From Russia With Love*. This Bondian toy c be valued up to $1,000 assuming its code book, calling car decoding machine, and rifle are intact. These two 007 "goodies" a probably the most renowned of all Bond merchandise. Othe include:

A unique 007 Lunch Box with thermos honoring *Goldfinger* a *Thunderball*; the James Bond AM Radio manufactured in the shape a 007; a James Bond arcade-sized Pinball Machine by Gottlieb; and series of space-age robotic vehicles marketed in Mexico by Matt These complemented Bond action figures that would drive su exotic modes of transportation as The Supermobile, Comman Gyrocopter, Laser Jet, and motorcycle.

Signals forecasting the boom of 007 marketing opportunit revealed themselves in the early 1960s when catchphrases such "Worthy of James Bond", "Styled Exclusively for 007!", and "A Me Fit for 007!" became prominent in advertising, employing the Jam Bond name to endorse goods already established in the marke place. The earliest memento directly tying in to the films was D. Comic's adaptation of *Dr. No*. This special release remains faithful the original story (enhanced by excellent artistry) although t

Facing Page: Original advertisement for the 007 race car set – a collectable which now commands up to $500.

Above: 007 computer games; electric drawing kit; pistol; horse trailer set; swim fins; Bond and Jaws dolls; *Goldfinger* puzzle; *Thunderball* Japanese underwater toys.

ence is subdued – Dr. No's death is amended so that it was less esome for younger readers. Trivia buffs may notice that only in U.S. edition are the "Three Blind Mice" inaccurately portrayed as ucasian. Originally sold for 12 cents, the coveted collectable now nmands prices of $150 or more. While this simple Bond item did c launch 007 as the 1960s icon he soon would become, it brought out an awareness of the Agent beyond the confines of the theater. By the time of *Goldfinger*'s 1964 release, the fuse on a merchandising nanza was already lit, soon to explode on crazed consumers. For a v dollars, lira, marks or yen, fans could transport themselves into e fascinating world of the famed secret agent. Quality products aring the 007 trademark were developed targeting all ages: For kids, Lakeside Industries' James Bond Electric Drawing Set ght entertain. For teens, James Bond Walkie-Talkies might be the wer for espionage needs. And the adults weren't forgotten: W.J. it's Underwater Sporting Equipment could be of use in searching SPECTRE Warheads.

ames Bond soon catapulted in popularity to become an industry to itself. Highlighting the merchandising barrage were firms offering variety of Bond treasures destined to become a part of the 007 stique. One was literally able to work, dress, play and drink in ndian style – courtesy of an amusing guide, "Every Man His Own 7".

From the world of 007 fashion, we were offered a line of men's toiletry accessories that "No Well Dressed Man Should Be Without", Exclusively produced by Colgate Palmolive, we could spruce up with 007 Hair Tonic, Cologne, Aftershave, Soap and the infamous Bond Deodorant! (Any one of these items can command $50 or more today.)

Adler Pants Co. introduced a line of men's 007 slacks, and the Harry Diamond Co. created 007 Dress Shirts, identifiable by a hang tag in the shape of a pistol; don't forget your 007 Shoes manufactured by Norvic Co (each shoe proudly displayed tiny "007"'s in the lining.)

Men's and women's robes and pajamas bearing the distinctive 007 logo proved to be successful for the Weldon Pajama Co. Completing one's haberdashery: personally tailored suits by Trimount Clothing; men's jewelry by Marvin Glass Assoc.; sunglasses by Beautiful Eyes in Optics (each bearing "For Your Eyes Only" imprinted on the lenses); and various swimsuits, T-shirts, neckties, raincoats and the obligatory "Spy" trenchcoat.

The most interesting and desirable by-products of the 007 phenomenon were the toys, games, and hobby crafts. Christmas catalogs were drenched with pages upon pages of 007 articles awaiting Santa's delivery. Milton Bradley was the first major toy company to capitalize on the Bond rage, releasing their 1964 James Bond 007 Secret Agent Board Game, introduced at the modest price of $1.49. Today, collectors must spend $30 or more in order to obtain one. The challenge of this contest was for "Agents" to accumulate points via spying in casinos, dark alleys and cemeteries. (Two editions of the game exist – the most desirable version depicts Sean Connery on the box.)

Milton Bradley also produced two superbly packaged games based on Goldfinger and Thunderball. In the former, players attempted to manoeuver their spies to safety inside Ft. Knox in a chess-like struggle. The latter required contestants to decipher secret signals uncovering SPECTRE's highjacked bombs. Other notable board games produced over the years include: Ideal's "Message From 'M'" game, forcing participants to do battle with Goldfinger, Dr. No and Largo. The James Bond Box, a 1964 British release similar in play to the U.S. game show "High Rollers" – contestants attempt to capture prizes through rolls of the dice. The James Bond Secret Service Game, released in 1965 by Spears in England, tested one's covert abilities in retrieving secret documents for a new rocket fuel.

Inspired by Thunderball was the Bond versus Largo Underw Battle Game. Released in the U.K. in 1965, this is an elabor produced and valuable Bond collectible. Inside the de-luxe g were two complete scuba armies each meticulously detailed. O handful of the games have surfaced over the years, comman prices of around $1,000!

Two more recent board games tying in with 007 have b manufactured in Europe: "James Bond Agentenspiel" (Germany), "James Bond Le Jeu" (France). The trend in the U.S. and the U.K late has been to concentrate on computer games, including miss involving a night time oil rig rescue (DAF); the raid of a sunken (FYEO); and the most recent, based on Licence to Kill.

A multitude of jigsaw puzzles have flooded the market over years, including several from Milton Bradley depicting various ac scenes based on Goldfinger and Thunderball. Unquestionably, rarest of these is the 20″ × 26″ Thunderball puzzle comprise 1,000 pieces. This double-sided jigsaw depicted a scuba-suited B alongside his ravishing ladies. On the reverse, is the seductive Don bathed in gold. Equally rare is the similarly designed Goldfinger pu featuring the film's cast. On sale for pennies in 1965, this jigsaw r sells for an impressive $100 bill.

An avalanche of puzzles flooded the market: Arrow's set of beauties honoring From Russia With Love, Goldfinger and Thunder H.G. Toys trio of The Spy Who Loved Me puzzles, depicting anim. battles between Bond and Jaws; an Italian set of rare, magnet Man With the Golden Gun collage-like puzzles.

Then there were the two dynamic Japanese puzzles boas gorgeous poster artwork from Moonraker and For Your Eyes Only; forgetting Britain's Hestar Company's set of three attractive puz based on A View to a Kill depicting Bond along with a bevy of lovely ladies.

A company specializing in 007 memorabilia during the golden ye of collectables was A.C. Gilbert of New York. In addition to B merchandise, the company also produced toys based on The M from U.N.C.L.E. By far their most memorable item was the "Jar Bond Roadrace Set", elaborate enough to carry a $50 pricetag in 19 The box containing this masterpiece of collectability was roughly size of Crab Key, and its contents were equally impressive. Driv tested their skills, with Aston Martins, no less, on a course of t curves, treacherous mountain climbs, and a most dangerous oil s The set now routinely commands prices of over $600.

Gilbert's forte, however, was in more affordable items. Introdu their "World of James Bond in Miniature", they released small ha painted spy figures representing Bond, his girls, villains and allies. S as a gift set of all ten figures, or in individual blister packs, t likenesses to the actors is remarkable with just a little poetic licer Retailing for 39 cents in 1965, they now sell for $10 each. Comp menting the figurines came action toy sets featuring Goldfinger's la table, Largo's yacht, "M"s bulletproof desk, and Dr. No's "breathing" tank (considerably less terrifying here, as the "flar consists of red wood "breathing" via a rubber band!).

Left: Rare U.K. *Thunderball* rifle; 007 wall clock; hand puppets; *Moonraker* model; 007 watch; rifle assembly kit; U.S. lunch box and radio in the 007 logo; various car replicas. From Japan: a 1981 puzzle, walkie-talkie set, speedboat toy and acrostar model.

...ing page: Japanese picture sleeves ...m 45 r.p.m. recordings of the Bond ...mes are prized by Bond collectors.

...ht: Talking target set; Japanese *Dr.* ...model kit; Gilbert Aston Martin; ...watch; prototype for Bond doll ski ...thes (never sold in stores); British ...edevil car set; *Thunderball* board ...me; Japanese *Thunderball* diver; box ...wrappers for trading cards; ...anese scuba figures display.

Seen on THE BEATLES abc network TV

52 WEEKS IN '66

JAMES BOND 007
EXCITING MINIATURE FIGURES AND ACTION TOYS

Another **GILBERT** Exclusive

Left: Trade brochure for 1966 line of Gilbert toys.

Facing page: the "Message from 'M'" game (the most opulent board game produced in the U.S.); Oddjob doll; 00 bubble bath; German handgun; computer game; figurine sets; weapon case; Japanese model of Lotus; candy cigarettes; unlicensed *Thunderball* "snow shaker"; and the classic Aston Martin from Gilbert.

The list from A.C. Gilbert is endless: 11-inch rubber handpuppets representing Bond, Largo and Oddjob, bearing a remarkable resemblance to their real life counterparts, even if Oddjob has caucasian skin tone on his hands, but a garish yellow tint on his face!

The James Bond Action Doll, marketed successfully with figures of Napoleon Solo, Illya Kuryakin and Honey West. Bond was equipped with a snorkel, mask, and swim-fins as well as a cap pistol which fired when placed in his hand. The box was beautifully produced, showing numerous photos and an excellent painting of Sean Connery.

Naturally, accessory sets of clothing and weaponry also awaited purchase. Introduced for Christmas, 1965, Gilbert spent $750,000 advertising their line of spy dolls. Accompanying 007, Gilbert offered the Oddjob Doll, complete with karate outfit and derby thrown in for "deadly" effect. The dolls sold for a mere $3.40 in 1965, but today you would have to part with around $200-$300.

The James Bond 007 Spy Tricks Outfit – a boxload of magic tricks performed with Bond's secret pistol, Oddjob's derby, 007 lie detector, etc. Largely due to the impressive packaging, this set of illusions sold for $5.95 in 1966 and may be worth $400 today.

The previously mentioned Aston Martin is one of the three most famous 007 toys ever – a *must* for fans and collectors. It operated on special 007 batteries, and was priced originally at $6.98. The car was reproduced by opportunistic competitors in "generic" models of varying degrees of quality.

The James Bond Spywatch offered not only the local and international time, but also concealed secret sighting lenses for "undercover usage". Over the years, a wealth of Bond timepieces have emerged. These include wristwatches that play the Bond theme as their alarm function, and wall clocks bearing Roger Moore's likeness.

Bond made his presence known during summer vacations via the creation of at least five different beach towels. The two most highly prized are the "007 James Bond" towel of 1965, featuring a huge depiction of Connery in a tux, gun posed in the familiar style; and the *Thunderball* towel of 1966 presenting 007 in a brilliant orange scuba suit and captioned LOO7K OUT!. These are valued at $200 each, although frustrated collectors who want to show off their treasures at the beach can do so for less expense ia the Gindi Company's 1981 beach towel line. The most attractive of these present Roger Moore in *Moonraker* against a blood-red background. Two other towels were created, but the likeness to Moore is not good.

Investment-wise, it would be difficult to top the popular line of Corgi die-cast James Bond vehicles manufactured since 1965. These beautifully made collectables are dollar-for-dollar the highest priced line of James Bond merchandise. Most notable was the replica of the Aston Martin DB5, popular enough to merit being named "Toy of the Year" in 1965 – is there any male over 32 years of age who did not receive this in their Christmas stocking! Various incarnations have existed since then. All are silver, except the original which was painted gold, and today sells for $500. As of 1991, newly produced versions of the Aston Martin are still big sellers for Corgi.

Other miniature Bond vehicles followed over the years: the Toyota from *You Only Live Twice* (modified with missile launching capabilities), the moon buggy and Ford mustang from *Diamonds Are Forever*, and the Lotus Esprit and various helicopters, space shuttles, etc., all commanding extravagant prices.

Most of these toys were smartly packaged with illustrated display stands, information, and photos from the films. A second line of smaller versions enjoyed release under the label "Corgi Juniors" and "Corgi Rockets". Although less elaborate, these blister-pack collectables can be every bit as expensive as their larger counterparts.

Rarest of all are the little-seen vehicles from *OHMSS*, including Tracy's Mercury Cougar, with and without ski racks; SPECTRE's Mercedes Benz; several of the stock cars featured in the film; and the bobsleds piloted by Bond and Blofeld. Individual items can bring up to $250. In 1983, Corgi released an Octopussy set consisting of the tiny Acrostar, and accompanying Land Rover and horse-trailer. Following Corgi's lead, Matchbox began producing Bond items in 1985, marketing a Rolls Royce and taxi from *A View to a Kill*. In 1989, they manufactured the smartest Bond collectable in years: a de luxe gift set of cars, planes and trucks from *Licence to Kill*, already priced at $50 on the collectors' circuit.

Another staple among young males is the model construction kit. James Bond was never neglected in this area, either. A Japanese company, Imai, issued some interesting and valuable kits of their own including the 007-SPECTRE Bomb Sled, the Bond Frogman kit, 007 in Aqualung and others obviously inspired by *Thunderball*. In the 1980s, Imai distributed some nicely packaged model kits of *Dr. No* and *For Your Eyes Only*. Two of the most famous firms to produce 007 models were Aurora in the U.S. and Airfix in Great Britain. Both companies released model versions of the Aston Martin DB5, each quite valuable today.

One of the rarest Airfix kits is a 1:24 scale exact replica of Little Nellie, the gyrocopter of *You Only Live Twice*, now worth a cool $400. Another Airfix kit depicted Bond's battle with Oddjob in Ft. Knox.

"If you don't give him 007 ...I will"

Now, dare to give him what he really wants – 007, the bold new grooming aids that make any man dangerous.

There's a 007 gift set for every assignment. The arsenal includes 007 After Shave, Hair Tonic, Spray Deodorant, Cologne, Shave Cream, Talc and Soap. Each has the license to kill... women.

Give him as much as you dare. But hurry. If you don't, someone else will.

Above: Colgate's 1965 line of men's toiletries promised to bring out the killer in each man.

Facing page: Bottled in Bond: 007 beer; drinking glasses, whiskey; martini glass; and promo poster for *The Living Daylights.*

pistol. The following year Lonestar released the elaborate Thunder Ricochet Rifle selling today for an obscene sum! In 1973, the comp tied-in to the release of *Live and Let Die* via a Super Action Pack containing a pistol with silencer, hand grenades, holster, badge, c finder, and a "communication device" (not so awe-inspiring a consisted of two cups tied together by a string).

One of the rarest toy guns is Crescent's Walther PPK issuec promote *For Your Eyes Only.* Aside from beautiful packaging, the painted silver with a dark brown hand grip, was realistic enough carry a warning not to use it on the street.

Another major distributor of Bond toys was Multiple Produ Aside from their famed attaché case, Multiple also distributed the Secret Rifle and Pistol Set; and the Personal Attack Kit, consisting hidden cap gun, a weapon to fire missiles containing secret messa and a 2-way holster. Its $3 selling price in the 1960s has increased fold. Multiple also offered the 007 Shooting Camera. Designed a ordinary movie camera, it fired golden bullets through its lens was contained in a de luxe carrying case.

Later items in the Bond arsenal were produced by Coibel Toy 1983. These included a wide range of exploding pens, coins spoons, a .45 caliber pistol, and a long 007 Thunderblaster Rifle. T showpiece was the Electronic Pop-Up Talking Target Game, wh darts were fired at likenesses of Bond villains. If a bullseye was scor a menacing voice boomed: "You got Me!". The set sold for expensive $27.95, but is worth many times that amount today.

Bond's value in merchandising was not lost on the food and liq industry. The United Rum Merchants of London distilled guarante "Licence to Sell" bottles of spirits brewed with a special blend "007 vodka". Although a comparatively low 65.6 proof, it undoubte had "a delivery like a brick through a plate glass window". The pou for this "Bottled in Bond" novelty was a pistol spout. Hoping achieve an even broader appeal, the National Brewing developed the "007 Special Blend", a beer that did not survive its marketing in the mid-western USA. The limited number of steel c containing the brew displayed several designs featuring beaut women and exotic locales, and a single unopened ale may fetch $2 today. There is, currently, a James Bond Brandy in Malaysia and a Bond wine is being tested in France.

If a Bond collector is fortunate to possess or obtain any of th tipples, what receptacle will be unique enough to serve it in? H about Pepsi Cola's set of four colorful drinking glasses designed promote *A View to A Kill?* Each glass features a scene from either Spy Who Loved Me, Moonraker, For Your Eyes Only* or *View.* On reverse, a brief synopsis of the film and the bold claim that "Ro Moore IS James Bond!"

We should not neglect to mention another mainstay of Bo collectables: trading cards sold with a piece of chewing gum st enough to challenge Jaws! In the U.S. the initial series of cards we distributed by the Philadelphia Chewing Gum Corporation depict scenes from the first three films. Curiously, the company refused mention the name "Pussy Galore" on the cards, choosing instead

Unfortunately, the model is somewhat marred by poor artwork and the figures resemble Laurel and Hardy more than Bond and his nemesis; nevertheless, this dubious collectable sells for hundreds of dollars. More appealing are Aurora's individual models of Bond and Oddjob, attractively packaged and selling for $250 each. Other models of a more recent vintage include Revell and Airfix's space shuttle from *Moonraker,* and kits of the Lotus Esprit.

If models alone could not satiate young boys' obsessions with Bond paraphernalia, then the quantity of toy armaments relating to 007 was enough to have satisfied the Allies in their invasion of Normandy!

Many firearms were produced by the British-based Lonestar company, which launched the arsenal in 1964 with a modest Bond

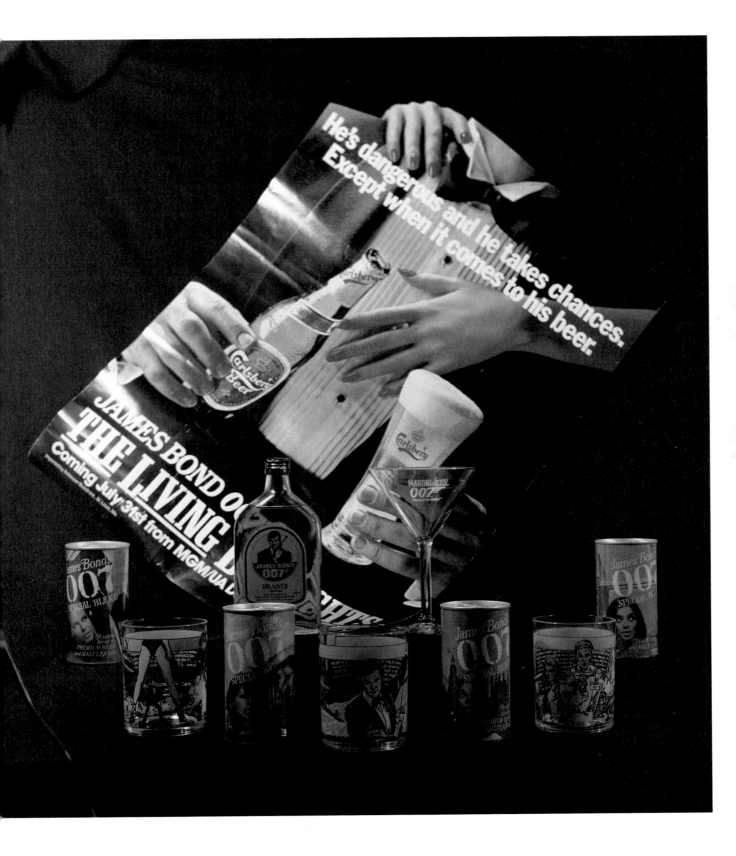

Gilbert action figures, toys and accessories.

The British "Bond vs. Largo" game is one of the rarest and most valuable 007 toys. Also shown: "Mini-Standees"; Bond card game; British board game; key-ring finder; computer game; walkie-talkies; space gun; Viewmaster reels; and the very rare Mexican-produced Land Rover.

MINIATURE... 52 WEEKS OF NETWORK TV

No. 16503 JAMES BOND in Scuba Outfit Packed 24 per carton, shipping wgt. approx. 2½ lbs.

No. 16506 GOLDFINGER Packed 24 per carton, shipping wgt. approx. 2½ lbs.

No. 16501 JAMES BOND in Formal Outfit Packed 24 per carton, shipping wgt. approx. 2½ lbs.

No. 16505 "M" (Bond's boss) Packed 24 per carton, shipping wgt. approx. 2½ lbs.

No. 16525 SET OF 10 MOVIE SPY FIGURES. Realistic 3¼" replicas of characters familiar to millions through the fabulous James Bond books and movies. They include: Bond himself in 3 different outfits; his secret service boss, M; M's lovely secretary, Miss Moneypenny; Domino, the feminine interest in "Thunderball"; and four famous villains: Goldfinger, Oddjob; Dr. No. Meticulously hand painted in correct colors with authentic molded details. Packed 12 per carton, shipping wgt. approx. 13 lbs.

Bond playing cards.

er to her as "Goldfinger's Female Pilot". Britain countered with a ilar set distributed by Somportex. Cards for *Thunderball* were also eased by the same companies, although the British set had its card .24 withdrawn as it depicted Bond punching a woman – actually e" was a SPECTRE assassin in drag. Nevertheless, the card was emed unsuitable for inferring that it was not improper to strike a y. This card alone is worth over $25, and the full sets of cards sell around $100 each. Indeed, the wrappers sell for $35-$50!

For *You Only Live Twice*, Somportex released a truly unique set of mm color slides on strips, complete with viewing mount. The est set of trading cards are those promoting *OHMSS* by Anglo nfectionery Ltd. Sold only in the U.K. these color cards represent e of the few merchandising links to George Lazenby's brief tenure 007. A complete set now sells for $250. Other gum cards tributed over the years included those for *Moonraker*, the most eresting being a set of small color cards enclosed with candy arettes, distributed solely in Scotland. The latest series of Bond ds were produced in Holland consisting of 100 small color cards ting *Dr. No* through to *Octopussy*. A follow-up set of 100 cards re issued for *A View to A Kill*.

On the music scene, classic tunes from the Bond films have been y exploited over the years. Complementing original soundtrack ums for each Bond epic have been picture-sleeve-45s from recent nd movies. Rarer still, are de luxe sleeves accompanying Japanese 7 singles in the 1960s. These often contained a sheet of photos and ormation about the film, and a collectors' edition record for *underball* was enclosed in a 12-page booklet jammed with otos.

As this chapter has illustrated, the manufacture of James Bond materials knows no bounds, and the collecting of such mementoes is stronger today than ever. Many collectors by-pass the more readily available articles and head directly for the near-impossibles like 007 wallpaper, and "Moonraker" sleeping bags (released only in Canada); while others attempt to gather anything bearing the 007 logo like Bond greeting cards, 007 bullethole auto decals, calendars, etc., etc.

Where does one obtain this type of memorabilia? One key source is through the James Bond Fan Club, which also has under its umbrella "The James Bond Collectors' Club News" (33 High Park Ave., Wallaston, Stourbridge, West Midlands DY8 3ND, England). Each periodical has an extensive selection of Bond merchandise and collectibles for sale. The Club formally sponsors James Bond Conventions where fans from across the globe travel to the U.K. to buy, swap and sell 007 treasures as well as interact with fellow enthusiasts and Bond stars. Addresses and suggestions of other outlets for Bond memorabilia can be obtained by writing to the authors: C/O Box 205, 261 Central Avenue, Jersey City, N.J. U.S.A. 07307.

JAMES BOND AND HIS GADGETS

If there is one thing more synonymous with James Bond than danger and sex, it is his legendary utilization of some of the most incredible gadgetry ever to appear on-screen. Bond's use of gadgets has been both lauded and denounced. Some fans claim the films lose their appeal when the script emphasizes realism over technology, while others maintain 007 sacrificed his personality by becoming a mere operator of hi-tech machinery. What no one can dispute is that a fortune was spent to insure all of the gadgets were feasible in real life. The emergence of the now familiar gadgets came as an attempt to modernize Fleming's stories and to put as many incredible thrills on-screen as possible. Despite the wide range of lethal devices employed in the films, there is one constant: they are inevitably provided by "Q", the dour and curmudgeonly genius who supplies the technology that has saved Bond's life on innumerable occasions. What follows is a comprehensive listing of the contrivances designed by the ill-tempered Einstein of Her Majesty's Secret Service.

Dr. No

The first James Bond film found 007 relying more on his wits than sophisticated gadgetry. The only weaponry dwelled upon is Bond's Beretta, which "Q" dismisses as a gun more "befitting a lady" (and not a nice lady, at that). Bond is re-equipped with a Walther PPK, reputed to have a delivery "like a brick through a plate glass window".

The 7.65 mm firearm, manufactured in Germany, comes with an 8-shot clip and accepts a Brausch silencer. Its introduction came at the suggestion of famed weapons master, Geoffrey Boothroyd and it remained Bond's trademark handgun until *Octopussy*.

From Russia With Love

For 007's second adventure, "Q" presents Bond with a "smart looking piece of luggage": an ordinary black leather attaché case. However, it is an ingeniously lethal piece of work. The case contains 20 rounds of ammunition in 2 concealed tubes, as well as a razor sharp throwing knife hidden in the side of the case. Inside, Bond finds a folding AR-7 sniper's rifle with a night-vision telescopic sight. More impressive is a teargas bomb disguised as a tin of talcum powder. It explodes if the case is opened incorrectly. As if this were not enough, the case also conceals 50 gold sovereigns (this was in the days before American Express!) – "A rather nasty Christmas present", quips 007. Other mechanisms utilized include one of the first pocket pagers (causing Bond to experience the frustrations of coitus interruptus); a "bug detector"; and a tape recorder disguised as a Rollifex camera.

Goldfinger

The gadgetry craze was truly launched with this third Bond film, also renowned for "fleshing out" the character of "Q" and establishing him as a major presence in the series. Touring "Q" Branch, audiences witness prototypes of hi-tech equipment being tested, including parking meters that spray toxic gas, bullet-proof body wear, and the most incredible automobile ever designed – the Aston Martin DB5. ("With modifications", deadpans "Q" in the understatement of a time).

The car was written into the novel after Fleming received the vehicle on loan from Aston Martin-Lagonda, Inc. In the book, the car

Bond is presented with a "nasty Christmas present" – the ingenious attaché case in *From Russia With Love*.

Mont Blanc company capitalized on
s version of their fountain pen.

James Bond (Roger Moore) receives a very special pen from Q (Desmond Llewelyn) as Vijay (Vijay Amitraj)
looks on in a scene from "Octopussy"

Montblanc saves James Bond 007!

Albert R. Broccoli presents Roger Moore as Ian Fleming's James Bond 007.
Produced by Albert R. Broccoli. Directed by John Glen. Executive Producer Michael G. Wilson.

OCTOPUSSY

as outfitted with a few unexciting modifications. On film, however, e producers had more exotic functions in mind and spared no xpense to provide space-age gadgetry for Bond's less than modest eans of transportation. Among the defense mechanisms found on e cinematic Aston Martin:

● Retractable bullet-proof shield – raised or lowered electronically from the trunk.

● Twin retractable .30 calibre Browning machine guns –

concealed behind the parking lights. The effect of firing guns was achieved by igniting trickles of acetylene gas that were discharged into the tube representing the guns.

● Revolving licence plates – syncronized in front and rear to accommodate three different countries.

● Smoke screen – emitted a cloud of fog from smoke cannisters that discharged into the exhaust pipe.

● Radar screen – enabled Bond to track an enemy with an active "homing device". A map display beneath the console

● Oil slick – built into the tail light fixtures, this feature allowe
up to ½ litre of oil to be sprayed onto the roadway.

Four vehicles were used, each with varying functions. Only one Asto
Martin was used for major sequences, while a second car was divide
into sections and used only for interior shots. A "standard" thir
version was utilized expressly in the scene wherein Bond demolishe
the car by slamming into Goldfinger's factory and a fourth car wa
built solely for publicity tours.

Less fantastic gadgets employed in *Goldfinger*, include a pair c
homing devices, one magnetized to attach to the car of the prey. Th
other fits snugly into the heel of Bond's shoe. The least technic
gadget at 007's disposal is also the most amusing – a snorkel-breathe
attached to a helmet with a decoy seagull perched atop.

Thunderball

Audiences so loved the gadgetry in *Goldfinger* that the fourth Bon
epic, *Thunderball*, vowed to give 'em even more. If the gadgetry her
was too plentiful, it was nonetheless impressive.

The famous Aston Martin reappears briefly in the pre-credi
sequence, harboring a new modification – a jet-powered wate
spray, powerful enough to disable the bad guys. The pressurize
spray, capable of a 75-foot range, was released through hose
connected to a jet pump contained in the car's trunk, adding 2,000 lb
to the car's original weight. Bond also utilizes a Bell-Textron Jet Pack
virtually a one-man flying escape unit, powered by a highl
concentrated peroxide fuel, allowing an aerial escape from pursuer:
The jet pack (on loan from the U.S. Army) actually worked an
allowed the user to achieve heights of up to 600 feet.

Like his gadgets, Desmond Llewelyn's "Q" had also become
popular mainstay in the series. Among the arsenal he reluctantl
supplies to a disinterested Bond:

● A Rolex watch which serves as a geiger counter.
● A radioactive capsule that emits a homing signal, later insurin,
Bond's rescue from an underwater cave.
● A miniature flare pistol.
● A cigar-shaped "rebreather" providing up to four minutes o
emergency oxygen. This device was originally designed as ar
innocuous "shroud", later replaced by this more exotic design.
● An Aqualung breathing pack which served to jet-propel the
wearer through the water. Additionally, it was equipped with a
speargun device to shoot bolts with exploding heads and emitte
a camouflage dye.
● A prototype Nikon underwater camera, which today can be
found in any store, but in 1965 was considered revolutionary. The
camera took eight shots in rapid succession.
● A Geiger counter camera programmed to click in the
presence of radioactivity.

allowed Bond to pinpoint his prey's exact location. (The map's
image was achieved through front screen projection, a technique
which is now widely available.)
● Tire slashers – this device consisted of a set of knives which
extended and retracted from the rear wheels, enabling Bond to
destroy the tires of a car driving beside him.
● Passenger ejector seat – this clever addition allowed Bond
quickly to dispose of unwanted company. A pilot's ejector seat
was used in the sequence in which a villain is sent soaring. In other
sequences, the standard passenger seat was used.

You Only Live Twice

this fifth Bond epic, 007 was dispatched to Japan, blessed with the est budget to date. The movie is but minutes old before the first device is seen – a canvas sail-cloth "shroud" in which Bond's rpse" is buried at sea. In actuality, Bond has been sealed in what ears to be the world's largest plastic sandwich bag, receiving gen via a closed-circuit rebreather which keeps air bubbles from aping (and having the ruse discovered).

The real hi-tech wonder of the film is Little Nellie, a tiny flying ogyro helicopter, copied from a prototype developed for the ish military in 1962. At only 9½ feet long, the craft could maneuver any standard helicopter (as SPECTRE would soon over) and could accelerate to 130 mph in 10 seconds.

The autogyro arrives in Japan stored in 4 alligator suitcases (imagine story "Q" had to tell customs officials to explain why his luggage tained a rocket-launching helicopter!). Once assembled, "Q" efly explains her various "idiosyncrasies":

● two machine guns fixed port and starboard.
● two rocket launchers firing heat seeking air-to-air homing missiles, powered by 96 lb thrust rocket motors.
● two flame throwers on either side of Nellie's tail, each with a range of 80 yards.
● two devices which created and dispersed a smokescreen.
● aerial mines dropped by tiny parachutes for use when Nellie is directly over her target.
● a flight helmet containing a movie camera and microphone/transmitter.

The famed Aston Martin displays its wares.

Bond and his *Thunderball* jet pack. ("No well-dressed man should be without one!")

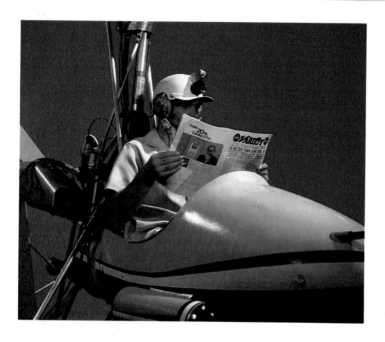

Connery catches up on industry news while waiting for his next scene in the Little Nellie battle in *You Only Live Twice.*

On Her Majesty's Secret Service

Gadgets are practically non-existent in this unusually realistic Bond epic, in which Bond relied on his ingenuity to survive. The technology of the previous films is summarily dismissed within the opening seconds of the film. "Q" hands "M" a vial containing "radioactive lint" appropriate as a tracking device when placed in an opponent's pocket. "M" drolly observes the need to track 007 instead and "Q" retires until Bond's wedding in the final moments of the film. Congratulating Bond and his new bride, "Q" offers, "if there's anything you ever need . . .". Bond humorously replies, "Thanks 'Q', but this time I've got the gadgets and I know how to use them!"

The one special device Bond does make good use of is a dual safe-cracking and photocopying machine. The suitcase-sized unit is equipped with a sensor that fits over a safe's· tumbler to calculate every conceivable combination until a "chirp" signals that the safe can be opened. (Characteristically, Bond peruses a Playboy while the device does all the work.)

Diamonds are Forever

For *Diamonds*, Sean Connery was back, and with him came the customary gadgetry missing from *OHMSS*. Among "Q"'s "goodies":

- Transparent artificial skin fingerprints, perfectly duplicati the fingerprints of an opponent.
- An electromagnetic r.p.m. controller operated by "(himself during his visit to Las Vegas. The device, worn as a rir adjusts the revolutions of a slot machine's cylinders, causing the to make "Q" a winner with every spin!
- An electric voice box, allowing one to imitate perfectly t vocal patterns of anyone else.
- A piton bolt gun which fires a steel-toothed peg attached tc strong rope, enabling Bond to scale Blofeld's hideaway atop casino.
- A bladed clamp that resembles a mousetrap, crushing . opponent's fingers when attempting to disarm Bond.
- Clusters of rockets installed under the hood of the Astc Martin DB5 by "Q"'s technicians. (Only on letterboxed vide versions can this be seen.)

Live and Let Die

Roger Moore's debut as Bond proved to be the first film not t include an appearance by "Q"; only his creations were displaye Among Bond's "travelling companions" this time around were Rolex watch that emitted a magnetic field strong enough to defle the path of a bullet when its winding button is pulled. (Bond finds more appropriate use by utilizing it to unzip his lover's dress.) It doe come in handy when 007 uses its bezel's buzz-saw feature to slic through rope binding his hands.

In Bond's toiletry kit, a bug detector awaits use, as does a hairbrus concealing a radio transmitter. Bond is also equipped with a speci shark gun designed so that the barrel and butt come apart and f innocuously into a case. The gun shot compressed gas pellets, whic caused its target to inflate and explode.

The Man With the Golden Gun

Several intriguing devices appear in Roger Moore's sophomor outing as Bond, although these are destined for the villain's disposa These include a car that converts into an airplane (achieved in par with the use of miniatures) and a fantastic 24 carat gold pistol wielde by Scaramanga. The gun is quite ingenious, assembled from ordinar looking wardrobe accessories. *Gun* also allows another brief visit t "Q"'s workshop, where a technician blows up an entire brick wall wit a rocket-firing 35mm camera mounted on a tripod. "Q" provide Bond with a truly "titillating" gadget – a third nipple, an identifyin abnormality of Scaramanga. ("Q" must have quite a good tim outfitting female agents with similar devices!) Less "abreast" of th times is a homing device disguised as a button on Mary Goodnight' frock.

Various paraphernalia (some unused)
from *Diamonds Are Forever*.

The Spy Who Loved Me

The gadget-crazy days of the 1960s were brought back with the 1977 Bond epic *The Spy Who Loved Me*. The most memorable piece of technology on display is Bond's latest automobile – a Lotus Esprit every bit the rival of the legendary Aston Martin. The Lotus is forever etched in Bond history as "Roger's car", while the Aston Martin is immortalized as "Sean's car". The Lotus displays its fascinating array of gadgets with a sensational car chase that takes Bond from the mountains of Sardinia to the depths of the Mediterranean Sea. So spectacular are the special effects in this sequence that it took 70 technicians three months of pre-production planning and five weeks of filming to finalize a scene occupying less than 3 minutes of screen time. When fullly equipped with the special gadgetry called for in the screenplay, the final cost topped $100,000.

As with the Aston Martin, several different models were utilized with varying functions according to filming requirements. The first vehicle was fully operational and was utilized in the scene in which Bond's car was pursued by a motorcycle and a helicopter. A second Lotus consisted only of the body frame, wheels and steering column. This was the actual car seen diving into the water. In order to propel this particular vehicle, which had no motor, a pick-up truck was used to push the car until it reached a speed of 60 mph to travel along a dock and hit the water. A third car was used for a sequence featuring the submerged vehicle's wheels retracting in favor of "fins", propellers and a rear rudder. This car consisted of nothing but hydraulic systems operated by a technician inside the Lotus. The fourth Lotus was actually able to travel underwater. It contained four motors and could accelerate up to 6 knots, although controlling the steering proved to be a nightmare for the driver (who was equipped with a diver's outfit and oxygen mask, as the car filled with water). To combat the poor visibility, red strobe lights were used.

Other features of the Lotus utilized by Bond include:

● A ballistic rocket used to destroy a helicopter. This was accomplished on-screen by mounting a projectile (actually some aluminium tubing) into a small tube which contained a scuba tank. A burst of air released by the tank propelled the missile through the water.

● A cement spray affixing to the windscreen of a pursuing car, making visibility impossible.

● An oil release mechanism, which on land provides a slick. Under water, the oil acts as a "smoke screen" to camouflage the movement of the vehicle.

● Harpoon guns which fire missiles from astern.

● A periscope for visibility and direction co-ordination while underwater.

Complementing Bond's aquatic arsenal was a newly developed "Wetbike", resembling a motorcycle on waterskis. Roger Moore is seen riding the bike sans stuntman, but not before having taken several un-Bondian spills in the sea during practice sessions.

The Spy Who Loved Me gives us a look at "Q"'s Egyptian workshop, hidden in a pyramid. Among the goodies on display are a serving tray that can decapitate a dinner guest. After seeing the device successfully demonstrated on a dummy, "Q" deadpans "I want that ready for Akmid's tea party". Other amusing gadgets include stools with ejection seats; Arabian smoking pipes that shoot bullets; cement firing double-barreled guns; and camel saddles with ejecting razor blades.

Other devices employed by Bond include a Seiko wristwatch which prints and displays a ticker tape message from "M"; a ski pole doubling as a high powered rifle; and a cigarette case and lighter housing a micro-film viewer.

Moonraker

For this 11th Bond film, agent 007 is literally sent out of this world. As one would expect, "Q" branch would have to work overtime in order to equip Bond with gadgets that function both on land and outer space. Among the "novelties" Bond is provided with is a wri bracelet that can fire cyanide-coated or armour-piercing darts. Bor also faces aquatic action in *Moonraker*, and must rely on two custor made motorboats provided by "Q". The first appears to be a standard Venetian gondola. However, when necessary, it can conve into a high speed motorboat and hovercraft.

Somewhat more plausible is the "Q" Craft, actually a modifie Glaston Carlson Scimitar, capable of ejecting mines and torpede launched by Bond. When he cannot avoid falling into the famed Igac Falls of Brazil, the boat provides a hangglider, lifting 007 over the fa to safety.

Back on land, we accompany Bond to "Q"'s Brazilian worksho where his staff is predictably testing new deadly "product lines Among them: exploding bolas, a sombrero-clad dummy that spli open to reveal a blazing machine gun; and a laser pistol that ca literally melt an opponent. Ironically, this entire operation is conceale within a monastery (no wonder there is so much concern about ho church contributions are utilized!). An additional item employed b Bond is a clever safe-cracking device disguised as a cigarette cas ("Q" is in trouble if Bond ever kicks the smoking habit). The cas contains an X-ray device that secures the proper combination for ar lock. A companion piece is a lighter which contains a mini camer bearing a "007" inscription (the center "O" serves as the lens!). "Q' final contribution to *Moonraker* is a new Seiko explosive wristwatc whose wind button houses a long fuse wire. Pressing the time se button causes a detonation.

ger Moore poses next to the amazing
crostar jet from *Octopussy*.

bove: The water ski from *The Spy
ho Loved Me* and *(Below)* The hang
der and lethal speedboat from
oonraker.

For Your Eyes Only

During the obligatory visit to "Q" branch, we see a phony "cast" for a broken arm springing outward with shattering force. Also on display s an umbrella whose ribs contain razor-sharp knives which slam round the user's neck when rain hits the device, and a computer onsole, the Identigraph, used to recreate 3-D composite features of uspected villains. By entering the relevant data, a reasonable likeness s immediately displayed and transmitted through Interpol. Seconds ater, a positive identification can be obtained.

For Your Eyes Only also marks an encore appearance by the Lotus Esprit, although it proved to be the car's swansong. In one cene, enemy agents scoff at a window sticker labeled "Burglar Protected". When they smash the window, however, sensors ontained within the sticker cause the car to explode.

Later, Bond is equipped with a replacement Lotus and amusingly nstructs a passenger not to touch any of the buttons, allowing the audience to snicker in contemplation of the potentially disastrous consequences if he did.

The only other notable gadget in *Eyes* is a wristwatch doubling as a walkie-talkie, which is also capable of transmitting digital message read-outs. This is put to advantage during a hilarious epilogue in which Prime Minister Thatcher believes she is congratulating Bond on a job well done when in fact she is speaking with a rather naughty parrot. Well, it plays much better than it reads!

Octopussy

Octopussy marked another return to the high tech world of the 1960s James Bond. This is apparent from the pre-credits sequence involving Bond's use of a mini-jet aircraft known as a Bede Acrostar. When planning *Moonraker*, Cubby Broccoli had read an article about stunt man Corky Fornoff, the inventor of this remarkable little craft. What impressed Broccoli was the fact that Fornoff had flown the plane through an amazingly narrow opening in an airplane hangar for a stunt used in a Japanese t.v. commercial. Cubby envisioned a similar stunt for *Moonraker's* opening but later switched the emphasis to skydiving, having been inspired by a sequence in Roger Moore's own superb war film *The Wild Geese*. The Acrostar scene was resurrected for *Octopussy* with Fornoff flying his own plane.

The Acrostar itself is the world's smallest jet plane. At 12 feet in length and 5 feet 8 inches in height, it weighs only 450 lbs with a wingspan of 17 feet. The aircraft can cruise at 260 mph and can obtain a top speed of 310 mph, reaching altitudes of 30,000 feet. As of 1983, there are only two of these planes in the world and both are owned and operated by Fornoff.

Among the less spectacular, but still impressive, devices provided by "Q" are:

● An attaché case with a false bottom to contain disguises and high explosives.
● An imitation Fabergé Egg containing a homing and listening

device. (Bond's special watch also acts as a receiver and direction finder for the homing device.)

● A Mont Blanc fountain pen which released a nitric acid mixture capable of dissolving all metals. The pen also has an earpiece which picks up converations "heard" by the Fabergé Egg's "bug".

● A mini-submarine disguised as a crocodile. This rather novel invention features a silent-running electric motor, buoyancy tanks to enable diving and surfacing, and a console display terminal in the croc's head. Oxygen tanks circulate air within the device. Included in the blueprint for this gadget, but never seen on-screen, are a periscope and a missile-launching system located in the "belly". Amazingly, there is still room inside for Bond, although the croc's dimensions probably exceed that of the entire Spanish Armada.

● A helium balloon operated by "Q", complete with a closed-circuit t.v. system and a huge Union Jack on the canvas. (With subtle identifiable markings such as these, it becomes easy to see why "Q" is not known for his discretion as a field agent.)

A View to a Kill

Roger Moore's final appearance as Bond saw him utilizing some of least spectacular gadgetry in the series. These surprisingly non-let "toys" included:

● "Snooper", a sort of alien house-pet/robot whose mo ments are controlled by remote radio signals. Snooper transm video images via cameras in his "eyes". He also sports retractable neck which enables him to capture images at vario heights. While this unit might make a popular children's toy would prove just a wee bit obvious if seen darting about the bo rooms of the Kremlin.

● A min-submarine disguised as an iceberg. Inside the appears to be little of practical use, although there are plenty alcoholic beverages and other temptations aboard to allow Bo to seduce his female fellow-submariner.

● A billfold which uses ultra-violet light to read previou

written material by picking up the indentations of pen marks on the underlying paper.

● A camera ring with a lens encased in its jewel.
● A pair of polarized sunglasses whose rotatable lenses filter out all sun glare.
● A shaver that doubles for a listening device detector.
● A credit card modified by "Q" Branch, allowing easy by-passing of window locks.

nfortunately, these devices are not utilized in an overly creative shion. Not to worry, for the filmmakers decided that with a new tor playing Bond in the next film, it was time to become more ealistic in terms of the script and the gadgetry.

The Living Daylights

or Timothy Dalton's impressive debut as Bond, he was afforded a ew and improved Aston Martin V8 Volante, a highly stylized dated version of its ancestor from the *Goldfinger* days. There are a w features both cars have in common: tire slashing devices (on alton's model, laser beams installed in the hubcaps do the job), and ulletproof body, engine and passenger compartment; a scanning gital radio receiving all police and military wavebands; twin missiles oncealed in the front "fog lights"; a jet engine booster making it ossible for the car to be propelled at incredible speed; tires with uds for driving on ice; convertible skis hidden under the doors lowing the car to be steered accurately on snow and ice; and a self-estruct mechanism Bond employs during a breathtaking escape.

At "Q"'s headquarters, we see the generally irritable genius in a rather playful mood. He demonstrates a portable stereo/cassette player that converts into a rocket launcher ("... Something for the Americans – called a 'Ghetto Blaster!'") and a sophisticated data base retrieving a number of suspects. We also see a rare glimpse of "Q"'s humor as he invites one of his staff to sit on a couch, only to have the piece of furniture literally swallow-up the hapless fellow.

The new Bond also gets the usual inventory of hi-tech goodies, including a key ring packed with "stun gas" effective up to 5 feet, activated by Bond whistling "Rule Britannia". An accompanying key ring finder carries a lethal explosive detonated if the need arises by a wolf-whistle generally used to express admiration for a pretty girl. Bond also utilizes a high powered rifle with armor-piercing bullets, attached to a preposterously large infra-red scope. Finally, there is also a pair of binoculars adapted for normal eyeglass frames.

Licence to Kill

Timothy Dalton's success as Bond led to his return in *Licence to Kill*, the most realistic Bond epic since *On Her Majesty's Service*. Items displayed as ideal for "the man on holiday" include an exploding alarm clock (presumably for very deep sleepers!), a toothpaste tube containing plastic explosives, and a cigarette box housing a fuse and detonator. Most interesting of *LTK*'s gadgetry is a signature gun resembling a movie camera with an "optical palm reader" located in the grip so that only Bond can activate the firing mechanism. We also see an instant camera that not only takes X-ray photos of its subjects, but also emits a laser beam.

cing page: Timothy Dalton's "wheels" the Aston Martin Volante.

Q" still coming to the rescue in *Licence Kill*, presenting Bond and Pam with ome deadly hardware.

EXPOSED! THE "LOST" 007 SEQUENCES

Scene 523. *The Man With The Golden Gun,* Exterior-beachfront on Scaramanga's Island:

"James Bond and Scaramanga stand back to back, their weapons raised towards the sky in preparation for a traditional duel. The men begin backing away from each other, but when the countdown hits "zero" each combatant dives for cover on opposite sides of the battlefield. "Now I know how you do it, Scaramanga!", shouts Bond in reference to his rival's unblemished record of victory in identical situations. "The secret of success is never take chances", counters Scaramanga, seconds before dashing behind a rock, prompting a shot from Bond's Walther PPK. "That leaves you five!" taunts the arch-villain, to which Bond responds "four more than you!" The stalking cat and mouse game continues, with each duellist attempting to expose his rival's position. Bond wastes three more shots in futile attempts to terminate his foe, while Scaramanga cunningly tries to lure Bond into his deadly "Funhouse". Bond expels his last bullet, firing at a hastily made "dummy" Scaramanga has fashioned of himself with a wooden plank, and articles of his clothing, stuffed with seaweed. When Scaramanga fires the one bullet in his famed Golden Gun, Bond assumes his nemesis is out of ammunition. Scaramanga grins as he loads another golden bullet into his gun's chamber and dashes into his Funhouse. Bond chases Scaramanga into the villain's lair, and the murderous trap which has been set for him . . ."

The success of each individual 007 film has been painstak[ing] achieved, resulting from innumerable revisions made thro[ugh] out the course of the project. Every Bond film undergo[es a] standardised evolutionary process from its inception as a basic [idea] of a screenplay, to a final shooting script; progressing to raw uned[ited] film footage; and ultimately emerging as a completed motion pict[ure]. Original concepts are changed or restaged to maximize the th[eme] while other modifications are prompted by unforeseen logis[tic] problems. Some sequences may be shot in their entirety, but [they] may be eliminated from the final print. The earlier extract from *Man With the Golden Gun* illustrates this case, although a portion [of it] does appear in the U.S. teaser trailer).

In most cases the changes tend to be sensible and benef[icial]. However, amidst an era of widespread interest in documenting [and] restoring "lost" script materials, wouldn't it be fascinating to disco[ver] some of those missing 007 sequences that may have existed on[ly in] an early draft of a screenplay? Well, you need wait no longer. N[ow], for the first time, we present a listing of many such script out-takes.

Even Bond aficionados may be enlightened to discover:

In *Live And Let Die*, the speedboat chase on the bayou intende[d to] show Bond and his pursuers disrupting a spectacular water sk[i] show, causing a pyramid of performers to spill into the water.

The invincible Jaws was to have died from falling into a furnac[e in] *The Spy Who Loved Me*.

The sequence in *OHMSS* where Bond purchases Tracy's wedd[ing] ring, originally included a glimpse of Irma Bunt watching from [the] shadows.

Left: Deleted fight scene between Bon[d] and Adam in *Live and Let Die*.

Facing page: German lobby card illustrating a deleted scene from *Diamonds Are Forever.*

View's original screenplay had Zorin manipulating the course of Halley's comet to cause worldwide destruction.

erally hundreds of revisions are made during the construction of :h Bond film, some simply reflecting changes to character's ntities:

Afghan leader Kamran Shah (The Living Daylights) was originally known as Ranjit.

Corinne Dufour in *Moonraker* was first named Trudi Parker. Her name change occurred upon the signing of French actress Corinne Clery. Similarly, the beautiful agent Aki in *You Only Live Twice* was originally named Suki. The revision came about to "honor" actress Akiko Wakabayashi, who ultimately played the part.

while many other script changes reflect substantial revisions to otlines originally envisioned:

In an early draft of *The Living Daylights*, Bond and Kara prepare to ditch the cargo plane they are piloting, but alter course when sighted by friendly military aircraft. Bond lands the plane on an aircraft carrier, skidding across the deck until it teeters on the edge. The plane plunges over the side, but its cargo netting latches on to the ship's derrick, allowing Bond and Kara to climb to safety.

The most notable alteration concerned the script for *Diamonds Are Forever*, whose original storyline found Bond menaced by the brother of Goldfinger! (Gert Frobe was even approached for the role). This confrontation was ultimately scrapped to allow the re-appearance of Blofeld, marking his third consecutive Bond showcase, as the film's main protagonist.

Further revisions centered on the climax of *Diamonds* which underwent extensive rewrites. An early script proposed a thrilling boat chase on Lake Mead, culminating with Blofeld trapped above

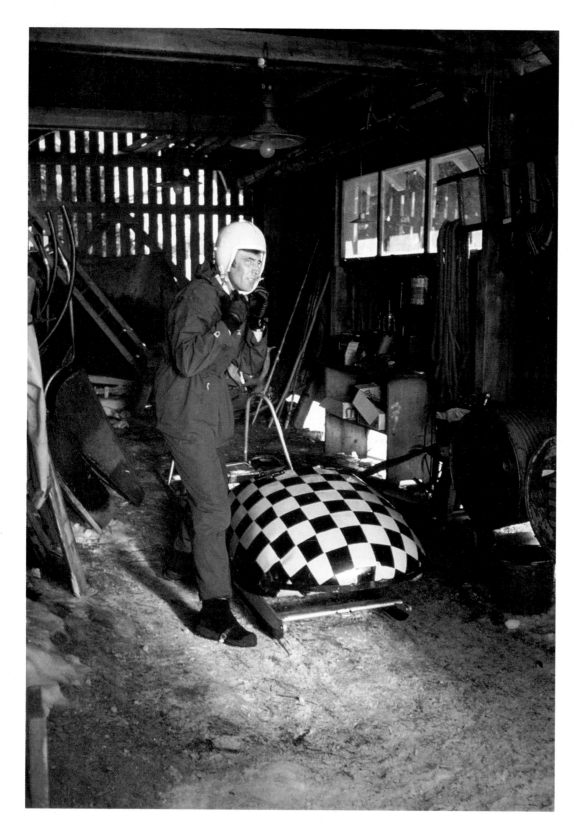

Left: In the original script for *OHMS*
Bond was to pursue Blofeld on a
snowshovel! Fortunately, it was deci
Bond was to utilize this bobsled for t
classic chase sequence.

Right: A deleted scene from the
"missing" beach shoot-out from *The
Man With the Golden Gun*.

oover Dam by an exotic fleet of vessels from the casinos, whose aptains respond to Bond's plea to "Do your duty for Las Vegas!" he finished script relocated the finale, suggesting an enormous elicopter battle on an off shore drilling rig.

During the fierce battle, U.S. frogmen were to dive from the tacking choppers affixing dynamite charges to the oil rig's supports. leanwhile, Blofeld escapes via his bathosub. Bond spots him and ursues the villain by commandeering a weather balloon, enabling m to fly over Blofeld's escaping sub.

Arriving onshore, Bond chases Blofeld into a salt-mining plant, timately thrusting the SPECTRE chieftain to his death in a granulator. urprisingly, this sequence was to be resurrected in *Live and Let Die*. lowever, while out location hunting, the scouts came across a arning sign cautioning: "Trespassers Will Be Eaten!", protecting a rocodile farm. The audacity of the sign so intrigued the filmmakers nat the original scene was abandoned in favor of a crocodile farm etting.

Not all changes to the scripts are as drastic. Often the transition etween script and screen involves minor alterations in method while emaining loyal to basic themes:

In *Dr. No*, a variation of the finale had Bond locating Honey, imprisoned in her room, posed with a bottle of liquor as a weapon. She faints in Bond's arms. Bond steadies Honey, while simultaneously catching the bottle before it smashes to the floor. Removing the cork with his teeth, he takes a swig, tosses it aside and carries Honey to safety.

In *Thunderball*, Bond initially escaped from Fiona and her henchmen in the corridor of his hotel. When a waiter passes wheeling a room service cart Bond clutches a cookstove as a weapon and flees, although Fiona manages to wound him in the leg. In the finished film, Bond escapes from Fiona's car by igniting a bottle of rum spilled by a passing drunkard.

The pre-credits scene for *The Spy Who Loved Me* was set at sea, with Bond and his paramour about to make love on a raft. Bond's pager indicates a signal from "M", and the agent steps off the raft onto a surfboard which he rides to shore and a waiting Jeep. The setting was later relocated to allow stuntman Rick Sylvester to demonstrate his talents on skis.

Similarly, *Thunderball*'s pre-credits sequence featuring the fight between Bond and the widow was originally set in an Oriental strip club/gambling establishment, with the villain posed as a cabaret girl dressed in a peacock costume. The final film changed the location to a funeral, and the peacock became a widow.

In *For Your Eyes Only*, Bond was to dump a huge mound of snow and ice from a truck onto the villainous hockey players. "A real snow job", noted 007.

In the same film, Kriegler threatens Bond with a huge block of marble, and then he steps on a loose floorboard which springs up, hitting him in the crotch. This causes Kriegler to fall through the window to his death.

In the climax aboard the cruise ship in *Diamonds Are Forever*, Wint and Kidd, posing as waiters, lure Bond from his stateroom under the guise of an urgent call. By the time Bond discovers the ruse, Tiffany is bound and spread-eagled on a bed, terrorized by a suspended vat of boiling oil. Bond springs into action and lowers himself through the cabin porthole. A fight ensues, culminating with 007 thrusting the hot oil toureen at Wint, scalding the villain's face and causing him to be impaled on an ice cornucopia. Bond tosses brandy on the flaming shish-kebabs wielded by Kidd, whose torso erupts into flames. 007 then tosses him through a port hole.

Bond editor and director Peter Hunt has informed us that only a minimum number of scenes were deleted from the early films, as budgetary considerations mandated that the script be "fine-tuned" before the camera rolled. Yet inevitable exceptions have surfaced:

In *OHMSS*, Bond visits Sir Hillary at the College of Arms only to discover a SPECTRE agent eavesdropping. Bond stalks and then eliminates the enemy in a rail station.

For reasons unknown, many European prints of *OHMSS* eliminate the entire sequence where Bond breaks into an attorney's safe in Switzerland to photograph secret documents. Some versions also omit the brief scene in which Bond's contact argues vainly with one of Blofeld's guards to gain access to Piz Gloria by cable car.

Left: Honey is staked out as fodder for Jamaican Land Crabs in *Dr. No*.

Right: "*En Garde!*" this action sequence from *Octopussy* was originally scripted for *Moonraker*.

In *Diamonds Are Forever*, Bond avoids his brush with cremation at the Slumber Mortuary, and commandeers a hearse which he races to the Tropicana Hotel and Casino. Screeching to a halt at the front door, Bond tells the startled doorman to, "Have whatever's inside [the hearse] sent up to my room!"

While some deletions did not radically affect the plotline, several edits may have created continuity problems:

During the gondola ride in *From Russia With Love*, Bond displays the reel of film shot by SPECTRE showing 007 and Tania making love. Bond holds a few frames to the sunlight and says, "He was right, you know" – a meaningless comment in the final print. In fact, he was referring to Red Grant's critique of the juicy footage – "What a performance!" – which was deleted from the film.

The death of Plenty O'Toole in *Diamonds Are Forever* is never satisfactorily explained due to a key sequence that was excised. Plenty returns to Bond's room after her unceremonious dump into the pool, courtesy of invading gangsters. She secretly observes Bond making love to Tiffany Case, and rummages through Tiffany's purse to obtain her address (presumably to exact some sort of revenge). Arriving at Tiffany's house, Wint and Kidd mistake her for Case, their next target. Plenty is murdered and again discarded into a pool, but this time with her feet encased in a block of cement.

Occasionally, sequences had to be amended due to reasons beyor the control of the filmmakers:

In *Dr. No*, Honey's predicament, as per Fleming's novel, was to b retained, showing her staked-out as human fodder for gia Jamaican land crabs. Although attempts were made to film th sequence, the crabs were considerably less enthused abou crawling all over Ursula Andress than human thespians might hav been, and, in fact, all of the crabs eventually died. A less inventiv situation was substituted with Honey facing the prospect c drowning. Fleming was outraged over the dropping of the origin concept, but the filmmakers pacified him by promising to shoc the "rats in the tunnel" sequence in the next Bond epic, *Fro Russia With Love*.

One obvious continuity error almost made it into the final cut c *From Russia With Love*, recalls Peter Hunt. Bond's taxi is trailed b Bulgarian agent, who in turn is tailed by Bond's friend Kerim Be Bond slams on the brakes of the taxi, causing the three cars t crash and sandwiching the Bulgarian vehicle, rendering it incapab of further pursuit. As Bond and Kerim are about to step into th car of another assistant, Kerim says to the villain, "My friend, that life!" Although the scene worked well, it had to be deleted when member of director Terence Young's family discovered a poir that had been overlooked: the Bulgarian had been killed by Bon earlier.

...me ideas, reflecting errors in judgment, occasionally surfaced; ...ankfully to be rejected at a later date:

The first draft of *Dr. No* featured the title character as the main protagonist's pet monkey. Bond confronts the villainous Buchfield, whose capuchin monkey, Lee Ying, sits perched on his shoulder. As Lee Ying displays a menacing grin, Bond realizes "*This* is Dr. No . . . how clever!"

When George Lazenby assumed the Bond role in *OHMSS*, a concept was briefly entertained to explain that Bond's new look was the result of plastic surgery, designed to alter 007's all too recognizable features. The idea was shelved as being patronizing to audiences.

...ccasionally, controversy necessitated compromises to avoid ...oblems with the censors:

To justify Bond's killing of Professor Dent in *Dr. No*, an alternative version was filmed showing Dent firing a remaining shot from his pistol, hitting the wall behind Bond. Bond simultaneously fires to kill Dent in self-defense. Director Terence Young argued for Bond's "cold-blooded" killing of Dent, whose gun is empty in the final version. However, several "excessive" shots by Bond into the mortally wounded Dent were deleted.

An underwater scene in *Thunderball* had Bond and Domino making love behind a mountain of coral. A huge explosion of bubbles rises to the surface, followed by Domino's bathing suit. Presumed to be too suggestive, the scene was discarded.

Tom Mankiewicz's script for *Live and Let Die* had the ethnic backgrounds of the two female leads reversed: Solitaire was to have been black, and Rosie Carver was to have been white. United Artists balked at the concept, thus the role reversal. Incidentally, while attending the film's première in South Africa, Roger Moore was shocked to discover the Bond-Rosie love scenes had been deleted by the censor.

In *Licence to Kill* Sanchez's grisly revenge against Lupe's lover Alverez is hinted at offscreen. The actual depiction of the removal of the man's heart was more graphically illustrated, but trimmed due to excessive gore.

Bond's original introduction to Pussy Galore in *Goldfinger* went something like this. Pussy: "I'm Pussy Galore". Bond: "I know, but what's your name?" The sequence was amended to Bond's responding "I must be dreaming!" It had been difficult enough to gain approval for use of Galore's first name.

The initial plot of *The Spy Who Loved Me* centered on an international terrorist organization which attempts to overthrow SPECTRE and replace its goals of larceny and blackmail with an all-out plot to decimate the world's population. The idea was scrapped as being "too political" for a Bond film.

Australian censors were offended by the intensity of the train fight sequence in *From Russia with Love* and trimmed the scene to a fraction of its original length. The scene in question is considered to be an example of near-perfect acting, direction and editing.

As recently as 1989, censors still incurred the wrath of Bond fans. In Great Britain, several seconds were snipped off scenes in *Licence to Kill* due to alleged excessive violence; notably, Sanchez's fiery death.

Time considerations are often responsible for sequences being trimmed or deleted. Peter Hunt related that he had exceeded the promised running time of *OHMSS* by at least twenty minutes. Heartbroken, he could not bear to cut any further scenes. The producers decided to let the influential manager of the Leicester Square Odeon Theater in London, where the Bonds traditionally premièred, to unwittingly act as arbitrator. Asked if any footage should be deleted to allow for an extra showing each day, his reply was: "Don't dare edit anything!" Thanks to this gentleman's desire to put art over profit, audiences can revel in the most leisurely paced, yet emotionally stirring Bond film to date. Nevertheless, not all Bond epics fared as well:

In *A View to a Kill* "Q"'s Snooper device penetrates Zorin's pumping station only to be attacked by a guard dog. Snooper responds by squirting a stream of fluid in the killer canine's eyes.

In *Live And Let Die* Bond greets his driver at Kennedy Airport but the man fails to give the proper recognition code. Bond's Walther prompts his contact's memory, and he utters a password referring to New York's baseball teams, the Mets and the Yankees.

Bond's somersaulting car in *The Man With The Golden Gun* was to have been pursued by police cars, only they ended up "in the drink" trying to emulate the 007 stunt.

Dr. No urged Bond to transmit a message to Leiter assuring him that Crab Key was "clean". In return, No promised a less painful death for Bond and Honey, arrogantly assuring them they would be kept alive only long enough to see his scheme succeed.

In *Diamonds Are Forever* a scene showed Bond wining and dining Plenty O'Toole in the restaurant of the Whyte House Hotel and Casino. Here, Bond rejects a wine as unsatisfactory, and is admired by a beautiful female harp player floating on a large "sea shell" in an adjacent pool.

In *Moonraker* Drax conducted a board meeting with his industrial cohorts in the blast chamber of the shuttle.

While the time factor plays a major role in scene editing (for example, the first version of *You Only Live Twice* ran over three hours!), it is gratifying that many such scenes are revived in later Bond films:

In the trailer for *Thunderball* Bond says: "The things I do for England", as Fiona begins to undress him. The line does not appear in the final print, however, although it does reappear in a similar scene with Helga in *You Only Live Twice*.

The "keel-hauling" scene from *For Your Eyes Only* was origina[l] slated for *Live And Let Die*, as the sequence actually occurs in th[e] novel.

The elephant hunt in *Octopussy* was originally scripted for *The Ma[n] With The Golden Gun*; and the pre-credit ski jump in *The Spy W[ho] Loved Me* had once been considered as a mode of escape f[or] Blofeld in *OHMSS*.

The Acrostar pre-credits scene from *Octopussy* was envisione[d] initially for *Moonraker*, as Bond and Holly would pilot Acrosta[r] above a South American river. However, before filming, the riv[er] bed dried up.

Moonraker's battle inside a Venetian glass factory was origina[l] written for *The Spy Who Loved Me*, set in an Egyptian antiqu[e] museum.

Bond's arrival via hang glider to Kananga's mansion in *Live And L[et] Die* was considered as 007's method of transportation to Marie[']s residence in the pre-credits of *Diamonds Are Forever*.

The rejected plastic surgery plot to introduce the new Bond [in] *OHMSS* formed the basis for Blofeld's doubles in *Diamonds A[re] Forever*.

Screenplay updates were often necessitated by a new actor assumin[g] the Bond mantle. As writing progressed, prior to the casting of a ne[w] Bond, "fine tuning" became critical to play up the actor's individu[al] personality and interpretation of the role. For Roger Moore, the *Liv[e] And Let Die* script was altered considerably to tone down its viole[nt]

Bond wines and dines the ill-fated Plenty O'Toole in this lost scene from *Diamonds Are Forever*.

Left: Nurse Pat Fearing returns Bond's mink-lined affections in this deleted scene from *Thunderball*.

Right: Bond examines a trick camera from "Q" Branch but the gadget never made it to the final print of *The Man With the Golden Gun*.

ects. The fight between Bond and Kananga was originally a more otracted and brutal affair. Keeping with Roger's lighter touch, the ene omitted the gore.

Love scenes, too, were altered. When it was determined Connery ght return as Bond, plans were made for Ursula Andress to appear as Honey Rider. But the idea had to be dropped as dress and Moore had no previous chemistry to which audiences uld relate.

e script for *The Living Daylights* was originally written with Roger oore in mind. When Timothy Dalton assumed Bond's licence to kill, veral key changes befitting his style had to be made. Most notable is the deletion of an elaborate scene set in Tangiers where Bond is rsued across rooftops. He sends one policeman plunging into a vat red dye ("Better red than dead" was the intended Moore-ism), en utilizes a small rug as a "flying" carpet, riding it along wires on a ephone pole, to the amazement of the crowds below. The scene ncluded with 007 grabbing onto a huge banner and dropping onto passing motorcycle for a convenient ride. These sequences were tually filmed, but were wisely shelved. Remember, Dalton was to a serious interpretation of Bond.

ot even "Q" Branch is immune to having its deadly playthings cised from the finished films:

For *The Man With The Golden Gun*, Bond was to possess a rocket-firing camera that also emitted stun gas and a a self-destruct device linked to the shutter speed selector. To 007's chagrin, the only thing it couldn't do was take pictures! Complementing the 35mm arsenal, was an exploding thermos exploited in the climactic battle against Scaramanga.

A close look at scenes reflected on the body of the "golden girl" in the credits of *Goldfinger*, reveals a device not seen on theater screens – a machine gun mounted in a Post Office truck.

A scene shot for *A View to A Kill* finds Bond in police custody in Paris, due to his reckless pursuit of May Day. As the desk sergeant documents Bond's possessions, he announces "one watch!" only to find it contains a garrotting wire; "one pen!" emitting a deadly acidic ink; and "one lighter!" discharging a flame-throwing device, almost scorching the sergeant's forehead.

In *The Living Daylights*, "Q" gives Bond a pen capable of duplicating writings made by any other pen; and in *Live And Let Die* Bond tests a shark gun by firing its gas pellet into the jaws of the prey. As the shark inflates and bursts, Bond quips "Wait 'till "Q" hears about this!"

Occasionally, a sequence is reshot when the screenwriters discover a more inspired idea:

In *For Your Eyes Only*, Bond drops the villain into a river, commenting "The party's a washout!"

Before it occurred to the writers to introduce a new Aston Martin in *The Living Daylights*, Bond and Kara were to escape from behind the Iron Curtain via a pilfered KGB automobile and an ice yacht.

The snake assault scene from *Live and Let Die* had the serpent leaping at Bond's mirrored reflection, whereupon the agent crushes it in a medicine cabinet. The revised scene shows Bond igniting the snake by using a cigar and an aerosol spray can.

Peter Hunt has confided that *You Only Live Twice* was to have contained three separate car chases; but then "Little Nellie" was discovered.

This chapter has presented only a fraction of the more entertaining and, perhaps, controversial out-takes from the Bond films. While the final screen versions have unquestionably been both financial and artistic successes, we continue to enjoy these "lost sequences", in the hope that one day, they may be restored on home video.

JAMES BOND BLOOPERS

No one is infallible – not even James Bond! Although the 007 films have traditionally been praised for their handsome production values, it is inevitable that in a body of work extending four decades a few mistakes or "bloopers" will surface. Some are quite obvious, but in fairness, most are so subtle that they become apparent only after many viewings. Indeed, you'll need the "still frame" of your VCR or laser disc player to spot many of these mistakes, or continuity errors. If readers can supply additions to this listing, their input would be welcomed. Now sit back and enjoy these SPECTRE-inspired slip-ups pertaining to our (almost) perfect, favourite secret agent!

Dr. No

A villain uses a megaphone to shout warnings to Bond as he hides in a ditch on Crab Key. At one point his voice remains magnified even when the megaphone is nowhere near his mouth.

Escaping a cell, Bond almost drowns in a series of seemingly endless airshafts, as cascades of water appear and disappear suddenly. He escapes by kicking the grillwork from a vent leading to Dr. No's laboratory. The existence of this vent, however, would have allowed the waves of water to exit into the lab, which is as dry as Bond's Martini.

As Bond awaits the arrival of Professor Dent at Miss Taro's apartment, there is a close-up of Bond fitting a silencer onto his pistol. While Bond is wearing a necktie in previous shots, the close-up shows that the tie is no longer present.

When Miss Taro gives 007 directions to her home, she tells Bond t[he] address is 239 Magenta Drive. Yet, when Bond later phones for a c[ab] he states the address as 2171 Magenta Drive, while Miss Taro nods [in] affirmation.

Prior to Dent's assassination, Bond tells him "That's a Smith a[nd] Wesson, Professor, and you've had your six [shots]!" However, t[he] gun Dent is holding is actually a Colt .45 with a seven-shot capacity.

Although Bond is assigned a Walther PPK as his new official handg[un] earlier in the film, he uses a Browning 1910 .32 caliber to kill De[nt.] This gun may have been substituted because it allows for ea[sy] connection to a silencer.

From Russia With Love

In both the British and American trailers (or "coming attractions"), t[he] name of every major cast member is mentioned, except for on[e] "minor" exception – Sean Connery!

During the Gypsy fight sequence, Bond is seen cocking his Walthe[r] PPK automatic pistol several times. This need only be done if blank[s] are being used. When live ammunition is utilized, the cocking proce[ss] is done automatically.

As Blofeld chastises Klebb and Kronsteen, his SPECTRE ring appear[s] on alternate hands.

In the main title credits, actress Martine Beswick is identified a[s] "Martin Beswick". (Ms. Beswick cannot have been too insulted as sh[e] later returned to co-star in *Thunderball*).

Bond opens the faucets to take a bath in his hotel suite. He [is] disturbed by a noise, which turns out to be Tanya entering his bed – [a] passionate evening ensues. However, he never turns off the faucet, s[o] where did all that water go?

Left: In this sequence with Prof. Dent from *Dr. No*, the length of Bond's sock varies from scene to scene.

Facing page: In this harrowing scene from *Dr. No*, Bond's life is threatened by a tarantula. However, in reality tarantula bites are rarely fatal.

Goldfinger

As Bond's plane plummets to the ground after depressurizing, the wires supporting the model of the plane can be seen. Also, the depressurization of the cabin would not automatically cause the plane to go hopelessly out of control.

After the bomb in Ft. Knox has been neutralized, Bond comments that in three more "ticks" Goldfinger's plan would have succeeded. However, the timer on the bomb indicates there are "007" seconds remaining to detonation, an afterthought of Harry Saltzman's requiring an insert shot of the countdown. Connery had already completed filming, and was unavailable to insert the revised voice-over, thus the blooper remained.

Casualties among the troops guarding Ft. Knox are revealed to be feigning death, as the fatal nerve gas was replaced by a harmless substance. Yet, we see numerous automobile wrecks that occurred along the depository's roadways. These could not have been arranged spontaneously without real loss to life and limb.

The gold supply in Ft. Knox is stored in such a way that the bricks of gold are stacked from floor to ceiling. In reality, gold is too soft a substance to be stored this way, and the bricks would be crushed under the tremendous weight.

Oddjob slays Tilly Masterson with his razor-brimmed derby. Yet, she is not decapitated, and there is nary a sign of blood despite the fact that earlier, the same chapeau severed the head from a statue.

In the epilogue, Bond is stunned to find that his plane has been hijacked by Goldfinger. Although it is implied that Bond, Goldfinger and Pussy are the only occupants of the plane, one can catch a quick glimpse of a Korean guard in the background as Goldfinger emerges from behind the curtains. After the plane depressurizes, widescreen prints of the film clearly show the guard inexplicably laying unconscious at Bond's feet.

When Bond glances in his car mirror, he noted the initials "T.M." on Tilley's riflecase. However, the initials are not reversed as they would be if he were viewing them in a mirror.

In the climactic fight in *Thunderball* observe the captain in the background. As Bond hits him, the captain's hat flies off, but due to an edit is in place again on his head by the time he hits the ground.

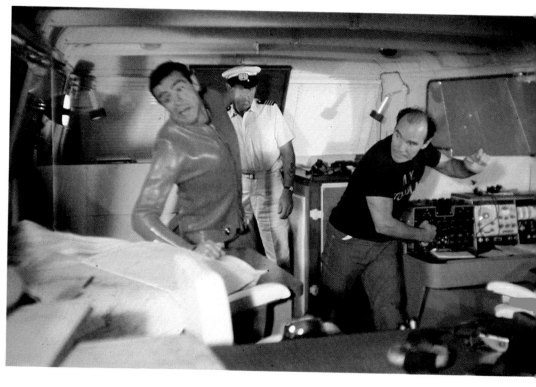

Below right: During this sequence from *Thunderball*, Felix Leiter's pants change from shorts to long pants, then back to shorts again.

As Leiter searches for Bond in the film's final scene, his helicopter is seen speeding through the sky. However, in a close-up none of the clouds in the background indicate any movement at all.

During the Ft. Knox assault, Goldfinger's henchman Kisch is disguised as a U.S. Army Officer. Yet, the stripes on his uniform are from the Air Force.

Thunderball

At one point, during Bond and Leiter's search for the Vulcan via helicopter, Leiter's voice is clearly that of Pinder, Bond's assistant in the Bahamas.

Bond is issued a "mini-breather" with an emergency four-minute supply of air. Yet, Bond utilizes the device for a far longer period during the climactic battle sequence.

When Bond swims to the secret rendezvous point for the SPECTRE frogmen, he has bare feet. Yet, when he rises from the water, he has footwear.

At several points during the underwater battle Bond's face-mask inexplicably changes color from black to blue.

When away from his hotel room, Bond leaves behind a mini-tape recorder to detect the entrance of any intruders. Presumably gone for hours, he returns and uses the device to find someone ha entered the room. However, the quantity of tape indicates it had th capacity to record for only a few minutes.

During the pre-credits sequence, Bond immobilizes pursuers b spraying a pressurized stream of water from a device in his Asto Martin. In reality, the car would have to contain water tanks large than the vehicle itself to make such a device functional!

nd, Domino, and a professor jump into the ocean moments before e DISCO VOLANTE explodes. Bond and Domino are rescued, but the e of the hapless professor is left unclear.

ring the spectacular Junkanoo parade one can observe several rchers carrying placards of decorated "007s". During the same quence, a dog can be observed "relieving himself" in the eground.

refully observe the opening gun barrel sequence. It appears as ough Bond almost stumbles during his gun-firing pivot, nearly using him to lose balance. The same sequence is repeated in black d white for *You Only Live Twice* and *Diamonds Are Forever*.

scene depicting Bond and Leiter in a helicopter reveals a reverse age, as evidenced by Bond's wristwatch being on the opposite nd and the part in his hair reversing.

You Only Live Twice

nd affirms to a contact that he has never been in Japan before. owever, in *From Russia With Love* Bond recalls a trip to Tokyo th "M".

hen Tanaka's helicopter implements a giant magnet to hoist up the ain's car and drop it in the ocean, Bond watches the entire affair on closed-circuit TV in his car. As there is no evidence of a second licopter, who could have filmed the incident?

nd does not correct Henderson when he orders 007 a Martini tirred, not shaken". 007 aficionados know he only consumes his artini if it is "Shaken, not stirred.".

uring a sequence set in Siberia, palm trees can be seen in the ckground.

nd is "murdered" when his "Murphy" bed snaps him up into the all and gunmen spray it with machine-gun fire. The action is part of a cret Service plan to deceive Bond's enemies into believing he is ead. If the gunmen use blanks, how can the police discover actual llet holes in the bed minutes later?

2"'s technicians remove the red propeller guards protecting Little ellie, yet just a few moments later we see the front guard still intact.

tering SPECTRE's volcano fortress, Bond is forced to flee a cave ue to the presence of highly poisonous gas. However, in the film's max, Bond and his allies are unaffected as they escape by swimming rough the same toxic cave.

Bond arrives atop Blofeld's volcano fortress with nothing but the clothes on his back. Seconds later he changes into a commando uniform, complete with bulky suction cups which he uses to penetrate the volcano. Not even Batman has a utility belt that elaborate!

On Her Majesty's Secret Service

Bond meets Blofeld wearing no disguise other than a pair of glasses. This dupes Blofeld despite their knowing each other from the last film. As for Blofeld's powers of observation, one might speculate that he had been a lookout at Pearl Harbor!

Blofeld claims proof of his ancestry is tied to a generic trait: lack of earlobes. However, it is quite obvious that Telly Savalas, who portrays the villain, is endowed with earlobes. Had they said that all of the previous Blofeld's lacked hair, Savalas's claims would have been indisputable.

When Blofeld is caught in the tree branch during the bob-sled chase, a close-up shows the branch around his neck. Yet, in the distant shot, his neck is clearly free and he is holding onto the tree with his hands.

As Bond plays at a gaming table, the cards he deals have white backings, yet seconds later the backings change to red.

Blofeld uncovers Bond's disguise when 007 mis-states the location of the SPECTRE chief's ancestral tombs. Blofeld says the true genealogist Sir Hillary Bray would know the correct location. In fact, Bond was actually repeating information given him by Sir Hillary.

Bond describes his personal Coat of Arms as bearing four bezants, or gold balls. Yet, in looking at the Coat of Arms, we see that there are only three bezants. This is actually a voiceover blooper, as lip-readers can see Lazenby enunciates the word three.

Diamonds Are Forever

In the pre-credits sequence, Bond is nearly assassinated by a villain lying in a mudbath. Obviously, a gun, submerged in mud for an extended period of time, could not have been relied upon to fire properly.

When Bond turns Tiffany over on the waterbed, one can observe she is wearing a "pastie" on her left breast.

Bond plants paste and glass diamonds inside the body of smuggler Peter Franks. Yet, they do not disintegrate following Franks' cremation. Shady Tree recovers them from the ashes.

Blofeld states that science was never his strong suit. Yet, in *OHMSS*, he is presented as a scientist/chemist.

During the pool fight, Bond is holding Bambi under the water with his right hand, but a second later he releases her from under his left hand.

During the oil rig battle, there are five helicopters – four identical, and a different one with Whyte. Two 'copters are destroyed in the battle. Yet, the three surviving helicopters are identical, including the one carrying Whyte.

During the moon buggy chase, a tire from the buggy can be seen bouncing into view. The axle broke five times, and when the blooper occurred, the buggy was actually lying immobile. Yet, in the next shot, the buggy's wheels are intact.

The most infamous Bond blooper occurs during the police car chase in Las Vegas. Driving into a narrow alley, Bond tilts his Mustang on two wheels to squeeze through the opening, only to have the car emerge on the opposite two wheels! Despite a last-minute continuity shot inserted to correct the blunder, the sequence is clearly a blooper.

During Bond's battle with Bambi and Thumper, a close look at the black villainess's dive into the pool shows her to be a different actress wearing a wig. Once in the pool, another glimpse shows her to be a Caucasian stuntwoman in makeup.

When "Q" continuously hits the jackpot in the Las Vegas casino, w the aid of his RPM Controller, the slot machines do not light up sound alarms as they normally would to indicate a big win.

Bond, imitating Bert Saxby's voice, is instructed by Blofeld to Willard Whyte. Later, the real Saxby shows up to carry out assassination. Since it was Bond who had spoken to Blofeld, how Saxby learn of the assassination plot?

In the side-show at the casino, the barker of the gorilla exh identifies the beast as originating from Nairobi, South Africa. In f. Nairobi is in Kenya.

The car Bond rents in Las Vegas has California license plates, inste of those issued by Nevada.

Live And Let Die

Rosie Carver screams at the sight of a dead snake in Bor bathroom. Her voice differs noticeably seconds later when s screams again upon discovering a voodoo warning, indicating c scream was an afterthought, and dubbed by a different actress.

The back of the Tarot cards featured in the film contain the numer "007". When Baron Samedi uncovers two of the tarot car foretelling Solitaire's impending death, they are not from the de used previously.

Left: At one point in this train fight fro Live and Let Die, a technician can be observed in the reflection of the window to Bond's left.

Facing page: Disguised as an alligator, Bond swims undisturbed through waters infested with the beasts. (Good thing for him it wasn't mating season!) Yet later in the film the thugs from Octopussy's palace are immediately eaten alive when they retreat through the same body of water. How did they initially swim to the palace without being eaten?

The Man With The Golden Gun

several points in the film, the voice of Bond's assistant, Lt. Hip, is bbed by a different actor.

nd and Goodnight are enjoying a romantic interlude aboard ramanga's junk when their encounter is interrupted by a phone from "M". How did "M" know of their whereabouts, and how did acquire the phone number for Scaramanga's vessel?

The Spy Who Loved Me

e song heard in Anya's music box transmitter is "Lara's Theme" m *Dr. Zhivago*, a work banned at the time in the Soviet Union.

Moonraker

Corinne dashes through the forest to escape Drax's Dobermans, e is alternately wearing sandals and boots.

ax's space station cannot be observed from earth because of its dar-blocking device. How could he build such a city in space livious to intelligence sources, when the device was not yet in use?

For Your Eyes Only

nd's bald, wheelchair-bound nemesis in the pre-credits is clearly earing a skull cap to conceal his hair.

ying *chemin de fer*, Bond is dealt a five and an ace. Yet, the croupier ounces that Bond has won by accumulating a count of nine.

n top of a staircase, Columbo and Kristatos fight for possession of e ATAC. Kristatos falls to the ground, while a frame later he is back p the staircase.

Octopussy

As Bond, attired in a white tuxedo, enters the casino a boom microphone erroneously appears at the top of the frame.

The Fabergé egg smashed to expose a listening device is explained as being a replica. In actuality, Bond had planted the device in the real Fabergé egg, which they have now destroyed.

The waters surrounding Octopussy's fortress are infested with alligators, as confirmed when a villain is consumed after falling into the water. Yet, moments before, he and his fellow thugs swam through the water to reach Octopussy's palace. Earlier in the evening, Bond navigated effortlessly through the same channel. Granted, he *was* disguised as an alligator, courtesy of "Q". If the costume was that convincing, Bond should have been grateful that the real 'gators did not seek him out for mating purposes!

A View To a Kill

Bond's taxi has its windshield shattered when 007 smashes through a road barrier. Later, the taxi is back in front of the same road barrier which caused it the loss of its windshield.

A long shot of Zorin's stable shows a large puddle of muddy water but later the ground is dry.

During the Eiffel Tower chase, Bond becomes entangled in May Day's fishing line. Although he is holding a gun in his right hand, an insert shot depicts him as having his hand free.

During the villain's attack on Stacy's house, Bond inexplicably fails to utilize his handgun. Instead, he grabs a rifle which he learns contains only salt. Yet, he continues to shoot at the villain's getaway car even though the gun is useless.

The Living Daylights

As Bond drives up to the Hotel Isle de France to confront Pushkin, his car bumps into a pedestrian. Bond apparently thinks his licence to kill extends to his driver's licence!

Licence to Kill

Bond drives up to the Key West airport, simply leaves his rental car in front of the terminal gate, and walks immediately to the ticket counter to check in for his flight. How was the car to be returned to its original location?

INTERVIEW WITH
ALBERT R. BROCCOLI

Albert R. (Cubby) Broccoli was already a well known producer when he entered a partnership with Harry Saltzman to produce the James Bond films, beginning with *Dr. No* in 1962. The partnership lasted until 1974, with *The Man With The Golden Gun* representing the last 007 film to be co-produced by both men. From *The Spy Who Loved Me* in 1977 Cubby Broccoli continued to produce James Bond films on his own and in later years enlisted his step-son Michael Wilson and his daughter Barbara as co-producers. The following interview took place at Mr. Broccoli's home in Los Angeles on December 5, 1990. Interwoven are occasional comments from Cubby's wife, Dana Broccoli.

Q: What led you to see the potential of James Bond onscreen?
A: Well, I had been reading Fleming's works and I was surprised that no one had made films of them. I really wanted to acquire the James Bond properties but I understood somebody already had the rights. [Writer] Wolf Mankiewicz said: "I know the guy who has the rights, but he hasn't been able to make a deal and there are twenty-one days left in his option." The next day, in came Harry Saltzman. I didn't want another partner after Irving Allen and I had broken up. I told Saltzman I wanted to buy the Bond books, but he dismissed the Bonds as a bit of nonsense, and said: "I'd like to go into business with you. I've got a property called *Gold in the Streets*. It's about going to New York and getting rich. Then I've got something else about a scarecrow who comes to life." I told him I was only interested in the Bond books. He finally said, "Why don't we do them together?" Well, I was afraid somebody else would acquire them, and I finally agreed to a 50-50 partnership.

I talked to Columbia about doing a film and they said if we could make it for $400,000 they would agree. I said, "You can't do a picture like this for $400,000." So when they didn't want to get involved, I got on the phone and called a friend of mine, Arthur Krim, who was looking for pictures for United Artists. He said to get on a plane and speak to a young guy [at UA] named David Picker, who knew about the Bonds, and was excited about the idea. When we got there, I thought we would have a meeting just with Krim and Picker, but there were nine or ten people there. In forty minutes, we made a deal for six pictures. As we left, Harry said, "We haven't got a deal. We don't have anything on paper." I said, "When you shake hands with Arthur Krim you *have* a deal."

Q: What were your impressions of Ian Fleming?
A: Lovely, wonderful man. He *was* James Bond. Fleming was not pleased with the choice of Sean Connery as Bond. He wanted a man called Roger Moore. I said "Ian, we don't want Roger Moore because he is "The Saint", and that may be difficult to overcome". He finally met Connery in Jamaica at Goldeneye [Fleming's residence]. They became very good friends, and Fleming liked him. In fact, United Artists had been pushing for somebody else for the role, and in that respect, Harry and I were in unison that Sean was the guy we were

going to use. We screen-tested a lot of people, but we didn't scr[een] test him. We had a deal with Connery before we had dire[ctor] Terence Young. When Terence heard we had cast Sean, he hel[d his] head and said, "Disaster! Disaster! Disaster!" I said, "It's a [fait] *accompli*."

Q: How did Connery come to your attention?
A: My wife Dana and I saw him in *Darby O'Gill*, where he playe[d an] idiot farmer, but he had balls. The actors we had screened were [too] effeminate. I said to Dana: "Do you think this guy is sexy?" She s[aid,] "He's a very sexy guy." We had to polish him up. He had been un[der] contract for a long time at Fox, but they never used him. Whe[n he] came to Harry Saltzman's apartment in London, he was real brus[que] and said: "I'm not doing any tests", and he kept pounding the tab[le. I] said to Harry, "This is the guy", although he looked rather unker[mpt]. So we made a deal.

We didn't pay him a lot of money [for Dr. No] because of [the] budget. He complained later, but we had paid him what he [was] entitled to. We started his whole career. I never had a problem w[ith] him until after he left our domain, and he started saying terrible th[ings] about me. I was the only one he could deal with, [as] he really ha[ted] Saltzman.

Q: Why were you not able to acquire the rights [to] Fleming's first Bond novel, Casino Royale?
A: The rights to *Casino Royale* had already been sold to Greg[ory] Ratoff and he was trying to make it with Fox, but he died before [he] completed a deal. I went to Charlie Feldman, an agent w[ho] represented Ratoff's widow, who said the rights were not availa[ble.] Eventually he [Feldman] got the rights himself, and came to me [and] said he wanted to make the picture with me. I told him I already ha[d a] partner. Half the rights now belong to Columbia and the other [half] belong to United Artists. (Feldman would eventually produce the [ill-] fated satirical version of "Casino Royale" in 1967.)

Q: Why was Dr. No chosen as the first film?
A: It wasn't. It was *Thunderball*, but there was a lawsuit going [on] between Fleming and Kevin McClory. Because of the litigation, [we] decided to do *Dr. No*.

Q: Is it true that in an original draft of the screenplay, [Dr.] No was a monkey?
A: It's true. I've got a leather-bound copy of the draft written [by] Wolf Mankcwitz and Richard Maibaum. After all the material we h[ad,] they very proudly show Harry and I this screenplay which was [not] James Bond. I said, "Forget it! That is *not* going to be the story!" We [sat] down and worked on the script together. Wolf was so annoyed w[ith] me, he asked to take his name off the script, which was a pity beca[use] he was a good writer, and contributed to the final screenplay. [He] later wanted his name back on the script, and I told him, "Everythin[g is] being printed now. It's too late."

: If the script had the character of Dr. No, as a monkey, ho was envisioned as the protagonist?

: I don't remember. [Broccoli asks his wife Dana to bring in the iginal draft]. This will only be the second time I've seen it!

: This (referring to the script) indicates the villain was med Buckfield.

: I wanted to bury this thing! It was a big laugh with Dick Maibaum, o's a good writer for Bond. But, no one would believe a story like s.

Q: Is it true Terence Young discovered Ursula Andress?
A: He also took credit for finding Sean! He was at the house the other day, and he's a lovely guy, but he didn't discover Ursula Andress **Dana**: He [Terence] wanted us to use Richard Johnson.
Cubby: I remember my wife and I saw a beautiful girl on television, who we wanted to use for *Thunderball.* So we had her come into see Harry, Terence and myself. Before I could get there, Harry and Terence saw her, and they said: She's too flat chested." You know who it was? Julie Christie!

Getting back to Andress, we couldn't find a beautiful girl who could

Broccoli (*left*), Saltzman and "new" Bond Roger Moore on the set of *Live and Let Die.*

act. I went through a lot of rejected photographs and I saw a picture of this beautiful girl with her hair wet – just as Fleming had written. Harry said: "How do you know she can act?" I said, "The way she looks, she doesn't *have to act!*" I called Max Arnow, who I worked with at Columbia Pictures, who said she talked like a Dutch comic! We were struggling, because in two weeks we were going to shoot the picture. I asked him to make a deal for her and send her to Jamaica. I told Terence, who said: "Another disaster!" [Laughs.]

Q: Is it true that you wanted to involve Hitchcock with the Bond films?
A: No, not at all. What happened was that Sean Connery started to get teed off. We had two deals: one for Bond and the other for non-Bond pictures. He didn't want to do the non-Bond films for us and said, "I want to do a picture with Hitchcock!" I said, I didn't know Hitchcock very well, but I would call Lew Wasserman to tell Hitchcock that Sean would like to make a film with him. [Connery was soon signed for the lead in Hitchcock's *Marnie*].

Q: Did censors pose any problems in releasing Dr. No?
A: Not as much as we had for *Licence to Kill!* The only thing they did concerning *Dr. No* occurred when Professor Dent tries to kill Bond in bed. But Bond is sitting behind the door, and gives Dent six shots. They made us cut out three shots.

Q: Was Cary Grant ever considered for the Bond role?
A: Cary Grant was a very dear friend of mine, and the best man at our wedding. He didn't want to do it. He said: "It's a good idea, and I like it, but I can't do Bond." And we couldn't have paid him the money – it would have taken up half our budget.

Q: Was Noel Coward really considered for the role of Dr. No?
A: Noel was always at [Fleming's house] Goldeneye, and I used to meet him there, along with all these élitists. I said to Fleming: "Why don't you see if he'd like to play Dr. No." The telegram returned and it said: "Dear Ian, the answer to your question about Dr. No is NO! NO! NO!"

Q: What are your recollections of From Russia With Love?
A: It was a terrific story and had everything. We were lucky in having a terrific cast – Robert Shaw, Lotte Lenya, and Pedro Armendariz. I recall the Orient Express fight was beautifully written, filmed and enacted. Sean was tremendous and Robert Shaw was terrific. We didn't know Pedro Armendariz was dying. Despite the pain, he went right on working. We gave him a farewell party. It was tragic, although he and his wife enjoyed it. He was a gun collector and he had this gun shipped to him at [the hospital] at UCLA. He then shot himself.

Q: Was Raquel Welch considered for the role of Domino in Thunderball?

A: I signed Raquel to do the part, but the young [Darryl F.] Zanu came to me and said it's important she does a film for Fox. H prevailed upon me, and we let her go and dropped the contra Faye Dunaway was also signed (as Domino), but she had a change heart and we let her out of it.

Q: What are your recollections of George Lazenby a OHMSS?
A: He could have been a good Bond, but the minute he signed u he became impossible. He now says he made a mistake. Occasiona he would call and say he wanted to do Bond again, but I said v couldn't do that. It was a good movie, though, with a good scri George did the best he could in the role.

Q: Do you have any memories to share regarding receivi the Irving Thalberg Award at the 1982 Oscars?
A: It was a big honour. (Pointing towards the mantle on which t award is displayed.) You can bring it over, if you like. It says "F consistent high quality in motion picture production". It was all ve nice. I was quite surprised and very happy at being honored by peers.

Q: What precipitated your breakup with Harry Saltzman
A: It was a mutual decision because we weren't getting along and wanted to do other things I didn't want to get involved with. So went his way and I went my way.

Q: What led to Timothy Dalton's signing for the Bo role?
A: Roger Moore had been playing Bond for thirteen years and both felt it was time for a change. We considered Pierce Brosnan ar Mel Gibson for the role, but we liked Dalton's acting and the way looked. We decided to change the style of Bond to suit Timothy an we feel he is a great James Bond.

INTERVIEW WITH
ROGER MOORE

Is it true you were originally considered for the role of [Jam]es Bond by Ian Fleming?

I have no idea. I had never met Ian Fleming, but I remember when [the] search for Bond was going on. I really wasn't aware of Bond until [then]. I was doing *The Saint* and *The Daily Express* was conducting a [sear]ch for Bond. However, since I was involved with *The Saint* I would [not h]ave been available, although Cubby told me later I had been on [the] short list."

You were asked, however, to play the role on subsequent [occ]asions.

Yes, before George Lazenby took over. at that time, they were [talki]ng about going to Cambodia, and all hell broke loose and things [were] postponed. Lew Grade decided to sell a series Tony Curtis and I [did — *The Persuaders* — which sort of precluded me from doing Bond. [The]y then had the search and came up with George Lazenby.

Although that was an excellent series, it wasn't a hit in [the] U.S. Is that why you were unexpectedly free to play [Bo]nd in Live and Let Die?

Well, the show was an enormous hit in Europe and is still quite [pop]ular there. However, its cancellation did allow me to do the Bond

Did you have any reservations about following in [Co]nnery's footsteps?

I didn't have any reservations, because, as I said at the time, four [or] five thousand actors have played Hamlet! Everyone had their own [int]erpretation. The only time I had any nervousness about what was [goi]ng to happen occurred after I had finished the film. I was in a car [hea]ding to London for our first big press conference prior to the [open]ening, and the nerves lasted about three minutes. I realized it was [rat]her like being on the way to a delivery room, and that kid's going [to] come out one way or another!

Did you consciously try to give the character your own [in]dividual style, as opposed to Lazenby, who adapted [Co]nnery's methods?

Well, Lazenby had a big disadvantage in that he hadn't been an [act]or before, but was a model. He did look good, and that is how he [ca]me into the role. I was already fairly well established, so I didn't [ha]ve that disadvantage. For *OHMSS*, I think Peter Hunt did an [ex]cellent job. I think the film was a very good episode in the Bond [ser]ies. Guy Hamilton learned from the experiences on that film, [ho]wever, and later said we would avoid doing anything that would [res]ult in my being directly compared to Sean. I never said anything [lik]e "A Martini — shaken not stirred!."

Is it true you "ad-libbed" much of your dialogue?

They were well-rehearsed "ad-libs"! They were particularly [pr]evalent on the films Lewis Gilbert directed. We used to have great

Suitably attired for action.

fun with Desmond Llewelyn, although I later had the co-operation of John Glen. For example, Desmond always hated wearing shorts! I would always allow him to overhear me say that the script should call for Desmond to wear shorts. It used to drive him mad! Most of the ad-libs were discussed in advance with the writer, the director and Cubby. We would sometimes shoot two or three versions, and whichever one worked, we would use. One of the best one-liners was written by Tom Mankiewicz for *Diamonds Are Forever*. Sean meets Lana Wood at a craps table in Las Vegas, and she says "My name is O'Toole – Plenty O'Toole". Sean replies: "After your father, perhaps?" Mankiewicz gave me a great line, which I loved as well, in *Man With the Golden Gun*. When I hold the sights of the rifle down on the gunmaker and say "Speak now, or forever hold your piece!"

Q: We understand there was always a spirit of co-operation among everyone on the set.

A: Yes, the series could not have gone on for this length of time without that co-operation and working together as a team. A lot of the original team have stayed with the series all the way through. For instance, Cubby was always very avuncular, and absolutely lovely to have around. He would always have the backgammon board ready. We had a running game going from my first film to my last.

Q: When you first signed on as 007, did you envisage you would be playing the role through seven films over a period of 12 years?

A: I didn't think I would go beyond two! I figured the films would have run their course. As it went on, people would ask me "How does it keep running?" Well, it was like a fairy tale for kids – basically the same story, and it must never change. People know what to expect when they go to see a Bond film. They pay their money, and get their money's worth. The sets are beautiful, the locations are glamorous, the ladies are lovely, the action is there – tongue in cheek, and very spectacular.

Q: Can you recall any stunts that placed you in personal danger?

A: All of them – like getting up out of a chair! In fact, in *The Spy Who Loved Me* a stunt involving a chair left me with 3 holes in my backside where most people only have one! Originally, I was supposed to be behind the chair, which was protected with steel lining. An explosion was to go on in front of it. I said there really wasn't any suspense, and it would be much more effective if I was sitting down. So I did. The explosion went off just a bit too soon, and now I need 3 toilets! It was very painful and embarrassing. I had to go twice a day down to the studio nurse and have the dressings changed on my backside!

Q: Were you an admirer of the series prior to taking over the role of Bond?

A: I hadn't seen all of them. Cubby and Harry were friends of mine. We used to sit around the (gambling) tables like real life James Bonds,

and that's how we met. They would sometimes show me the film the Audley Square screening room. I think Sean was terrific. Y later, when we were both doing our Bond films simultaneously, would see each other and commiserate with the discomfort of it you know, what they were doing to him and what they were doin me in terms of the stunts, and all that. Sean and I are now tryin find a film in which Michael Caine could be involved. I think it wo be a mistake for Sean and I to play up "The Two James Bon however.

Q: Do you have an opinion of Timothy Dalton's interpr ation of 007?

A: I must tell you the truth – I have not seen them, and for a v good reason. Knowing that I would get asked questions like that, always desperately honest. If I didn't like the performance, I d know how I would answer. I do know Timothy, and he is a very, v pleasant chap and a good actor.

Q: Do you have a personal favorite among the films in series?

A: Among the ones I did, *The Spy Who Loved Me* was the o enjoyed best. I think it was the one where all the elements worke had the right balance of locations and humor. I also enjoyed wor with Lewis Gilbert tremendously.

Facing page: Roger Moore relaxes in a chair honoring his alter ego on the set of *Live and Let Die*.

INTERVIEW WITH
KEN ADAM
PRODUCTION DESIGNER

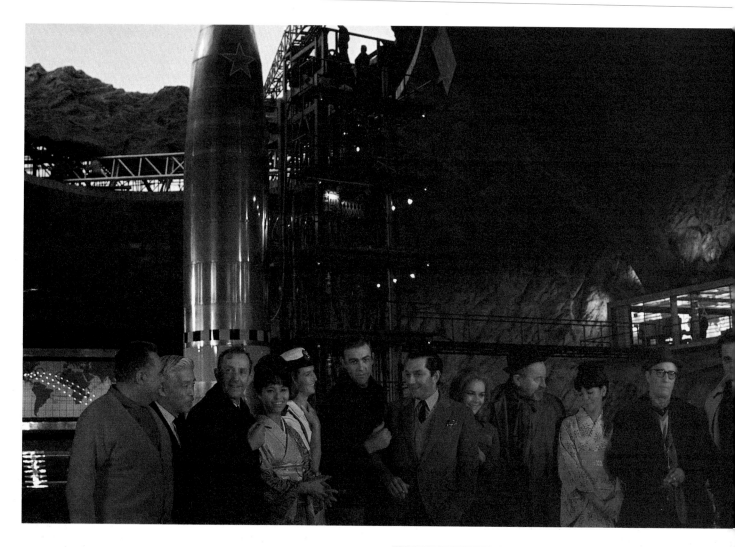

Adam's breath-taking volcano set for *You Only Live Twice*. From left to right: Harry Saltzman, Teru Shimada, Freddie Young (cinematographer) Akiko Wakabayashi, Lois Maxwell, Sean Connery, Ken Adam, Karin Dor, Jan Werich (the original Blofeld), Mie Hama, Lewis Gilbert, and Cubby Broccoli.

Q: *Of all the Bond sets you've created, which one gave you most satisfaction?*
A: Difficult to say, but I think the films at the beginning of the Bond series. I like *Goldfinger* and at the same time I liked the interior of Ft. Knox, and the laser room in Switzerland.

Q: *Is it true you were not given access to the real Ft. Knox?*
A: With the help of Robert Kennedy they allowed me to visit the site, but of course I wasn't allowed inside.

Q: *Someone once said that your version was probably much more exciting than the actual Ft. Knox!*
A: I hope to think so. I believe in what I call "heightened reality" or "stylization", and I knew the gold vaults at the Bank of England. Because of the weight of gold, it is never stacked more than a few feet high, but I decided that in Ft. Knox – the largest depository in the world – I would build it as high as I could. [The filmmakers] loved it, I

think. The interesting thing was I got a number of letters from people all over the world saying how was it we were allowed inside Ft. Knox when the President of the United States wasn't even allowed in!

Q: *What would you say was your most challenging or complex set for any Bond film?*

Well, that was the volcano [for *You Only Live Twice*]. We went Japan expecting to find some of the locations Fleming had talked out, and very much to our surprise found nothing. Then in uthern Japan, on an island called Kushu, we came across this region th six or seven volcanoes and it almost looked like a moonscape. at triggered off all sorts of ideas and, one evening, while we were discussion, I can't remember if it was me or Cubby who remarked Vouldn't it be interesting if the villain for the story would have his adquarters, or launching site, inside an extinct volcano?" We all ought that was a great idea, and Cubby said: "Get to work, Ken!"

: How did that idea finally get transformed into the ctual set?

: Well, I always start anything I design with a sketch, however much scribble it might be, and then it becomes a little more elaborate, and en we start building what we call an art department model – a 3-D odel. We showed it to Cubby and Harry Saltzman and Lewis ilbert. They became stimulated by the idea. Cubby asked me how uch it was going to cost and I said, "Well, I can only give a uesstimate' but I would say round about one million dollars." This as a big slice of any film's budget in 1966. Cubby didn't blink an eye. nd then the ball was in my court, which I suddenly began realizing as a gigantic responsibility.

: When the set was finally complete, were you involved ith setting up camera angles and making suggestions?

: Oh, yes, very much so and I had great support from the ameraman and director of photography Freddie Young, who loved

: How many technicians were employed in the con- truction of that set?

: If you talk about all the construction, labour and outside ontractors who supplied more than 700 tons of structural steel, I vould say there were about 400 people employed. We did it very uickly; the set was built in about three-and-a-half-months.

: One of the great mysteries is why that set was not ominated for an Oscar. How do you feel about that?

: It didn't bother me. It was strange. The only nomination for a ond picture was later on, for *The Spy Who Loved Me*. Until then I hink – certainly in the United States – people felt it was not proper since] the films were so commercially successful.

: Have budgetary constraints ever compromised your vork in the Bond films?

: No. Obviously, one is forced to compromise to some extent, but n the Bond films, I must say I was in the fortunate position to almost ave *carte blanche*. On the volcano set, I knew if everything worked, I vas a hero. But, if things didn't work, and I spent that kind of money, d never work again!

You try to cover yourself by calling in civil and structural engineers to make calculations, and see that everything's safe. We had a full size helicopter flying, and a rocket ship taking off through the artificial lake which was almost seventy feet in diameter and had to slide open. So one worked under enormous pressure and strain, but fortunately I had a first class team of collaborators with me. You progressively get more daring with what you try.

Q: How did you become involved with the Bond films?

A: I had worked for Cubby before on a number of films, one of the most important of which was *The Trials of Oscar Wilde*, for which I received the Russian Film Academy Award. Harry had met me in Italy while I was working on other films, so they both knew me, and so did the director Terence Young. We did the first Bond film, *Dr. No*, as a very low-budget picture – one million dollars.

Q: Why did you not continue with From Russia With Love?

A: Stanley Kubrick had seen *Dr. No* and was quite impressed by my work. It was the first time in a long time that a film expressed a slightly larger than life, tongue-in-cheek design, but also a reflection of our electronic era of computers, etc. So, he called me and offered me *Dr. Strangelove*, and that's why I wasn't available to do *From Russia With Love*.

Q: What is your favorite set from a Bond film?

A: In terms of design, my favorite eventually, was *The Spy Who Loved Me*. I started by experimenting with new shapes and new forms; with Atlantis and the interior of the supertanker. I decided not to make the same error as on the volcano, where I did all the structural work, and then it had to be pulled down because from the exterior it didn't look "very attractive" to the locals. So, on *The Spy Who Loved Me*, I built this stage at the same time as I built the set: the interior of the LIPARUS supertanker with the nuclear submarines. The stage has, I think, been one of the most successful investments by UA because, even though it wasn't a soundstage, it was so big it was used by all the big American productions that came to Europe.

Q: What were Sean Connery and Roger Moore's reactions to seeing some of these magnificent sets?

A: Oh, I think they were very excited by the sets, and working in these surroundings. Although perhaps sometimes they felt a little overwhelmed that the sets were overshadowing their performances. Both Roger and Sean were great personal friends of mine. One of the anecdotes I remember was on *Diamonds Are Forever*. Sean was a passionate golfer, and so was the director Guy Hamilton. Everybody was talking about golf, but I quickly got very bored. So, I made a $175 bet with Sean that provided he give me a reasonable handicap, and two weeks to learn the game, I would win against him. So, it became the talk of the whole studio. But, of course I lost! Sean was a very good golfer, but he was so nervous, he nearly gave me the game!

INTERVIEW WITH
TIMOTHY DALTON

Q: What inspired your interpretation of James Bond?

A: That's simple. I just went back to the books. The early movies were really quite close in spirit to the books. They really weren't special effects or gadgets movies. They were very popular, imaginative thrillers. They stretched the boundaries of believability but they still were contained within believability. Fleming made you believe this guy could do these things. Those books were the inspiration for the early movies, and the early movies were the foundation for the entire series. [In those] Bond seemed to me to be a much more human and real personality – kind of multi-dimensional.

Q: We understand that prior to The Living Daylights you had been approached to play 007?

A: There was a time when Sean Connery gave up the role. I guess I, alongside quite a few other actors, was approached about the possibility of playing the part. That was for *On Her Majesty's Secret Service.* I was very flattered, but I think anybody would have been off their head to have taken over from Connery. I was also too young. Bond should be a man in his mid-thirties, at least – a mature adult who has been around.

I was not approached for *Live and Let Die,* but there was a time in the late 1970s when Roger may not have done another one, for whatever reason. They were looking around then, and I went to see Mr. Broccoli in Los Angeles. At that time, they didn't have a script finished and also, the way the Bond movies had gone – although they were fun and entertaining – weren't my idea of Bond movies. They had become a completely different entity. I know Roger, and think he does a fantastic job, but they were different kinds of movies. Roger is one of the only people in the world who can be fun in the midst of all that gadgetry. But in truth my favourite Bond movies were always *Dr. No, From Russia With Love,* and *Goldfinger.*

Q: What were your impressions of the other Bond actors – Connery and Lazenby?

A: Well, Sean was bloody good. As for Lazenby, *OHMSS* was a better film than most people give it credit for; and Lazenby had the problem that I wouldn't go anywhere near, which is taking over from Connery. You couldn't take over from him. Lazenby was okay, but inexperienced. I'm not going to knock him, and the film is one of the best.

Q: Did you have concern about taking over the role after Roger Moore's popular reign as Bond?

A: Not so much, because I've now been the fourth Bond and it's become a tradition that the movies go on with other actors in the part. I also believed at the time, and I think it was Mr. Broccoli's wishes, that we move away from that style of movie, so we'd be coming in with a movie that was different. The danger, of course, is if people don't like that style. You know, as well as I do, that some people say they prefer Connery's Bonds and others prefer Moore's Bonds – the world is pretty much divided, depending on who you

grew up with. Whichever way you look, there are two wonderf[ul] powerful precedents. So, no matter what I did, the movie could[n't] have failed very badly. The result was better than could be expecte[d.] Some people didn't like it, but the majority did like the change.

Q: Wasn't The Living Daylights written in a rather gener[al] style, as it was not certain at the time who would [be] playing Bond?

A: It was, so it had varied elements of what they had been doing. B[ut] it did bring it back to a much more human story. There was a goo[d] involvement with the girl. It was maybe a bit complicated as a stor[y] towards the end, but you could see the direction we were going in.

Q: Did you have much input in modifying the Bon[d] character?

A: Not really. Any good actor comes up with ideas, and there is [a] creative forum of discussion, but it's within the parameters of th[e] script. The same was pretty much true of *Licence to Kill,* although [I] would have liked to see more humor. Not silly or camp humor, bu[t] good, mature adult humor.

Q: Do you enjoy the atmosphere on a Bond set?

A: It's a great atmosphere, but people don't play jokes too muc[h] because we're working on a $30- or $40-million movie with a toug[h] and tight time schedule with 18-hour work days. There is goo[d] humor, but everybody on the project wants their contribution to b[e] the best possible.

Q: Have you ever received any advice from either Sea[n] Connery or Roger Moore?

A: I've only met Sean once, and that was very briefly. But Roger [I] know, and I think he's a great guy, but he didn't offer advice.

Q: Connery has been quoted as saying that the future o[f] James Bond is in good hands with Timothy Dalton.

A: I'm very pleased, but he started it you know, so it started off i[n] very good hands!

Q: Do you enjoy performing your own stunts?

A: For an action film to involve an audience, you've got to get [a] camera in somewhere. You've got to make the audience believe tha[t] the man they're identifying with is there in the middle of the danger. Now, that doesn't mean to say you do all your own stunts – insurance companies and directors wouldn't let you. They want to finish making the movie, which they cannot do if there was an accident. We are surrounded by top class, professional people who are totally skilled a[t] what they do. We usually find a way to get me in there at some point, so an audience really does believe it. For instance, in *Licence to Kill* [I] did most of those scenes on the trucks. But I wouldn't do anything that was foolish or dangerous, because that would be stupidity.

n's Bondian debut in *The Living*
ghts.

Did you do much rehearsing in preparation for your
ut as 007?

I didn't do any rehearsing. I had just finished *Brenda Starr* in
erica, on a Saturday. I caught a plane which landed in London on
day, and started work on the Bond movie on Monday morning.
or time available for rehearsals – forget it!

Is there anything you'd like the future Bond films to
centrate on?

Personality. Much more character. One of the problems of
ving Bond is that he becomes the instrument or vehicle through
ch a hi-tech adventure story is told. That can be a problem, as it
often mean that the other characters are much better defined.
en these movies started, we were in the forefront of innovation.
've got to stay in the forefront, which is tough to do. We've got to
e great stories, and Bond has to be fleshed out a bit more.

The Timothy Dalton Bonds downplay the gadgetry.
uld you like that trend to continue?

I think so. It's nice to have one or two gadgets, but again, you've
to go back to the early films. I can't think of a gadget in *Dr. No.* In
m *Russia With Love*, there was the watch that was a garrote, and

the briefcase. They were fun and interesting, but they were not in
there for their own sake. The car with the rockets in *Goldfinger* was
great, but let's sort of draw the line about there, because you mustn't
trust that the gadgets are going to get Bond out of a tricky situation.
Ultimately, it's got to be down to the man getting *himself* out of the
situation, because that's what I believe an audience will go with.

Q: What has been the most rewarding aspect of playing
Bond?

A: Going to a cinema full of people who are watching the movie,
and seeing how much they love it. That really is the best aspect,
because that's why you do it. It's tough for everbody when you're
making a Bond movie. Since I'm right in the center of it, I get both
praise and criticism that I don't deserve because that work comes
from others. But, there's no question that the guy playing Bond is out
there on his own. You're kind of alone in a position of strange
responsibility. You're responsible for the work of others as well as
your own – whether it's good or bad. The way our unit has been with
me – certainly in anything that's tough or dangerous to do – makes
me feel so safe and secure. They're great, great people, and they've
made my life so much easier. That level of support from the entire
unit and crew is fantastic. The same goes for Cubby Broccoli; I like
him as a man, and I have a great deal of respect for him as a producer.

INTERVIEW WITH
MAURICE BINDER

Maurice Binder began his association with the James Bond series in 1962, with the first epic, *Dr. No.* In addition to designing the trend-setting main titles, Binder also created the famous gun-barrel opening, used in each of the succeeding Bond films. He was also instrumental in the creation of many of the film's trailers and advertising posters. Regarded as the premier artist in the field of main title designs, Mr. Binder continued to work on the James Bond series through *Licence to Kill* (1989). This last interview was recorded only weeks prior to his untimely death in early 1991.

Q: How did you first begin your relationship with the Bond series?
A: I had done the main titles for *The Grass is Greener* and they went over with a big bang. Broccoli and Saltzman were in the audience and they asked me if I'd like to do the titles and the trailer for a little film called *Dr. No.*

Q: How did you create the famous gun-barrel opening sequence?
A: That was something I did in a hurry, because I had to get to a meeting with the producers in twenty minutes. I just happened to

have little white, price tag stickers and I thought I'd use them as shots across the screen. We'd have James Bond walk through fire, at which point blood comes down onscreen. That was about twenty-minute storyboard I did, and they said, "This looks great took a couple of hours to film it at Pinewood. I used Bob Simmo Sean's double, to do the gun-barrel scene, as it was a silhouette. Th I got Martine Beswick for the dancing, and the three blind beggar did all of that against a white-background.

The gun-barrel itself was a real gun-barrel. I borrowed a gun fr a shop in Piccadilly. We had to open the barrel so we could lo through. We put the camera at one end and photographed it. V were having a dreadful time, and Trevor Bond said, "Maybe should do some pinhole photography." So, we punched a hole i piece of cardboard, and one end would come into focus, but t other end wouldn't. Later when we went to Scope, I had to reshoc with Sean. Roger Moore always played practical jokes [filming his g barrel sequences]. Once, he turned around and let his pants down.

Q: Who created that unique electronic sound over t main titles of Dr. No?
A: Well, the film itself had Dr. No working with computers,

Maurice Binder directing title-song performer Sheena Easton in the credits sequence of *For Your Eyes Only.*

pple the rocket. I thought we should have computer sounds on the les. I looked for where I could get the sound effects, and they said ere was a lady in Surrey who had been doing experiments with ectronic sound. She sent me a couple of selections which I then ed. I then wanted to use a big bang to follow the shot, so I used the cond stanza of the James Bond theme. When it came to Sean onnery's name, that's when I used the first stanza of the theme and it in the "007s".

Monty Norman, composer of the Bond theme, heard it and went azy saying, "I've got to fix that!" But it was too late, because esident Kennedy wanted to see the picture, and United Artists was nding the print to the White House. The President loved it and ept running it for all of his friends.

Q: Why were you not involved with the main titles for rom Russia With Love and Goldfinger?

A: We were having a bit of an argument about the logos, and I really dn't want to go into it; but they came back to me and we agreed at I loan my assistant Robert Brownjohn for those two titles. Trevor ond knew how to implement Brownjohn's ideas.

Q: How did you create the underwater motif used in the main titles for Thunderball?

A: In the pre-credit sequence, Bond's Aston Martin sprays the illains, and the screen fills with water. I thought it could lead into the irls swimming around, so I shot them in an underwater tank, in ilhouette. These were two gals who swam professionally in ightclub tanks, but they said they didn't want to swim nude. I told hem that if they wore bikinis, it wouldn't quite work. As a ompromise they agreed to makeup as dark as possible. Then they valked out on the deck of the tank, absolutely nude and said: "This is ot us. We're unrecognizable."

We photographed them underwater against white panel and I did he bubbles against a black velvet background. It was all shot in black nd white and I put the color in optically.

Q: Were there any censorship problems with the glimpses of nudity in that title sequence?

A: In Spain, they were very prudish at that time and they censored he title sequence. Yet, I had an easier time in those days than I do oday! When ABC Television runs the Bond films, they're always inicky about the titles, and they ask what they can do to cover up ome of them. By this time, they've been in all the theatres, on cable elevision, and suddenly it's being censored.

One night I watched *The Man With The Golden Gun* and the whole itle was censored. On *Thunderball* they scanned the titles. I now do a eparate title for television and video. On *You Only Live Twice* you ee the girl's nipples in the titles, yet I couldn't get away with that on *A View to a Kill!* I had to throw out some of the most beautiful title sequences you've ever seen!

Q: Can you relate any anecdotes which took place filming the titles?

A: On *Golden Gun* we were shooting at Pinewood with model Carolyn Cheshire, who did several of the titles. She was turning around, and her pubic hair stuck out. I said, "The smoothness just isn't there!" She replied "I'm not shaving! Take this brush and see if you can get it down." Well, given the opportunity, I started brushing! I suddenly feel someone behind me, and it was Roger and Cubby. Roger said to Cubby, "If you're the producer of this picture, *you're* not getting the perks!"

Q: Why was Sheena Easton shown in the titles of For Your Eyes Only?

A: I thought this girl was beautiful, and Cubby agreed it would be great to show her in the titles. Originally, the first words of the title song began with the lyrics, "Put me down! Put me down! Put me down!", to segue in from the pre-credits sequence in which Bond drops the villain down a chimney. I was furious, and I told the composer, Bill Conti, that the first line of a Bond song should begin with the title. He said "You're right", and rewrote the song.

Q: What was your working relationship like with Paul McCartney on Live and Let Die?

A: He said he wanted to see some of my titles and I ran them for him and Linda. I told him since the theme was voodoo I'd like him to have several fast sections where we could have the girls writhing with their hands up and dancing. That's the way he wrote it, and it's a pleasure to watch. I love the transition from the eyes of the real face to the eyesockets in the skull.

Q: As you also designed many of the trailers, can you verify the existence of the "lost" Christmas trailer for Diamonds Are Forever?

A: Yes, I did that. I set a little Christmas tree up in the studio. Connery is seen walking inside a Christmas ball, then he turns and fires and we move in on it, and it becomes the logo. I used a female voice saying something about the film being a Christmas gift.

Q: Did you use film clips from preceding Bonds to link George Lazenby's main title to others in the series?

A: I think that was obvious. I had to match him in with other pictures. I showed the clips inside the figure of an hourglass. If you notice, Lazenby is seen jumping on a clock hand to hold it back, then we drift back in time and see the previous film clips. Of course, the one character I couldn't show in that sequence was Sean!

Q: Is there a contribution you've made to the series of which you're most proud?

A: *Dr. No* because it was so different, and *For Your Eyes Only* with Sheena Easton singing the song.

INTERVIEW WITH
VLADEK SHEYBAL

The following are excerpts from an autobiography Mr Shebal was preparing. Sadly, he passed away before completing the work.

In 1963, there was a telephone call from my agent: "A film script for you arrived." He sounded excited. "To direct the film?" I asked with pleasure. "No!" he laughed, "to play a part!" I felt disappointed. Little did I know while unexcitedly tearing open the envelope that this film would change my whole life. The title was *From Russia With Love*. I read it, and I hated it. I didn't care about my part, either – Kronsteen, a world famous chess player. One short scene at the beginning, then toward the end two short meaningless scenes. And then my death: being kicked by a spiked shoe with poison. What a ridiculous thing to invent!

When I conveyed all this to my agent, he said, "Listen, young man. Every English actor in the world would seize this opportunity without hesitation!", "I am sorry," I said, "I don't want to be involved with this rubbish." A few hours later my phone rang. I couldn't believe my ears. It was Sean Connery [an acquaintance of Sheybal's through Connery's wife Diane Cilento]. He was hissing at his end: "You complete idiot! How dare you turn down this part! Do you realise it will shift you instantly to an international film status? It was I who suggested you to the producers! You are going to play this part!" He slammed down the receiver. I took a deep breath and dialed my agent, telling him: "Yes, Peter. I will play it."

It was at a costume fitting that I first met Lotte Lenya. She smiled warmly at me and said: "I know you are going to play Kronsteen. I am Lotte Lenya. I am sorry it is me who is going to kill you with my spiked shoe, but I hope we will become friends in spite of it."

She sounded disarmingly sincere. "Are you the famous Lotte Lenya?" I asked, "I heard your fantastic Brecht songs from the record, of course . . . I didn't know you are going to play Rosa Klebb. How fantastic!" Everything started looking better and easier now.

My car went through the impressive big gate of Pinewood Studios. There was Sean waiting for me, with a big smile. He said, "Welcome to James Bond! You won't regret it, I promise!" [Later] I walked into the studio and saw the large set. My heart missed a beat. It was fantastic! All around us the chess players were sitting and watching hundreds of extras: women wearing splendid evening gowns, and men in black ties. I suddenly felt lost and shy, with all these extras whispering "Who is this actor?"

Then Terence Young arrived and we were introduced. I was so nervous I couldn't remember my few simple lines. But Terence whispered to me, "Don't fret. All will be okay. You look splendid in your suit. I shall give you plenty of close-ups. Just look at me and I'll guide you through it." He was always behind the camera as if hypnotizing me. I started to regain my confidence. And as predicted, my face appeared in big close-ups on the screen, starting an international career which would run over the next three decades.

Within the next few days, I started filming the scenes with Lotte Lenya. As I write I am looking at photographs from those scenes. Funny. I was so slim and Lotte so vicious and evil as Klebb. In real life,

she was the sweetest person I've ever known and we became friends for years to come.

She was in a way so pure and naïve as an actress that one day Terence Young said to her, "Lotte, turn your face a bit toward the camera." She looked quite lost – like a little girl – and asked, almost in tears, "I'm sorry Terence, where is the camera?" The camera is the most central and important thing in actor's lives. In America, they almost kill to get on the camera. And here is this frail woman, this great performer, literally not knowing where the camera was! At this moment, I wanted to hug her.

I didn't have any scenes with Sean, but he would often pick me up by car to have a dinner with he and Diane. They lived at the back of Shepherd's Bush. They bought an old chapel and made it up splendidly inside. His son Jason was already born, and I remember bouncing him on my knee. Sean was a family man, in the Scottish

Double-feature lobby card with Sheybal and fellow SPECTRE villain Lotte Lenya.

dition. We would come from the studio, and Sean would shout to ane, "We are hungry!" Then, he would seize little Jason into his ms slump in an armchair, and shout again "Where is my beer?" I ed these evenings with them.

For my death scene, Terence Young looked at me for a very long ie, then said, "I want you to die like James Cagney was always ing. Slowly. Very slowly. I want at first an expression of being zzled. You didn't expect this to happen." He would whisper during e filming, "Vladek, slow it down. Slide down slower . . . slower."

One day, Harry Saltzman started redirecting my dialogue. I played scene exactly as before. [After an altercation] Harry shrieked, "I n going to fire you!" Saying, "I fire myself," I turned and started to lk off the stage. I heard Lotte's voice: "Harry, you stop it. Vladek is ht. He cannot play the scene like you suggest." I thought, "Bless u, Lotte," but I knew I was finished with it all. I proceeded to the

dressing-room and started taking off my jacket. There was a knock on the door. It was Terence Young, who said, "In the whole of my career, nothing like that happened. And now you, who are not a star! I admire you, but we must finish the scene. Sean is now speaking to Harry, You will play the scene *our* way. Harry is not going to be on the set." I came back to the studio and I saw the smiles all around, and there was Lotte's gentle hug. I completed the scene.

Later, I heard that Harry swore that Vladek Sheybal will never be in his films. Well, a few years later I was offered a part in *Billion Dollar Brain* with Michael Caine. Michael, always being philosophical, said "Well, they always hate or love each other in films, but if they need you, they'll take you." "What are you talking about, Michael?" I asked. He pointed toward the director, Ken Russell, and a short man in a heavy fur coat. "That's Harry Saltzman. He's the producer of our film!"

INTERVIEW WITH
PETER HUNT

Q: *What led to your involvement with* **Dr. No?**
A: I had been acquainted with the director, Terence Young, since I was sixteen, and he had directed Cubby Broccoli's first picture, *The Red Beret* [1954]. I later did some special work for Cubby Broccoli and Irving Allen, on some film they had shot in Africa. I also knew Harry Saltzman, and one night we were having dinner. At the time I was working on a film called *On the Fiddle*, with Sean Connery. Harry began talking about how he was going to make these Bond films with Cubby Broccoli. They were discussing who was going to play Bond, and I sent up a couple of reels of Connery. Whether that influenced them or not, I don't know, because they were considering other actors. Anyway, they asked me if I would be the editor, and I agreed.

Q: *What type of style did you hope to achieve with* **Dr. No?**
A: Well, I wanted to make it like it was a paperback. They were glamorous for everybody who was ordinary and middle class. But [the producers] were hamstrung for money. Remember *Dr. No* was not big and extravagant. Also, you must remember that in the early 1960s, the cinema was inundated with "kitchen sink dramas". The style of filmmaking in those days was a slower process. We have become so accustomed now to "crash cutting", where Bond says, "Right, goodbye," and he is immediately in his next scene.

Initially we had problems with certain scenes that couldn't be shot because of rescheduling and bad weather. I started to make the thing work as a thought process from one scene to the other, without actually showing it. Terence was very encouraging.

Q: *Did you know that Terence Young has called you one of the great editors?*
A: Really! Well, I could compliment him the same way. I think he is a grossly underrated director. He was absolutely the image of James Bond. He gave those films the visual style. Through his encouragement, I was lucky and was able to give them the pacing. The combination of these two elements really started a new trend and style in filmmaking.

Suddenly, the Bond films were like a great breath of fresh air. You enjoyed it, and you came out feeling like James Bond. The humor gradually evolved, through the substance of the people making the films. I think the producers also have to be complimented. Their job is to put together a group of people, who can work superbly, and come up with a desired result. Broccoli and Saltzman were absolutely ideal for that. They brought together a very good group of people, and encouraged them; that was their real talent. They were great to work for, and very generous.

Q: *Were there any disagreements over the way certain scenes should be edited?*
A: We didn't really quarrel about anything – somehow it all worked very well. The producers were reasonable, and when you looked again at the things they queried, you would say, "Oh, I see what they mean!"

Q: *The Orient Express fight in* **From Russia With Love** *edited as impressively as, say, the shower scene in* **Psycho** *How long did it take to construct that battle?*
A: I think we had it scheduled to shoot over three days, then I put together in a loose form. There were various little pieces I thoug could be better, like maybe someone should shoot the bulb out, c put their foot through a window. Then we went back and sho another half day. Connery and Robert Shaw did a lot of their ow stunts. We had two handheld Airiflex's and one studio camera on The composition of the two carriages with the double doors wa very good, so we could take one side out and go through. I alwa maintain that the people in the compartments on either side mu have been deaf!

Q: *As you edited over the years, did you see Sean Conner maturing in the role?*
A: Absolutely! Up until *Dr. No*, you must remember, Sean was ver much a supporting performer. Over the years he has grown into tremendous actor. On *Dr. No*, he was particularly helped by Terenc Young. Sean had never played this type of suave character before He was more a jeans-and-sweater man. So, Terence took hold c him, bundled him off to his own tailor, and dressed him in style.

Yes, Terence was the water that made Sean grow.

But by the end of *You Only Live Twice*, Sean had not only grow tired of the films, but there was a pervading air of animosity. For wha reason, I've never been able to find out. But, I think Sean wanted t diversify, and of course, look what he has today.

Q: *Were there scenes shot, which were excised from th final prints?*
A: Well, in *Dr. No*, there was a scene where Honey was staked ou and around her were thousands of crabs, but unfortunately they a died! Nobody really knew how to take care of them; also they don move very fast. We shot the sequence but I cut it, and it was neve seen by the public.

In *OHMSS*, we did take out a whole sequence where Bond finds ar object on the desk of Sir Hilary, and traces it to a spy who is listening in to their conversation. We started to shoot it, and then decided i wasn't necessary.

Q: *How did you acquire the director's chair for* **OHMSS?**
A: By that time, I'd worked with Broccoli and Saltzman for elever years, including *The Ipcress File* and *Call Me Bwana*. I was supposed to direct *You Only Live Twice*, but they went with Lewis Gilbert. I go very sulky, and said, "I'm not going to work any more for you." They gave me a holiday with pay, and I went around the world. In Japan, met up with Cubby and Lewis, and Broccoli said, "Why don't we give Peter the second unit to do?" Eventually, I did the second unit, and ended up editing as well.

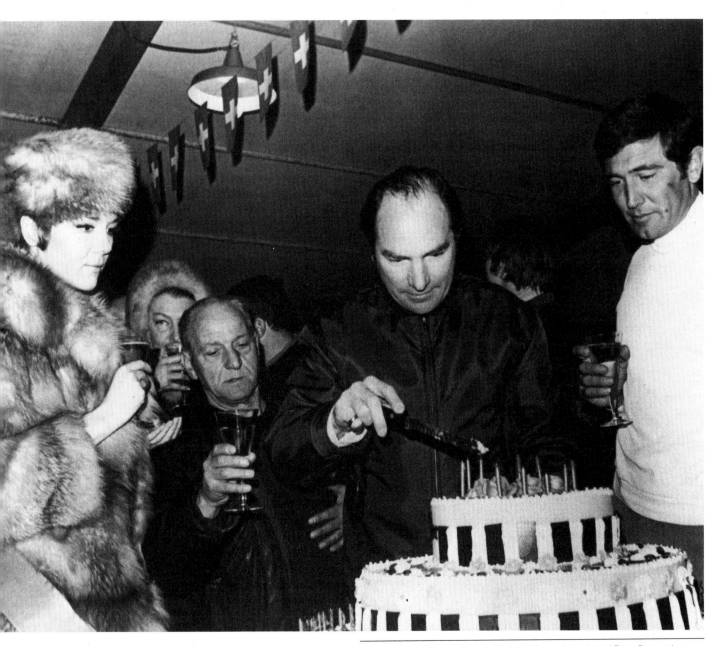

Peter Hunt celebrates a birthday with guests George Lazenby and Diana Rigg on the set of *OHMSS*.

Tell me about the Little Nellie helicopter battle?

Well, Little Nellie wasn't my idea, but the helicopter chase was, d grew out of a proposed car chase. We were using helicopters to d a castle as in the book, and we weren't able to find one — there n't any castles in Japan! We flew over a national park where there e twenty-one of these monster volcanoes, and they looked ctacular. I thought, "Why can't we have a helicopter chase instead a car chase? We ought to incorporate this great visual picture in the n." When we got back to London, we found this squadron leader o had built the Little Nellie helicopter.

Q: With OHMSS was there a conscious effort to get away from the emphasis on technology?
A: Yes, absolutely! I felt we had gotten too much into the gadgetry, and were losing our storyline and the style we had created. I felt we

must not become imitators of our imitators. *OHMSS* was one of Fleming's best novels. I was insistent that we not fluff it out with gadgets, but stay with the storyline. I had the support of [screenwriter] Richard Maibaum, and Simon Raven, who also worked on the script. Thank goodness – I think it works.

Q: What was your reaction to having to find a new James Bond?

A: Well, we wanted a new, young, up-to-date type. United Artists and the producers decided they wanted to carry on with Bond the way it was, and we looked for a young Sean Connery type. A good hundred people were considered for the part; I recall Ian Ogilvy and John Richardson. Roger Moore was discussed, but he was about to start *The Persuaders*, so we couldn't get him. It was Cubby who found Lazenby. George was quite a well known model and had done commercials for Big Fry's chocolate that became popular in Europe. Lazenby's name was discussed, and then later he met Broccoli at his barber's and they talked. George should have gone on – he would have been a very creditable Bond. Unfortunately, he was very misled by the people he trusted, who should have known better – agents, friends, and advisers. I thought it was my job, as director, to instill in him a great deal of confidence. But he was very good, and he took direction very well. I did have to employ all sorts of tricks, and be kind and loving and nice, and sometimes be horrible.

Q: What qualities did George Lazenby possess that led to his being cast as James Bond?

A: The physical appearance of the young man was tremendously good. I cut together ten minutes of film – romantic scenes and fights, – it looked tremendous. The physical side of him was excellent; the acting side of it was a gamble. But I felt confident I could make him James Bond.

Q: What is your opinion of OHMSS as a film?

A: It's the most satisfying film I've been able to complete. I was able to get my way in most cases, and do the things that I felt right. The producers never knew, until the very end, that the running time would be two hours and twenty-five minutes. I was very deceitful! There are no extra frames in that film, and it's a magnificent piece of editing, even if I do say so myself! Harry kept asking me, "What's the running time?" and I kept saying, "Oh, Harry, it's about two hours!" When I had to eventually tell him the truth, I thought he would go through the roof! "No way! You have to lose twenty minutes! We can only get in four showings instead of five per day!", he said. I told him, "Keep the cinemas open twenty-four hours a day, like we did with *Thunderball!*" In the end, it went out as I wanted.

Q: Was it always intended to retain the novel's tragic ending in the film?

A: No, but I was adamant about it. However, if George Lazenby was to continue as Bond, the film should have ended at the wedding. The next film would have started with the shooting of Tracy as a pre-sequence. By the way, we should give kudos to that magnific actress, Diana Rigg. She was not the first choice for the role. H and I went to France to see Brigitte Bardot. We had dinner with twice, and then she announced she had signed a deal to do a west with – Sean Connery! [*Shalako*].

Q: How did you discover the location for Piz Glo [Blofeld's Alpine fortress]?

A: We couldn't find a suitable location. We were in St. Moritz heard they had built a new skiing center on the Schilthorn in Murr They hadn't finished the construction work, and in fact had only b the external shell. They were also erecting the cable car installati We were offered the complex for free, if we agreed to furnish interiors. We also built a temporary helipad, but it was never ta down.

Q: Why did Donald Pleasence not continue as Blofeld OHMSS?

A: Donald Pleasence is a fine actor, but I wanted someone w would play it more realistically. If you look at him [*You Only Twice*], you never see him move anywhere. I had to cut movements, as he just "minced" everywhere. In fact, it was a par of what I tried to achieve with Blofeld. I really liked Telly Sav [*OHMSS*] as Blofeld.

Q: Did you find George Lazenby difficult to work with?

A: No, we had a few ups and downs, but no more than I would h with anybody. I took George and Diana [Rigg] to dinner, really to her opinion of Lazenby. She said he was fine and she loved him [the role], although they did have a few minor differences. These we petty things that were blown up into a lot of nonsense. Unfortunat George was ill-advised, and his career just didn't take off. He alw had a good sense of humor, and I'd certainly consider working w him again.

Q: What are your favorite Bond films?

A: *From Russia With Love* and *OHMSS*.

Q: Would you like to direct another Bond film?

A: Yes, I think I would at this stage. It would be interesting.

INTERVIEW WITH
LOIS MAXWELL

Q: How were you cast as Moneypenny?
A: I had always been an actress and had done a lot of work. Then I got married and had two kids. Unfortunately, my husband suddenly became very ill and looked as though he wouldn't be saved. I called Terence Young, whom I had worked with before, and Cubby Broccoli, who was a friend of my husband Peter, and said "I need a job as soon as possible." Although my husband recovered, Terence and Cubby called to say they wanted to talk to me because they were going to make *Dr. No*. They asked if I'd like to play Miss Moneypenny or Sylvia Trench. I read the scenes, and didn't fancy myself in James Bond's pajama top, hitting golf balls down the hallway. So I said, "If you allow me to give Moneypenny a background, and not force me to wear my hair in a bun, and horn rimmed glasses, with a pencil over my ear, I'd like to play her."

Q: Did you envision the series would become so successful?
A: Never! We saw a rough cut and to our amazement, we were not only thrilled but were also laughing. We realized the humor made it stand apart from cops and robbers pictures. That excited the imagination of the world.

Q: What was your impression of Ian Fleming?
A: I liked him very much. He was sardonic and amusing – my type of man and very much like my husband. There was a wrap party at the end of *Dr. No* and he said, "When I wrote Miss Moneypenny, I envisioned a tall, elegant woman with the most kissable lips in the world. You are her!"

Q: Can you describe your own feelings about the relationship between Bond and Moneypenny?
A: I think they had this delightful long holiday weekend together, and certainly appreciated each other's qualities. She knew that if she married him, he would break her heart. He knew if he allowed himself to fall in love with her he would never get his "00" because he would be bottled in domesticity. I still believe that even after his many flings, they still went off together occasionally.

Q: What was your relationship like with Cubby Broccoli, Bernard Lee, and Desmond LLewelyn?
A: Cubby is one of the nicest men I've ever met. He has always been a gentle giant. I like him enormously. I thought Desmond and Bernard were terrific – and excellent actors! We used to have the same crew, and every two years it was like rejoining a family.

Q: Do you think the part of Moneypenny has been sufficiently developed over the years?
A: No. I suggested, when Sean came back in *Diamonds Are Forever*, that Moneypenny be sent on assignment in Las Vegas. I envisioned a scene wherein this little Cherokee [plane] lands and a female figure walks out, and you are not quite sure who it is. But that night at the roulette table, Bond suddenly sees Moneypenny. She peels a micro-

Lois Maxwell as Miss Moneypenny, "the girl with the most kissable lips in the world", on duty in *You Only Live Twice*.

dot containing Bond's instructions off one of her freckles, and places it in 007's hand. The next morning, you see the Cherokee take off and there's an almighty explosion – the villains have bombed her. Cubby said, "No! No! No!" I said, "I'd much rather be blown up in an explosion than be superannuated."

Q: What was your impression of Sean Connery?
A: He is a thoughtful, very talented man who doesn't embrace fools gladly. However, by *You Only Live Twice*, he was terribly fed up. He was even cross with Bernard Lee and I during shooting, because of the film we made in Italy with his brother Neil [*Operation Kid Brother*], who was clearly exploiting Sean's name and reputation. At one point he said, "You are betraying me." I said, "I am not. I am getting a bigger part than I ever had in the Bond films." At a press conference in

Rome, Neil was in a very uncomfortable position as reporters tried to exploit competition between the brothers. I told Neil that if he was asked a loaded question, to kick me in the ankle and *I* would answer it. When Sean came back to do *Diamonds* he gave me a ride back to London. He said, "I have to thank you for protecting my brother and I. Without you I'm sure he would have gotten into trouble. I'm sorry I was rude to you." I saw Sean last about five years ago, when I was a guest at Norman Jewison's tennis party.

Q: What are your recollections of George Lazenby?
A: I liked George, but he was badly advised to not sign a five-picture deal. I told him he was out of his mind and he should sign it immediately and start being a good boy.

Q: You've always enjoyed a close friendship with Roger Moore, have you not?
A: Roger named his son after mine. When we were doing *The Saint*, I took my son Christian to the studio and introduced him to Roger. Roger said, "Christian! What a perfect name. If we have another son we'll name him that." We knew each other from our days at the Royal Academy of Dramatic Arts. One time, he played *Henry* V and I played his uncle with a long red beard! We were great pals even then, at age seventeen. We still write each other. As Bond, he had a very hard act to follow, and he did an excellent job, although he's best at playing Cary Grant-type comedy roles. The best dramatic role I've seen him in was as the mining engineer in *Gold*. He was marvellous in that.

He played endless jokes on the set of the Bond films. In *Octopussy*, I was supposed to introduce Bond to my beautiful assistant, Penelope Smallbone. Instead, I referred to her as "Penelope Smallbush". Roger said, "Oh, Miss Moneypenny, I know where *your* mind is!" Well, they were falling out of the gantries laughing. We couldn't shoot again for half an hour! Talk about a Freudian slip!

Q: Do you have any favorites among the Bond girls?
A: Ursula Andress was marvelous; so was Diana Rigg. Carey Lowell and Talisa Soto were wonderful, although *Licence To Kill* was too violent for me!

Q: What is your favorite Bond film?
A: I liked *From Russia With Love* very much, and Peter Hunt's *On Her Majesty's Secret Service*.

Q: What was your reaction to leaving the series?
A: One night Cubby called up and said, "I'm sorry, Lois, but we won't be using you in the next Bond film. I wanted to tell you myself, and didn't want you to just get a letter or hear about it in the press." That was very kind of him. I said, "Well, I realize it would be sort of silly to be making goo-goo eyes at Timothy Dalton!"

However, I want to play "M"! Bond can arrive in Moneypenny's office to find a new secretary. He says, "You're not Miss Moneypenny!" She looks at her watch and says, "Commander Bon you are late for your appointment with "M", and you'd better get there immediately!" So he goes thru the padded leather door, ar there is the big armchair with its back turned to him. It swings aroun and there is Moneypenny, who says to him, "Synchronize you watch, Commander, and never be late again!"

I thought the public would really like it. Cubby said, "It isn't going work, Lois, because traditionally, the head of MI5 has always been man." I replied, "Traditionally, the Prime Minister of Great Britain ha always been a man!"

On duty aboard "M"'s sub in *You Only Live Twice*.

INTERVIEW WITH
DESMOND LLEWELYN

How did you initially become involved with the Bond [film]s?

I presume the man who played Major Boothroyd in *Dr. No*, Peter [Bur]ton, was not available. I knew the director, Terence Young, [bec]ause I worked with him on a film called *They Were Not Divided*, [so] when my name came up, he must have said, "Okay, let's have [him]".

So you had no indication this would be a source of [em]ployment over the next thirty years?

A: Good God, no! I remember *Dr. No* got the most terrific notices. My wife came home saying somebody told her what a marvelous film it was, and that Bond was either shooting somebody or was in bed with a woman. The press just loved it, but when the second Bond film came up I really didn't think anything of it – just another job! Then there was the enormous success of *From Russia With Love* and *Goldfinger*. After that, I was in another film directed by Terence

Llewelyn enjoys some Bond-like perks in *Octopussy*.

Young [*The Amorous Adventures of Moll Flanders*], and I remember asking him, "Am I going to be in the next Bond film?" He didn't know.

Q: Terence found another Thunderball participant in Moll Flanders – Molly Peters.

A: Good Lord, was she in that? I met her recently at a Bond Fan Club convention at Pinewood. It was quite fantastic because they had absolutely every gadget, and a whole studio just full of Bond stuff. Quite amazing!

Q: What are your recollections of the various Bond actors?

A: Well, both Roger and Sean were great personal friends of mine, but I've known Roger much longer than I've known Sean. I go back to the television series *Ivanhoe* with Roger, and I had met him again in Rome when I was doing *Cleopatra*. Roger had a terribly difficult job, because as the posters said: "Sean Connery IS James Bond." He managed to turn Bond into a completely different character. You'll find that people who saw Sean first, don't like Roger, and vice versa. Sean was very ambitious and wanted more of a challenge. Of course, look how successful he is today.

As for poor old George Lazenby, he wasn't an actor. He was just picked out, and I heard that somebody once said to him, "You're now a star – behave like one." He most likely read all the stories about how actors were supposed to behave – partying, and arriving late on the set. He was not professional, but I'm not blaming the man; because he'd never been on a film set before and didn't know anything about it. It turned out to be a very good movie, thanks to Peter Hunt's direction and editing. Many people, familiar with the books, prefer Timothy Dalton's interpretation. He has gone back to Fleming. Again, Timothy had to be different from Sean and Roger, as no actor likes to copy another. Dalton is fantastic. He's made Bond into a real character.

Q: How was the antagonism between Bond and "Q" developed onscreen?

A: Well, in *Goldfinger* I'm seen working at a desk with a lot of gadgets. Originally, I stood up to greet Bond, and Guy Hamilton said, "No, no! You don't like this chap! He treats all your inventions with contempt!" As soon as he said that, the entire scene fell into place. It made the relationship much more interesting. The way the scene was written, it was obvious Bond did treat "Q" with contempt and didn't appreciate his inventions. Sean, of course, played the whole thing as though it were rather a waste of time, and that it was holding up his drinking time. He was always in character and kept fidgeting. That helped me keep genuinely irritated. I wanted to say, "Stop fiddling! I can't remember my lines!"

Q: Do you have a favorite Bond film in terms of how your character is presented?

A: Well, I was very lucky in *Licence to Kill* because the role of "Q" was enlarged. It's also the film I've made the most money from! The next largest part was in *Octopussy*, and there again, one trie[d to] establish a waspish relationship between Bond and "Q". But wher[e one is] just seen in the workshop demonstrating things, there isn't much [one] can do.

I had a very good scene in *Thunderball* with Rik Van Nutter as F[elix] Leiter, who was seen playing cards. Half-way through the sce[ne] Bond leaves "Q" to talk with Leiter; this irritated "Q", as I was in [the] middle of explaining the gadgets. It was quite a nice little scene, [but] the editor told me we had to cut it. My reaction was, "I have a sm[all] enough role, why cut me?" He said, "We are cutting down the scen[e] with Van Nutter, and, unfortunately for you, he's in that one."

Q: Did you have any problems adjusting to the vari[ous] Bond directors?

A: No. They are all brilliant directors. I had more contact with J[ohn] Glen, because he is a personal friend of mine. Terence I knew v[ery] well, but I hadn't seen him in so long. I think that Terence was m[uch] more responsible for the success of the Bond films than anyb[ody] knows. Terence is almost a Bond himself. Guy Hamilton, too, is [an] extraordinary director, but a very reserved man whom I didn't ge[t to] know as well as the others.

Q: Can you recall any amusing anecdotes from the set?

A: On *For Your Eyes Only*, I was having difficulty with my script – [as] usual! John Glen came up and said, "We have a good idea. We['re] going to put in a new bit – can you learn this quickly?" I looked a[t it] and said, "For God's sake, this is complicated gibberish! I coul[dn't] possibly learn all this in time." He said, "Of course you can." I sp[ent] the whole of lunch trying to study this bloody stuff, and when I fin[ally] said I thought I knew it, John and Roger burst into laughter. Ro[ger] *always* took full advantage of my difficulty in learning lines!

Q: To what do you attribute the phenomenal success [of] the Bond films?

A: I suppose I can quote Ian Fleming when he was asked w[hat] constituted a good 007 thriller. He said, "Give Bond the right cloth[es,] the right background, the right girls. Set your story in the m[ost] glamorous of places. Describe everything in minute detail and ta[ke] the story along so fast that nobody notices the idiosyncrasies, a[nd] you'll have a success". I think Cubby Broccoli has followed t[hat] formula. Cubby also says they have added a Hitchcockian eleme[nt.] For example, when you have a climax, you have another, and [then] another!

Q: After playing "Q" for so many years, do people ev[er] mistake you for your onscreen counterpart?

A: Oh, yes! But the thing is, I know absolutely nothing about gadg[ets] and they always go wrong for me! It's most embarrassing! If I go int[o a] shop to get my watch repaired, they will look at me and say, "Ca[n] *you* fix it?"

INTERVIEW WITH
MICHAEL G. WILSON

Michael Wilson has literally grown up with the James Bond movies. Starting as an Assistant Director and extra on *Goldfinger*, Mr. Wilson has made significant contributions the Bond series as both Producer and Screenwriter. The following interview took place at Leavesden Studios in England during the final weeks of production on *GoldenEye*.

Q: Given the fact that your background was initially in engineering, law and finance, how did you become involved with the creative aspects of bringing the James Bond films to the screen?

MW: Well, you know this is a family business and I am Cubby's stepson. The first time I got involved with the film business was in the summer of 1964, during my first year of law school. The day I arrived in England, I found that Cubby was going to the U.S. to do the location work for Ft. Knox. I drove out to the studio with him, and in the car he said "You know I can use an Assistant Director." I didn't even have a jacket with me. I was just in my shirtsleeves. He said, "It's too bad you don't have your passport with you." I said, "I just happen to have it in my back pocket!" So, I went back to the U.S. with him and worked on the Fort Knox scenes for about three weeks with Guy Hamilton and about 25 people. In those days we seemed to be able to do those scenes without hundreds of people.

Q: Were you intimidated at having these responsibilities thrust upon you so unexpectedly?

MW: I think I was too excited to be intimidated. I was just trying to do what I could to help out. I was an assistant and I was responsible for running around doing all the odd jobs...

Q: So, you are featured in Goldfinger as an extra...

MW: Yes, I'm in the film as a Korean with Pussy Galore's Flying Circus. I run around getting them ready for take off. I think I'm also in the film as Bond in a shot in which he is taken off by Oddjob somewhere.

Q: Following this screen debut you returned to law school. At what point did you decide to go into the film industry again?

MW: In 1974, I was a partner in a law firm and I had been working more and more on the family business. There were certain tax problems and there were situations in which it became clear that Harry Saltzman and Cubby were going to come to a parting of the ways. So I took a leave of absence for two years to come over and negotiate that situation between Cubby and Harry, as sort of an in-house lawyer. Norman Tyre was the General Counsel, but I handled these negotiations on a daily basis. Slowly, I started moving into the production area.

Q: What led you to pursue a career as a screenwriter?
MW: That came much later. I spent two years dealing with Harry

and we went through a lot of problems with the company and finally in 1976 we resolved them. At that time, we started *The Spy Who Loved Me* and I went off and supervised the underwater unit. You could say I was getting my feet wet, such as it was. I worked with Derek Meddings, who was the special effects supervisor and model builder. When we did *Moonraker*, I started to do some writing because there was a problem with finishing the script. We were actually shooting, and it had to be rewritten and I helped out there. It was kind of interesting, and I enjoyed it. On the next film, *For Your Eyes Only* I worked so closely with Dick Maibaum, Screenwriter, that he said, "My God, I think we should be collaborators."

Q: Richard Maibaum was certainly a master of his craft and responsible for bringing so many qualities to the Bond films. What was your working relationship with him like?
MW: I certainly learned a lot from Dick. He was a great writer and a great friend. We had a relationship where we wrote very much together. We usually "hop-scotched" with each other. We'd sit down and go through story conferences together, and afterwards he would say, "I understand this one really well. Why don't I take a crack at it?" And sometimes I would say the same back to him. We would send the pages back and forth and we'd discuss it between us. It was really a day-to-day collaborative effort.

Q: What elements of Ian Fleming's Bond have you consciously tried to incorporate or avoid in the scripts you have written?
MW: Well, Fleming's interpretation of Bond changed over time. If you look at *Casino Royale*, it resembles a film noir. It's about Bond becoming a seasoned veteran, losing all of his illusions. In the last half of the book, there is a certain horrid edge to it. Bond is a somewhat embittered character. Fleming lightened him up as the books became more popular. I guess we probably went with the lighter interpretation of Bond. I think how we write for Bond is very much affected by the actor who is doing the role. Roger Moore plays it one way, Sean Connery plays it another. The same with Timothy Dalton and Pierce Brosnan. Each one is a leading man, and they bring their own personality to the character. They are not character actors. They do not take on the characteristics of the character. They have very strong personalities and I don't think that can be ignored in the writing. Script writing is written for one performance. Theatre writing is written for multiple performances for different kinds of people with different kinds of interpretations. But in a film, you cannot ignore who is starring in it.

Q: Why has Bond continued to prosper with five different actors in the role of 007?
MW: Bond has such a universal appeal, which is even greater than the person playing the part. That is a very important characteristic. I think the films have succeeded because Cubby and Harry — and then later Cubby alone — insisted on the best production values.

Michael G. Wilson with Cubby and Da[n]
Broccoli at the premiere of *Licence to Kill*.

The audience has never been let down and they know that they are going to get a certain quality of film. I think the films have a certain prestige and a certain expectation. As for the individual actors, Sean Connery certainly set the character and is a legend in the role, obviously. I think that the first person who is successful in the role, as Sean was, puts up a huge hurdle for the next person to overcome. There is a tremendous expectation. I think that Roger Moore wisely did not try to imitate him but came up with his own interpretation. As did Tim and Pierce.

Q: Let's talk for a moment about On Her Majesty's Secret Service, which has had a renaissance in recent years both as a film and for George Lazenby's performance as Bond.
MW: I think people have always thought that the film had a tremendous story and had the scope to be the greatest Bond ever. The complexities of the plot and the characterizations were particularly good. The idea that Blofeld, having everything, still wanted to have social recognition and a title was the Trojan horse that allowed Bond to get in there and attack him. It's always been a story which everyone thought had a lot of potential. I think it was a tremendous challenge for George Lazenby – a man who had never acted before – to live up to Sean Connery. I can understand at the time why the audience may have felt disappointed. But I think you're right. In retrospect, the audience seems to look at the film as a single entity, almost isolated from the previous films. They see the

story for what it is. They've taken a much kinder view of George.

Q: What will be unique about the character of James Bon[d] in the 1990s?
MW: We have had a new team of writers, a new director and w[e] have had a lot of time to think about it. I think this Bond is pret[ty] close to the Fleming Bond but in contemporary terms. We hav[e] tried to make him an even more complex character than befor[e]. There are more conflicts with the villain and the situation. We hav[e] allowed ourselves to question the very need for his existenc[e]. Everyone he meets is undercutting him, whether they're friend o[r] foe. That's the world he lives in. That's the contemporary world. A lot of the support people that Bond had in the 1960s has given wa[y] to a lot of antagonism even in his own camp. So these are th[e] challenges he has to face today in the world and I don't think we'v[e] pulled back from them.

Q: To what do you attribute the longevity of Bond['s] popularity?
MW: Bond has become an evergreen character. Like Superma[n,] Batman and Sherlock Holmes. These are enduring characters. Ther[e] will always be Bond films. How long it might be between Bond film[s] and what form they take, I can't say. But he's such a well establishe[d] character, that there will always be the potential for Bond films.

INTERVIEW WITH
GEORGE LAZENBY

George Lazenby was a model with no prior acting experience when he was cast as James Bond in *On Her Majesty's Secret Service* (1969), replacing Sean Connery who temporarily left the series after *You Only Live Twice* (1967). Upon leaving the Bond series, Lazenby found that the big, starring roles he anticipated did not materialize. However, in recent years, *OHMSS* and his performance have undergone a renaissance with critics and public. Many consider it the best entry in the Bond series. George Lazenby continues to act regularly on television and in feature films.

Q: So much has been written about the tensions on the set of OHMSS. We'd like to ask you if you have any pleasant memories of the film?

GL: There are quite a few. First, I was very happy to get the role. Four months previously, I didn't think I had a shot. As time went on and I saw people drop by the wayside, I thought I had as good a chance as anybody. I knew the director, Peter Hunt, was on my side and as it turned out, he got what he wanted. I was a Bond fan myself, and you get illusions – delusions – that you can play it better than anybody else. I had tough shoes to fill. That didn't bother me, however, as I had nothing to lose.

Q: To obtain the role, is it true that you patterned yourself after Sean Connery and then introduced yourself to Cubby Broccoli at his barber's?

GL: Well, that's partly true. I went to Sean Connery's barber to get my hair cut the way his was cut, and it so happened that Cubby Broccoli was in the chair behind me. When I left the barber shop, Cubby apparently said, "That guy would make a very good James Bond, but he is probably a very successful businessman and wouldn't be interested."

Q: Can you explain why you only appeared once as James Bond?

GL: I had some bad advice at the time from a guy named Roan O'Reilly, who ran the pirate radio station Radio Caroline. He also managed the Beatles for a week after Brian Epstein died. I felt he knew more about life and the world than I did. He told me it wasn't a good idea for me to do another James Bond. He felt James Bond was over. He said "There is a new era coming. Look at all the hippies. They're not interested in conservative people like James Bond. They're more into *Easy Rider*." So I was convinced that it was Connery's gig and not mine, and now that I was famous I was better off on my own and doing other things. Then I found out that the industry shunned me.

In recent years, Lazenby has finally received the acclaim he deserved for his performance as 007 in *OHMSS*.

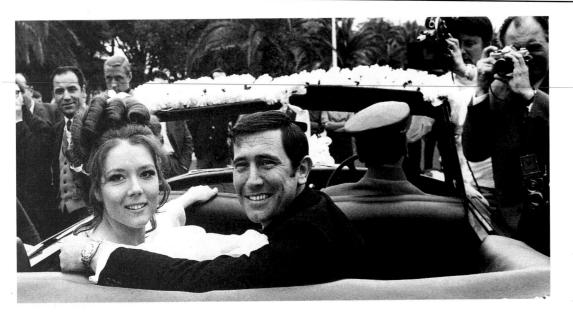

The world press converged on Portugal to record the wedding of James Bond (George Lazenby) and Tracy (Diana Rigg).

Q: What was the basis of rumours that you and Diana Rigg were feuding on the set?

GL: We really didn't get along that badly. I was like the cheeky young kid on the block and she was like the old hand who knew all the tricks. I wasn't listening to her and it pissed her off. I just wanted to go my own road. She felt I could have been a lot more clever at it, and she was probably right. "The Feud" was a lot of crap. For instance, the story about eating garlic before a love scene. What happened was, she was having lunch at the commissary a few tables away from me. Because of all the press, she yelled across the room, "Hey George, I'm having garlic for lunch. I hope you are!" The press blew it up to: "DIANA RIGG EATS GARLIC BEFORE LOVE SCENE." We were actually getting on well that day, and preparing for the proposal scene in the barn. Diana's performance was great.

Q: Looking at the film today, is there a scene of which you are particularly proud?

GL: Actors never think they do it well enough! I thought I did the scene where Diana Rigg dies pretty good, but today I think I could have done it better. I think the first take was better, but I cried. Peter Hunt said, "Let's do one without the tears. James Bond doesn't cry!"

Q: Can you recall any scenes from OHMSS that did not make the final cut?

GL: There was a scene when I was at the College of Arms and a guy was spying on us. I chased him over roof tops and through the streets of London. The villain got away and that leads to why we thought Blofeld might have some information. They thought it would be better if Blofeld didn't know so they chopped that sequence out. I recall I pulled my shoulder going over a wall, and I had to do a fight scene the next day.

Q: Did you favor downplaying the gadgetry in OHMSS in favor of more human emotion?

GL: I think it was a good idea, in retrospect. Peter Hunt wanted it to be based more on his direction and the acting rather than the gadgets. Some of these directors, if they are not sure of something, they just blow it up. But Peter didn't want to fall into that category. He fancies himself a director, and he is pretty good, I think.

Q: Do you have any recollections about the montage love scene over which Louis Armstrong sang "We have all the time in the world?"

GL: Well, the song is wonderful, although I tried to get Blood, Sweat and Tears to do the music on the film. If you check back to 1969 the year the film came out, the group had five hits in the hit parade. Today, I love Louis Armstrong's version of the song, and now I can understand why they wanted to use him. You have to be older to understand the soul of the man.

Q: Which were the most dangerous stunts you performed?

GL: The fight scenes, which went on forever. That one in the bell room was a bitch because they were using real bells. They got rid of the fake bells because every time we hit them, they would fly all over the place and wouldn't look real. So, they put the real bells back in and I wound up with lumps all over me from banging into those things. Now, as for dangling from the cable car, that didn't bother me because they had a harness on me. The wire went up inside my sleeve and I was hooked on by my hand, anyway. I could actually let go and still hang there, although it was a couple of thousand feet off the ground. In the studio, I had boxes underneath me so when I was crawling along the cable inside the wheelhouse, I wasn't hooked on. They showed me how to crawl commando style along there and when they'd say "Cut!", I'd just drop onto the boxes. I actually enjoyed it. They hated me for it, because they'd have to stack them all up again!

Q: Why do you think the Bond films have been so successful for 30 years?

GL: Well, I think they're a total fantasy. I don't know what the later ones are like because I haven't seen any since my particular film. But I might just sit down and watch them all one day, who knows. I think the success is that you know you'll have a good time and get a lot of fun for your bucks.

MISCELLANEOUS QUOTES

Clifton James
(W. Pepper in *Live and Let Die* and *The Man With the Golden Gun*)
uring the filming of *The Man With The Golden Gun*, there is a
ne between myself and an elephant. The scene was written to see
. with the elephant, and later discover J.W. in the water. As it
pened, on 'Action!' the damned elephant butted me into the
g [canal]. The camera was rolling and they kept it in the picture – I
w have a collection of elephants people have sent me; everything
m ivory to wood."

Jimmy Dean
(Willard Whyte in *Diamonds Are Forever*)
orking with Sean Connery in *Diamonds Are Forever* was indeed a
rning experience for me. Watching him act was very enlightening;
having him work with me, behind the set, on my golf swing was
en more enlightening. Immediately after the picture, my irons were
best they've ever been. All in all, it was a fun thing."

Molly Peters
(Nurse Patricia in *Thunderball*):
or me, working with Sean Connery was exciting. He is a man of
eat integrity, honesty and patience – I liked him. He was very
otective toward me. Terence Young ... elegant, refined, with

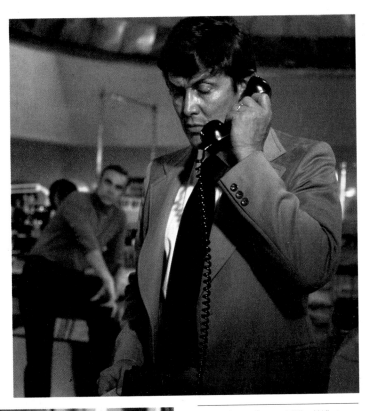

Above: Jimmy Dean as Willard Whyte in *Diamonds are Forever*.

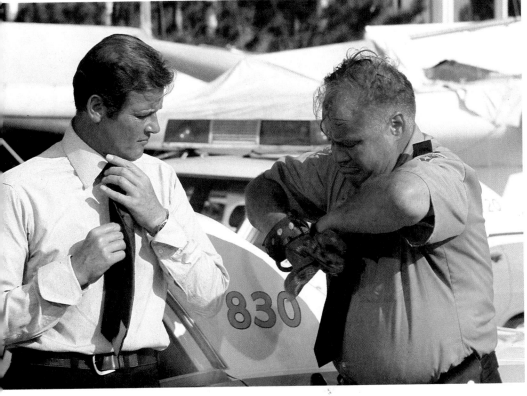

Left: James' Sherriff Pepper bumbles his way through an attempted arrest of 007 in *Live and Let Die*.

tongue-in-cheek humor; 007 off the screen – a lovely man. The girls were all beautiful, all pleasant. We helped promote *Thunderball* at a Brazilian film festival in Rio.

I think Adolfo Celi was well cast as Largo; his appearance exactly fitted the description given by Ian Fleming. *Thunderball* was a wonderful experience. I was never aware that the Bond films would become such a phenomenon – part of cinema history. May they long be so!"

Rose Alba
("Widow" in *Thunderball*)

"You asked for an amusing incident – as you probably know, my scenes were shot in France. On our return, Sean Connery took me to dine in an Italian restaurant. I had recently moved to a new address along with some furniture. Sean escorted me upstairs, and immediately rearranged everything … bookcases, Ottoman, China cabinets, dumbwaiters, beds – all heavy stuff. I cannot imagine why he did it. It certainly proved how strong he was. By the way, he departed after that."

Honor Blackman
(Pussy Galore in *Goldfinger*)

"Regarding *Goldfinger*, I remember when Gert Frobe and I, hav merely shook hands, stepped onto the veranda (the exterior farm Pinewood). Gert said to me, 'Louisiana, I believe'. We both sat dov and he started the dialogue – I was totally baffled. I didn't understa a single word, and tried to look cool waiting for him to stop speak (whatever language it was), and then I launched into my first line a hoped for the best. The whole scene was played like this. What was actually saying was: 'Operation Grandslam will make you a v rich woman.' But it was his very first attempt at English and it v quite unintelligible. He was dubbed in that film, of course.

"The other rather amusing episode, was the fuss everyone kin made about placing bundles of hay in the appropriate place, so t when Sean threw me [judo], I should be safe. I had just spent ye playing *The Avengers* on television in which I did all my own fighti and I had to do it 'keen' enough live in the studio on a cement flo In any case, I got hurt, but the way that scene ended was compensation prize!"

Left: Alba as the deadly "Black Widow widow is about to be "greeted" by 007 in *Thunderball*.

Top right: Mollie Peters and Sean Connery try without success to convince *Thunderball* director Terence Young that "three's a crowd"!

Right: Honor Blackman displays her considerable charms as Pussy Galore in *Goldfinger*.

FOR YOUR EYES ONLY
TRIVIA FACTS ABOUT THE WORLD OF 007

So after 30 years of James Bond films, you thought you knew everything there was to know about the world's most popular secret agent with a licence to kill? Well then, try some of these on for size:

● Ian Fleming once described his ideal choice to portray James Bond as none other than composer Hoagy Carmichael!

● The James Bond producers once denied a merchandising request for 007 condoms!

● Harold Sakata (Oddjob) represented the U.S.A. in the 1948 Olympic Games as a weightlifter.

● In order to accommodate crowds, New York's Paramount Theater ran *Thunderball* 24 hours a day!

● The 17th Bond film, *GoldenEye*, is also the name of Ian Fleming's Jamaican retreat.

● On the Bond set, the liquor that was used in key sequences consisted of ginger ale (for champagne), watered down coffee (for whiskey), and pure water (for 007's vodka martinis)!

● Composer John Barry was associated with the writing of all but 5 of the Bond films' title songs. Curiously, the 007 songs nominated for Oscars were those not composed by Barry!

● TV's Batman, Adam West was considered for the part of 007 following Connery's resignation after *You Only Live Twice*.

● Sean Connery was reputed to have worn different hairpieces for the love and action scenes.

● More than 75% of all filmgoers have seen *Goldfinger* at least once.

● The character of "M" as the crusty naval head of *Her Majesty's Secret Service* was based on a similar character known as "R" in the 1930s Hitchcock film, *Secret Agent*.

● Before Roger Moore even spoke his first line of dialogue as James Bond in *Live And Let Die*, he had to be rushed to the hospital, suffering from a kidney stone attack.

● *OHMSS*'s Blofeld, Telly Savalas, included a "no-flying" provision in his contract. Unfortunately for Telly, the provision made no mention about cable-car rides for access to location work atop the 10,000 ft. Schilthorn!

● Principal photography on *From Russia With Love* ended in Istanbul 2 days before a major revolution erupted in Turkey!

● *A View To A Kill*, was the Bond song which topped the charts in the U.S. Paul McCartney's *Live And Let Die* nearly reached the No. 1 position, stalling at No. 2.

● Following "Jimmy" Bond's appearance on the small screen in 1954's Casino Royale, courtesy of the Climax Mystery Theatre, plans were initiated 3 years later, to bring Bond to the big screen with actor Terence Cooper tipped for the role of 007. The project did not come to fruition. However, Cooper would in fact appear as one of the many 007s in Charles K. Feldman's 1967 spoof, *Casino Royale*.

● Ian Fleming despised movies, and for pleasure saw only 2 in his lifetime, *Cavalcade*, and *Gone With The Wind*. He did however sit through the first 2 Bond films long enough to grudgingly give Sean Connery his approval.

● 3 of the 4 Avengers girls also made appearance in 007 films: Diana Rigg and Joanna Lumley in *OHMSS*, and of course Honor Blackman in *Goldfinger*. (Coincidentally, *Avengers* star, Patrick MacNee also appeared in a 007 film as Tippett in *A View To A Kill*).

● *Goldfinger* himself, Gert Frobe, was a child prodigy as a violinist.

● While utilising the famous jet-pack in *Thunderball*, Connery had to wear a special Dacron suit whose colour would not fade due to the contact with the jet-pack's fuel.

● Ian Fleming assigned the rights of each 007 film to a particular member of his family in lieu of a will, so that each could profit by his assigned film.

● Whenever anything would go amiss on the set of *Live And Let Die*, invariably a member of the crew would shout, "Send for Sean" as a joke.

● Over 2,000,000,000 people have paid to view a James Bond film!

● Only Desmond Llewellyn "Q" has appeared in 007 films starring each of the 5 different James Bonds.

● Despite each actor's fluency in English, most of the early Bond girls' voices were dubbed; as were the villains, Goldfinger and Largo.

● Movements of the steel arm worn by Julius W. Harris (Tee Hee) in *Live And Let Die*, were controlled by the actor's breathing.

● Academy Award nominee and wife of Sean Connery, Diane Cilento, doubled for actress Mie Hama in a diving sequence for *You Only Live Twice* when the latter came down with a bout of poor health. Cilento was outfitted with a black wig and bikini identical to Hama's.

● By 1971, it was deemed unfashionable for 007 to smoke, hence throughout *Diamonds are Forever*, Bond does not light up. (He would take to smoking cigars in the next film when Roger Moore took over the role).

● Sharks obtained for Largo's "Golden Grotto" pool came from the Miami Seaquarium at a cost of $500 per shark. These were transferred each day from an off-shore vessel to Largo's estate.

● The amazing Acrostar, seen in the pre-credits of *Octopussy* was originally intended for use in *Moonraker*, slated for a "Little Nellie"-like battle sequence in and around Brazil's Angel Falls. The sequence was dropped when the falls' riverbed dried up!

● *Raiders Of The Lost Ark* was the result of Steven Spielberg's intense desire to direct a James Bond film.

● Because of 007's sexual exploits, the Salvation Army once demanded a scene showing Bond "using protection" be included in the films.

● *OHMSS* was originally scheduled to star Sean Connery and Brigitte Bardot. (The two would team together in the western, *Shalako*).

● Red Grant was a real character, a boatman in Jamaica, whose name was pinched by Fleming to give identity to his ruthless executioner, Spectre.

● When Lotta Lenya greeted Sean Connery after her appearance in a Broadway play, she proceeded to kick him in the shin, mimicking their famous scene together years back in *From Russia With Love*. Both enjoyed a chuckle.

● It is action-arranger Bob Simmons who appears in the opening gun-barrel sequence in *Dr. No*. This same sequence is repeated in *From Russia With Love* and *Goldfinger*.

● Carole Boquet was offered the role of Holly in *Moonraker* but was unavailable, having just signed for *That Obscure Object Of Desire*. She would take the lead in the next 007 feature as marine biologist, Melina Havelock.

● For *You Only Live Twice*, producers paid local fishermen $100,000 to keep their boats onshore for the duration of filming a scene at a small fishing village in Japan.

● Both Sean Connery and Cubby Broccoli shared one macabre thing in common - coffins. Broccoli at one point had worked as a wholesaler and Connery as a coffin polisher.

● Frank Sinatra was considered for the role as 007 in Charles Feldman's *Casino Royale*. Sinatra remarked that one would have to be crazy to compete with Connery!

● CIA director Allen Dulles assigned a research and development team to determine the feasibility of 007's homing system as designed by Q Branch for James Bond's Aston Martin.

● While preparing for *Thunderball*, Cubby Broccoli was invited to dinner by old friend Anita Ekberg. At dinner, Broccoli announced that the new Felix Leiter would be none other than Rik Van Nutter, Ekberg's husband.

● During the explosive climax to *The Living Daylights*, the Moroccan airfield (representing Afghanistan) was left open to civilian flights!

● To lend a feeling of nostalgia to the new 007 film *Live And Let Die*, it was suggested that Ursula Andress re-appear in a cameo as Honey Rider. The idea was dismissed as it was deemed improper that she resume a relationship with a "different" Bond.

● Howard Hughes was an extraordinary 007 fan whose price for the use of his Las Vegas Casino Hotel for Bondian filming was a 16mm print of the latest 007 adventure, *Diamonds Are Forever*.

● The real Major Boothroyd was indeed a weapons expert who offered Fleming advice on Bond's arsenal of guns.

● In protest against having their sacred grounds filmed for a James Bond film, monks shrouded their hilltop monastery with their dirty laundry. (Commented Moore, "Don't they know I was 'The Saint'?").

● Richard Kiel, as Jaws, was only able to stand his prop steel dentures for 5 minutes at a time.

● The beach sequence wherein *Dr. No's* men spray the island with machine gun fire from a launch at sea had to be redone when a detachment from the US Navy who were on leave, entered the bay to find out what all the firing was about.

● *Moonraker's* parachute/skydiving opening took 5 weeks and 92 jumps to film in its entirety. Each jump allowed only for 1 minute of freefall before filming had to be stopped.

● Rehearsals for *Thunderball's* intricate underwater battle took place in a shopping mall parking lot.

● Sean Connery's favorite James Bond film is From *Russia With Love*.

● It was *Goldfinger's* director, Guy Hamilton, who suggested Oddjob's hat be made lethal by equipping it with a razor brim.

● 007's producer, Cubby Broccoli was raised on an uncle's vegetable farm in New York. It was this uncle who introduced the vegetable to America.

● *The Spy Who Loved Me's* Vernon Doubcheff was cast principally because it was thought that he would make a great corpse! It is Jaws who kills the Egyptian club owner during the dervish dance sequence.

● The "Golden Girl" idea in *Goldfinger* was prompted by a real life incident in which a Swiss fashion model painted her skin for a promo and later died because of skin asphixiation.

● Ursula Andress was offered the role of Honey Rider w a "wet T-shirt" photo of her was discovered.

● *From Russia With Love* director, Terence Young double as Pedro Armendariz when ill-health prevented him continu with filming.

● A public letter writing campaign brought back Richard as Jaws in *Moonraker*.

● The summer before *OHMSS* was to commence filming Switzerland, the Swiss army placed explosives high up in the mountains to prepare for the avalanche scene.

● Adolfo Celi paused long enough between connecting flights to pick up some reading material which turned out to Fleming's Thunderball. Ironically, that same week, he was notifi about a meeting with Eon concerning his interest in a film ro for *Thunderball*.

● A 24 hour guard had to be posted on Pinewood Studi Fort Knox set so that workmen could not heist the (phony) gold bars as souvenirs.

Bond and Grant in the classic battle to the death aboard the Orient Express. Sean Connery and Robert Shaw did most of their own stunts in this sequence shot at Pinewood.

THE JAMES BOND FAN MOVEMENT

The international appeal of James Bond is amply illustrated by the thriving organizations throughout the world dedicated to the celebration of the Agent 007. Since this book originally went to press in 1992, the authors have received countless requests from Bond fans the world over inquiring as to how they can join the clubs and correspond with others who share their hobby. There are numerous magazines and clubs devoted to Bondmania, none of which are officially licensed or run by Eon Productions. However, the film-makers have been very cooperative with the fan movement and consequently the club magazines often enjoy advance photos and information on upcoming Bond films.

The James Bond Collectors Club: PO Box 1570, Christchurch, Dorset, BH23 5YH, England. Contact: Dave Worrall. Publishes the 007 News, a magazine devoted to collecting 007 memorabilia - past, present and future - as well as the latest information on new films and events.

The James Bond 007 Fan Club and Archive: POB 007, Addlestone, Surrey, KT15 1DY England. Contact: Graham Rye. Publishes the 007 Magazine, a glossy periodical covering the entire universe of the Bond phenomenon through interviews, critiques and rare photos.

The Ian Fleming Foundation: PO Box 6897, Santa Barbara, California, 93160, USA. Contact: Michael Van Blaricum. A non-profit organization devoted to preserving and promoting Ian Fleming's legacy and writings. The foundation publishes Goldeneye Magazine, which covers the Bond phenomenon in film and in print. The IFF also archives many of the props and vehicles from the 007 movies.

Club James Bond 007: BP 6090, 69468 Lyon, cedex 06, France. Contact: Jerome Nicod. Publishes the slick Bondmag, a French language magazine (with supplements in English) featuring the very latest in-depth news and photos about the new Bond films, as well as analysis of classic 007 epics.

In response to the overwhelming number of inquiries, asking how to obtain vintage James Bond collectables, most of the above club magazines have 'swap shops', merchandizing offerings and classified ads. Other prominent sources for rare toys, posters, games, books and records are:

Spy Guise Catalog: Dept. B, Box 152, Dunellen, New Jersey, 08812, USA. (US fans can also join any of the aforementioned European fan clubs through this address.)

Bond Collectibles: 966 US Highway 1, Avenel, New Jersey, 07001, USA.

Novice collectors be warned! The value of Bond memorabilia continues to soar, and in order to afford some of the rarest items, you might just have to design your own raid on Fort Knox.

Connery rehearses sending Bruce Glover away with "his tail between his legs" on the set of Diamonds Are Forever.

THE MARKETING AND PROMOTION OF A VERY SPECIAL AGENT

Only one man could destroy a Caribbean Island;

Only one man would drive a car with an ejector seat

Only one man could turn off an atomic bomb, blow up a volcano,

hold a helicopter in a suitcase, a rocket on his back,

artillery in one hand, and a beautiful woman in the other!

ONLY ONE MAN ! ! ! ! ! !

"WHO ARE YOU?"

[asks the alluring female voice, oozing sexuality]

"BOND – JAMES BOND!"

[responds the sophisticated gentleman spy]

(FROM A 1971 PROMO FOR "DIAMONDS ARE FOREVER")

Promoting secret agent 007's fabulous exploits with hard-hitting, attention grabbing tactics is vitally important in alerting legions of cinemagoers that: JAMES BOND 007 IS BACK!

The marketing staff's attempts to communicate this message to the receptive public via theatrical highlight footage (trailers); advertisements, TV and radio spots, posters, photos, etc. One vital marketing strategy is to invite the press to meet the stars on the set. There is still something magic in the phrase "exclusive interview".

Developing promotional methods to pave the way for 007's emergence onto theater screens has always presented a formidable challenge. Of tantamount importance for Bond's debut, was creating audience awareness of this fantastic secret agent, as well as his real-life alter ego – the relatively unknown Sean Connery. Weeks before the première of *Dr. No*, a series of stark teaser ads appeared in newspapers, presenting fictionalized statements made by each of James Bond's gorgeous girls: "I've known men from the CIA and Scotland Yard," declares a seductively posed Ursula Andress, "but wait till you meet that master of undercover operations – James Bond!"

Other inspired promotional gimmicks included an amusing script copy prepared for America's radio airwaves which boasted that "There has never been a man like Bond ... making Mickey Spillane look like a grandmother."

Another example of marketing braggadocio exhorted: "Make it a point to meet James Bond 007 battling Dr. No, a power-mad scientist with a fantastic secret, a mania for torture and a lust to kill. Dr. No has set a trap to murder James Bond – ace secret agent with a passion for wine and women. If you've never seen a motion picture that keeps you on the edge of your seat then see *Dr. No* packed with hot thrills and cold chills."

Exploitation materials identified Bond by a mysterious code number 007: explaining that the 00 granted Bond a Licence to [kill] "where he chooses, when he chooses, whom he chooses." Fr[om] London to the Caribbean, Bond developed "the technique of love [into] an art – and the art of murder to a science!" Further exposition i[nto] Bond's mystique was offered by theatrical trailers (works of ar[t] themselves, created by main title designer Maurice Binder). The[se] allowed fantastic three-minute previews into the exciting and dea[dly] environment of 007; blending astonishing live action sequences w[ith] suspenseful narration. Different trailers were made to appeal [to] various international markets. For example, the U.K. trailer for *Dr. [No]* features narration by Sean Connery, while the U.S. trailer attem[pts] (non too subtly) to exploit the JFK mystique by referring to 007 [as] "the favorite of millions from Hong Kong to Hyannisport!"

In those early, heady days of Bond's cinematic beginnings, ev[en] Sean Connery was sufficiently enthused to make extensive p[ro]motional tours, always accompanied by three luscious Bond-lad[ies] blonde, brunette and redhead. One publicity stunt involved an Ital[ian] casino where "James Bond" would break the bank at baccarat, [to] garner coverage around the globe.

Upon its initial release, United Artists' plans for the future of Jam[es] Bond were almost as deadly as those devised by Dr. No himself, a[s] the movie premièred unceremoniously and simultaneously at dri[ve] ins dotted around the U.S. When it proved to be a major hit [in] Europe, news of the film's success quickly spread and *Dr. No* w[as] belatedly given a nationwide release in the U.S. Broccoli and Saltzm[an] always resented the initial handling of their "masterpiece" and insist[ed] upon their own independent marketing team for future Bond epics.

Among the unsung heroes who can be credited with so brillian[tly] designing the series' classic ad campaigns are Jerry Juroe, Sa[m] Cooper, Derek Coyte, and the late Mike Beck and Tom Carlis[le.] Donald Smolen oversaw the advertising campaigns and most of th[e] posters from the 1960s through the late 1980s. Today, Jo[hn] Parkinson heads the worldwide licensing efforts, and vetera[n] publicist Gordon Arnell oversees the international publici[ty] campaign.

Riding the whirlwind success of *Dr. No*, 007 had less difficulty bei[ng] promoted for his follow-up outing, *From Russia With Love*. "Jam[es] Bond is BACK!" was the theme of the marketing campaign, noti[ng] that "only the second James Bond film could be more exciting th[an] the first!" Two amusing ads appeared in newspapers across the U.[S.] targeting those who had already seen *Dr. No* (citing them [as] "members of the 69,000,007 James Bond fans living in a world [of] hot-blooded excitement!"), and those not having seen the first 0[07] adventure, noting that they "were unprepared for Bond's soph[is]ticated mayhem", and advising them to "join the Bondwagon!"

Promos for *FRWL* warned that this time the masters of murd[er] would be pulling out all the stops to assassinate James Bond. Rad[io] listeners became aware of 007's new adventure through a series [of] exciting spots with a humorous slant:

Smersh Leader: Take a letter to James Bond. (Dictating) Dear Mr. Bond. You've had it! In the *Dr. No* caper you proved yourself to be the strongest, smartest, most secretive agent in the world. However, in *From Russia With Love* it'll be a different story! This time, we'll destroy you. First, we'll tempt you with the most beautiful women in the world, and then we'll BLAST YOU, STRANGLE YOU AND BOMB YOU! Kindest regards, etc., etc.
Secretary: Do you really mean all this, sir?
Smersh Leader: Of course, we mean it.
Secretary: Poor James!

. . . if that was humorous, now for some suspense . . .

Three times a week, the Orient Express screams over the plains of Yugoslavia and Greece; its locomotive roaring like a wounded dragon; roaring so loudly that it drowns out the sound of James Bond fighting for his life. Fighting a giant hulk of a man; fighting with fists, elbows, feet, knees, karate, and finally the hidden knife. All-around athlete ... expert pistol shot. Vices: women. Code number: 007. British Secret Agent James Bond coming "From Russia With Love!"

With *FRWL* receiving universal acclaim, the stage was set for the next Bond thriller, *Goldfinger*, to blitz the world, catapulting Bond to mega-stardom with a broad, red carpet release, and rapid-fire promotional campaign: "James Bond is Back in Action! ... Everything he touches

bove: Space Shuttle-sized "teaser" arquee for *Moonraker*.

ght: A cardboard Bond sees more tion than the average male, as denced by this publicity pose for *Octopussy*.

turns to excitement!" (In fact, everything he touched turned to box-office gold). *Life* devoted its cover story to the film, with a gold-gilded Shirley Eaton tempting readers. An amusing tie-in to *Life*'s stunning issue was a promo spot featuring a husband who discovers his wife has covered herself in gold paint. ("Just like James Bond's golden girl in *Life* magazine!" she coos).

Husband: Are you going to start with that James Bond 007 again? We had to change our licence number to 007 after *Dr. No*, our apartment number to 007 after *From Russia With Love* and furthermore . . . (he gradually becomes aroused) that doesn't look half bad!
Wife: What are you waiting for? Get a brush!

Goldfinger helped pioneer the theory of releasing major films in massive saturation bookings, rather than the traditional method of using select theatres to build word of mouth. This method generated enormous box-office in a short period of time. Yet, *Goldfinger* did not lack the red carpet treatment. For the New York première, a major media event developed when an armored vehicle transporting the print was accompanied by two beautiful, and armed, golden girls. The public ate it up.

Goldfinger's promotion extended to the music world with Shirley Bassey's highly successful title song. By December, 1964, everyone

was familiar with Messrs. Bond and Connery, and his third 007 ef was the first to feature Sean's name above the title, on a brillian constructed advertising campaign emphasizing the golden aura of th film. Imaginative gimmicks included a set of four theatre door pan depicting life-size replicas of Bond's luscious "babes".

Pre-recorded interview packages, sent to local radio station enabled hosts to ask questions of Sean Connery in order to simula actual interviews with the star. Commercial spots blitzed the airwav with feverish action sequences from the new film. Multi-colun newspaper ads boasted: "Held over – 5th week!" proving that Bonc staying power was not limited to the boudoir.

It's been said the key to any marketing program is to achieve fo specific goals: get attention; hold interest; arouse desire; and obta action. The campaign for *Goldfinger* succeeded triumphantly on levels. With the film firmly established as a classic of suspense, actic and thrills, the time seemed right to capitalize on a re-release of *L No* and *FRWL* via double feature.

"Double the Danger! Double the Women! Double the exciteme with double 0 seven!" blared the ad campaign. An amusing prom spot simulated a Hollywood première where Dr. No arrives ar renews his vow to destroy 007 (to which a polite location reporte offers his best wishes and good luck). Rosa Klebb then appears ar responds to an interview request with a karate chop. As dated these gimmicks appear today, they enabled the double bill

Left: In this early publicity stunt, "Bond girls" distributed movie tie-in editions of Fleming's *Dr. No* novel.

Above right: Two armed golden goddesses deliver prints of Goldfinger to a premiére engagement.

gross competing films on their *initial* release, as well as paving the
 for lucrative reissue strategies for upcoming Bond films.

While theater goers were relishing the previous 007 adventures,
cipation was simultaneously building for the mega-budget fourth
d epic, *Thunderball*, which was receiving a goldmine of publicity
n international magazines covering the filming in the lush
amian locales. *Esquire* devoted a large number of pages to an
ance "peek" at the fantastic gadgetry and special effects, while
h *Life*, and *Look* also featured cover stories. More risqué was an
tic pictorial in *Playboy* centering on photospreads of Bond's
men from past to present (with text by Richard Maibaum),
pled with a controversial interview with Sean Connery.

Emphasizing the girls, gadgets and guns, the ad campaign stressed
t *Thunderball* would exceed all previous Bonds in the area of sheer
ctacle. It also inspired some short-lived promotional stunts, such as
 plan to have "Bond" fly to the New York première on the
ous jet pack. Sadly, the stunt was canceled as it could have created
ious traffic disturbances (although in New York, it's unlikely anyone
uld have even noticed!)

More successful were the print ads and posters, featuring
mented drawings of Bond in action, on land, in the air, and under
 sea. The *double entendre* motto was "James Bond Does It
erywhere!" – especially at neighborhood theaters where *Thunder-*
 proved to be even more phenomenally successful than its
ckbuster predecessors.

Following the philosophy that "Bigger is Better", the producers
led out all the stops to insure the ad campaign for *You Only Live*
ice, would launch 007 into box-office orbit. Promotional devices
luded a volcano-sized billboard over the Astor Theater on Times
uare, depicting the various ad campaigns for the film. The primary
tif was a spectacular painting by Frank C. McCarthy showing Bond
lking virtually upside down within the SPECTRE volcano. McCarthy
o devised two supporting campaigns with Bond in Little Nellie and
ing serviced by Geisha girls while in a tub.

Sean Connery, fearing typecasting, was not comforted by a
blicity campaign that screamed "Sean Connery IS James Bond!"
e rationale for this pronouncement was to counter the competing
7 mega-budget spoof *Casino Royale*. United Artists wanted to
mind audiences that there was only one *real* James Bond, and *Twice*
s the legitimate continuation of that legacy. The film's trailer (and
aser poster) also reinforced this strategy by effectively tying-in
ghlights from all the previous Bond epics and reminding audiences
at: "Twice is the *only* way to live!"

A series of promo spots based itself on the premise that, "No
atter what the odds – *they* haven't got a chance against 007, James
nd – Sean Connery!" One ad found Bond battling four heavily
med SPECTRE helicopters spinning through the skies in a dance of
ath. A second spot pit 007 against fifty hardened karate experts
th hands that could slice through rock! The third ad found Bond
unter-attacking a spacecraft manned by precision killers, in the
ack infinity of outer space.

On Her Majesty's Secret Service presented the publicists with
perhaps their most challenging mission ever: exploiting a film where
the new James Bond would be an unknown actor – whose first 007
epic would be his last. Clearly, it would have been futile to spend
significant sums building audience identification for George Lazenby's
limited reign as Bond. Instead, the marketing campaign stressed the
fantastic action sequences and promoted the traditional character of
Bond. The media promos prominently featured the name of James
Bond, with nary a mention of the actor who portrayed him:

> Who could race down a mountain doing 60 m.p.h. on one ski?
> Who would hang from a steel cable that spans a 2,000 ft gorge?
> Who would try and outrun a Swiss avalanche?
> Who would hitch a ride on a speeding bobsled?
> Who would stand in the middle of a time bomb and take pictures?
> Who else but James Bond!

The advertisements shouted, "Far Up! Far Out! Far More! James
Bond 007 is Back!" A teaser campaign was developed to build an air
of mystery around the new Bond. Months before the film opened,

advance posters graced theatres depicting a silhouetted 007 – his face devoid of all features – surrounded by the omnipresent bevy of beauties. The main poster for the film – brilliantly depicted by artist Frank McCarthy and Robert McGinnis – did justice to Lazenby by prominently displaying him on skis, evading an army of SPECTRE assassins. However, "James Bond 007" received the above-title billing, with George's name listed among the other cast members.

Life magazine spotlighted the talent hunt for the new 007 with an article inviting readers to guess who, among the five finalists, had won the role of the decade. The magazine ultimately reveals it is George Lazenby, and featured a dynamic photo of the new Mr. Bond seated with Martini and pistol.

Most of the publicity accorded this fine film was sadly relegated to the tabloids, which had a field day fueling highly speculative stories about a feud between Lazenby and Diana Rigg. One paper dedicated a forum for the battle, with letters and responses from both "combatants" strategically printed in alternate issues. The studio made efforts to downplay such rumors through some open end interviews, which gave no indication of Lazenby's debut as Bond being his swansong as well. These efforts, however, failed to propel *OHMSS* into the Bondian box-office stratosphere.

To counter critics' comments that the Bond series was a dying enterprise, United Artists pulled out all the stops with Sean Connery's return engagement in *Diamonds Are Forever.* "HEEEEEEEEEE'S BA ! ! !" screamed marketing communiques, promising Connery brought "his own special brand of excitement with him." An amu Christmas teaser trailer opens to the familiar strains of "Jingle B as the camera moves to an ornately decorated Christmas t "Darling, for Christmas. it's diamonds . . ." notes the sensual v over. Zooming into one of the Christmas balls, the image of appears in the gunsight. A girl's hand removes the ball, purring because diamonds are forever." Inside the ball, Bond jumps and at the audience and "Jingle Bells" is suddenly replaced by the fan chords of the James Bond Theme. A pool of blood descends the screen, as the trailer previews the tenth anniversary advent for 007.

The poster for *Diamond*s, by artist Robert McGinnis, has Conr flanked by two buxom showgirls, with a satellite of diamonds in background. Immediately before going to the printer, however, painting was doctored to correct a subtle error: the world's lead chauvinist was actually below the two damsels. In raising the chara of Connery through last minute cosmetic surgery, McGinnis rece recalled, "If you look carefully at that poster, Connery has an aw long neck!" Nevertheless, the film was a smash, prompting trade in *Variety* touting: "The greatest three day gross in the history motion pictures!"

Left: An extremely rare prototype of poster art for *OHMSS*. While the background spectacle was retained, new art work of Bond and Tracy was substituted.

Facing page: A rare view of the underwater battle art from the *Thunderball* theatre poster.

With Connery hanging up his shoulder holster, once again, after *Diamonds*, the search was on for yet another James Bond. With the selection of Roger Moore as 007 number three, the promotional campaign concentrated on Moore's well-established image and did not stress this was another *new* James Bond. Fans were reminded that Moore was closer to Ian Fleming's concept of Bond than Connery had been. The television spots and trailers promised audiences that this time there would be more . . . "much more – Roger Moore!" *Live and Let Die* pledged both a livelier and deadlier Bond adventure with: A beautiful Italian spy; seven killers, a vodoo witchdoctor; a living corpse; a gorgeous double agent; five planes; twelve cars; ten acres of land; a wedding reception; a double-decker bus; a fleet of speedboats; a sea of crocodiles; a beautiful sorceress; a man with a steel arm and a retired navy landing craft . . . all against one man!

Live and Let Die assigned James Bond on a worldwide manhunt where the body count was going up. The producers hoped the box-office revenues would do the same, and they succeeded in bringing a contemporary freshness to the series. An avalanche of press coverage centered on 007's seduction of a gorgeous black CIA agent. The concept was still considered avant-garde and some Italian promotional materials were altered, so the young lady's skin took on a Caucasian hue.

Moore was always the good soldier in terms of helping to promote the film. He even wrote a diary of his experiences on the set, which was later published to coincide with the movie's première. In the book, Moore confesses of having no privacy off the set, due to the omnipresent army of international reporters and photographers, each with the uninspired question of how Roger's Bond would differ from Sean's.

Playboy, the foremost endorser of the Bondian lifestyle, featured a photospread of the new Bond girls *sans* any onerous clothing. Roger Moore proved Bondian double standards existed offscreen as well by declining a similar offer to pose nude for *Cosmopolitan*. Of extraordinary promotional value was Paul McCartney's great composition for the *Live and Let Die* title song, ultimately becoming an enormous hit, soaring to Number Two on U.S. charts.

Above: The rare "villains" U.S. one-sheet poster for *Golden Gun*.

Right: Unused "teaser" poster with the original release title for *Licence to Kill*.

Live and Let Die successfully insured 007's triumphant explosion into the 1970s. The film performed briskly at the box-office, and the producers could be assured that they were retaining their loyal audience as well as developing new 007 Bondmaniacs throughout the world.

For his ninth adventure, the marketing strategy centered on flashbacks to Bond's past glories with ads reminding viewers that "James Bond has taken you on eight of the most exciting adventures of your life!" continuing with the warning, "Now, he's on a collision course with the most dangerous man alive – *The Man With the Golden Gun*." Two interesting teaser posters were used to promote *Gun*. The first featured notorious villains of Bond's past and warned it was now the evil hit man Scaramanga's chance to terminate agent still for *From Russia With Love*.

7. The second, and more striking poster, presented a schematic of [ar]amanga's fantastic golden gun. Both were considerably more [ins]pired than the art for the main campaign, which was disturbingly [sim]ilar in design to the poster for *Live and Let Die*.

[*Golden*]*Gun* was cross-promoted with a wide variety of products, including [ev]erything from Nikon cameras, to Westinghouse kitchens and [G]uinness Stout. The films also contains obvious plugs for Sony prod[uc]ts, as exemplified in a scene where Bond lingers in the doorway of [an] electronics store, filled with nothing but the latest in Sony tech[no]logy. The film generated less than smashing revenues in the U.S., [alt]hough it was more successful in other markets. Sensing a need to [re]-invigorate 007 for American audiences, the marketing team put [th]eir full energies into the next Bond epic, *The Spy Who Loved Me*.

The summer of 1977 represented a critical period in James Bond's [sc]reen lifespan. Film critics speculated that 007's exploits had run their [co]urse; U.S. enthusiasm for Bond was sinking; and fears persisted that [au]diences would bring about what no Ian Fleming villain could: the [de]ath of Her Majesty's top Secret Service Agent.

A bombardment of advertising pounded home the point that *Spy* [w]ould be "the Biggest, the Best – Bond and Beyond!" Bond number [10] fulfilled its promise to deliver more dangerous villains, more [b]eautiful women, more fantastic gadgets, and more spectacular action [t]han any movie you've ever seen!" Practically every commercial [d]uring prime-time television and radio carried promos for *Spy*. One [s]uch spot was hosted by Roger Moore himself: "My name is Bond – [Ja]mes Bond. Since we've first met, you've joined me on nine of my [m]issions. My latest, and if I'm not careful, my last, will take me to new [h]eights of adventure, new depths of danger, and new areas of [e]xcitement. It won't be easy, but every job has its rewards. In this [c]ase, its *The Spy Who Loved Me!*"

Spy was the first to intone that Roger Moore IS James Bond; [g]ranting him billing on par with Connery in *You Only Live Twice*. For [th]e "new image" publicity campaign, world famous artist Bob Peak [w]as hired to design the off-beat and effective poster design. The [fi]lm's main theme, "Nobody Does it Better", was a smash hit on [in]ternational radio, courtesy of Carly Simon's splendid vocals. The [u]sual cross-promotional tie-ins were abundant, with everyone from [th]e Royal Navy to Seiko watches participating. For the first time in [m]any years, a wide range of 007-related toys swamped stores, and

magazines gave an abundance of publicity to Moore's memorable co-stars – the stunningly beautiful Barbara Bach, and the not-so-beautiful Richard Kiel as "Jaws".

Curiously, the initial release of the film was restricted to select theaters, as opposed to the standard wide release pattern accorded the previous Bond films. Word of mouth was hot, however, and the strategy built great interest in the film, as theaters could not accommodate the crowds. For the first time since *Twice*, rave reviews were quoted in the newspaper ads. *Spy* proved the old magic was back, recalling the Bondmania days of the mid-1960s. Bond could still hold his own, even in the age of mega blockbusters like *Jaws* and *Star Wars*.

Even before the next Bond epic, *Moonraker*, was released, the project had the inevitable air of success all over it. "Other films promise you the moon – *Moonraker* delivers!" boasted the television spots. The latest Bond benefited both from the success of *The Spy Who Loved Me* and also the international rage for science fiction epics spawned by *Star Wars* and *Close Encounters of the Third Kind*.

Strange as it may seem to die-hard Bond fans, who bemoan the film's abundance of slapstick, a key element in *Moonraker's* success was the return of Jaws – by popular demand! "Where all the other Bonds end, *Moonraker* begins!" shouted the appropriately cartoonish advertising poster. 007 did everything outer space could offer, backed by the largest promotional package the series had ever seen.

The huge publicity effort included a range of six theater posters, a teaser featurette titled "James Bond in Rio", dozens of radio and TV spots (with and without reviews of the film), pages of newspaper ads. Hundreds of photos were sent to the press (most other films confined themselves to a handful of such stills).

The film also benefited from publicity surrounding a week-long tribute to the series at the prestigious Museum of Modern Art in New York. Here, Bond classics were unspooled in the same edifice that housed the works of Picasso; Cubby Broccoli and his team made personal appearances to talk to fans and the press. The film's release was complemented by the usual cottage industry of 007 toys and novelties. All of this, combined with very favorable reviews, helped to launch *Moonraker* as the top moneymaker of the series. Fittingly, it also inspired the ultimate tribute – a *Mad* magazine satire titled "Moneyraker!"

Two years later, another Bond classic was unveiled that continued the box-office blitz. Smaller in scope, *For Your Eyes Only* still maintained the superb quality, allowing the ad campaign to brag: "When it comes to action, adventure, romance ... nobody comes close to 007!" *FYEO* contained one of the most controversial advertising campaigns of recent decades – one that angered many feminists. The offending artistry (ceremoniously dubbed "the legs art") had, as its foreground, the lower half of a taut female torso, with the *derrière* prominently displayed in a bikini bottom (reversed to increase the sex appeal). Between the girl's wide-open legs is the figure of James Bond, tuxedo-clad and posed for action. Several periodicals succumbed to the conservative outcry, by airbrushing boxer shorts over the bikini bottom! Further controversy erupted when a number of models claimed to be the proud possessor of the gorgeous "gams". The argument was settled when it was verified the luscious limbs belonged to New York model, Joyce Bartel.

The film achieved further notoriety when it was discovered that one of the lovely extras seen bikini-clad by a swimming pool, was in fact a male who had undergone a sex change operation. The tabloids exploited this, building the actress – Tula – into a star of the film no less, when, in fact, she is barely noticeable. The producers needn't have felt embarrassed, as "Mr." Tula was sufficiently well-endowed to have been a hit pin-up, some months earlier, in a British "skin magazine". This is the type of free publicity which marketing departments can only dream of.

FYEO marked the last time promotional materials generated for television appeared on film stock. With the emergence of cable television, the music video networks and the growth in popularity of the VCR, more sophisticated marketing packages surfaced. A greater emphasis was placed on the development of the Electronic Presskit – an elaborately packaged publicity tool that offered a *tour de force* for film promoters. The kit comprised interviews with the cast and crew, trailers, newsclips, music videos, and was used by TV stations to create a maximum interest.

The first electronic press kit was developed for the thirteenth Bond film, *Octopussy*, a film whose *double entendre* title made it a sure-fire box-office hit. For the first time, the female lead featured almost as prominently in the ad campaign as Bond himself. Maud Adam's title character was a natural for the promos: "*He* has a licence to kill; *She* doesn't need one; now, the excitement, the thrills, the adventure, the action are at an all time high. This is the one you've heard about: This is *Octopussy!*"

Artist Daniel Gouzee fashioned a seductively enticing poster featuring Bond being embraced, from behind, by Octopussy – her tentacle-like arms both caressing and menacing him. It's a striking piece of art, and proved to be an effective centerpiece of the ad campaign. A teaser poster featured thirteen James Bonds in a row, signifying the number of screen adventures 007 had experienced to date. The film continued the tradition of extravagant promotional opportunities, as only Eon could accomplish. As with most recent Bonds, the film was the subject of a Royal Première attended by their Royal Highnesses Prince Philip, Prince Charles and Princess Diana. The event was telecast on British television, to the delight of legions of 007 fans.

Once again, Seiko watches became the centerpiece of give-away contests, while the main theme, "All Time High", recorded by Rita Coolidge and written by Tim Rice, received enough airplay to allow it to become a standard today. In England, Smiths' Crisps allowed hungry Bond fans to obtain a 007 watch. They also organised competitions with James Bond albums and videos as prizes. Nabisco gave away "Octopussy" stickers in their Shredded Wheat cereal boxes. A wide range of international souvenir programs, magazines and books tied into the film, completing a successful promotional campaign – *Octopussy* became the highest grossing James Bond film to date.

Roger Moore's swan-song as 007 in *A View to a Kill* managed to overcome mixed reviews from critics, who complained that perhaps Mr. Moore had gone a film too far. This problem posed a challenge for the marketing department: how does one keep youthful moviegoers interested in a 33-year-old film hero portrayed by an actor in his late 50s? One way is to enlist the services of a hot rock band to insure the title song is a smash hit. Cubby Broccoli was approached by Duran Duran to allow them to contribute a song for the upcoming film. While it's doubtful Cubby had a credenza full of their records, he knew a good promotional opportunity when he saw it. The title track became an international smash, eventually becoming a number one song on the all-important music video network MTV in the U.S. A clever and very successful video linking the band to clips from the movie in a mini-Bond scenario, was also a great success. Duran Duran premièred the song at a Royal charity event and brought down the house. An amused Prince Philip, politely feigning an appreciation of the sweating rockers, is a memorable image.

In the U.S. Whoppers Candy featured an aggressive campaign highlighted by give-aways of the teaser poster and a free trip to Pinewood Studios. Canada Dry awarded tickets to advance screenings of the film, as well as a slew of other prizes ranging from new cars to a trip to San Francisco. A nationwide network of radio stations held "James Bond Première" nights on May 23, 1985 – each station promoting the film and giving away tickets to lucky callers. Crunch 'n Munch snacks gave away sets of Ian Fleming novels, and Bollinger Champagne issued a special James Bond poster to coincide with their own contest. Michelin Tires had their sales people wear buttons that read: "Michelin Saved James Bond in *A View to A Kill*", and issued a large 007 poster announcing a contest which gave away a new Alfa Romeo. Pepsi distributed 007 glasses as part of a trivia contest.

Each of these promotional opportunities was explained in a marketing guide presumably sent by "M" to MGM /U.S Field Operatives. Among the instructions contained therein: "Further information on what is planned to make this the biggest, boldest, box-office booming Bond in history is contained in this missive. DO NOT DESTROY IT! When you've got an adventure like *A View to a Kill*, everyone should be in on the secret."

Britain, promotions were no less prevalent or inspired. Philips tronics, Smiths Crisps, Matchbox Toys, and Wright's Soaps, e among the many major firms clamoring to become part of er Moore's farewell appearance as the world's most popular et agent.

1987 came a new James Bond adventure – *The Living Daylights*, ring a new James Bond, Timothy Dalton. The freshman 007 was a household name, and therefore did not benefit from an already blished persona as had Roger Moore. Dalton did possess dentials that made critics generally agree he might be the best r to take on the Bond role, although he had to develop his own e of playing 007.

he Eon team knew from the start that light comedy would not be ton's forte, and wisely encouraged him to bring Bond back to the cs: a potentially ruthless detective who pursued his missions with vavering intensity. To illustrate the point, a teaser campaign ured a poster of a deadly looking Dalton, pistol at the ready, ide a tag line which read "James Bond at His Most Dangerous." In U.S. it read: "The Most Dangerous Bond. Ever."

n extensive analysis of marketing costs indicated that the film's y $5.5 million marketing launch in the U.S. should be spent thus: 7% on newspaper ads; 31.6% on regional TV ads; 28.9% on onal TV spots, 6% on radio and 5.8% on miscellaneous marketing npaigns. This strategy differed significantly from campaigns employed previous Bond films, but it centered primarily on the most fitable way to promote the movie. The standard print campaign in U.S. was dominated by an ad depicting Bond aiming a gun at a uty in her nightwear.

Merchandise tie-ins in the U.K. included a very extensive cross-omotion with high tech items from Philips Electronics, which arded replicas of "Q" Branch's electronic key-finger ring. Nabisco uded 007 stickers with their chocolate biscuits; Unigate furnished e tickets with their Farmer's Wife orange juice cartons; and record npanies made the most of the title song by rock group a-ha.

Two "official" movie books were issued for hardcore Bond lectors: *The James Bond Movie Book*, and *The James Bond Movie ster Book*. In the U.S. Bollinger Champagne once again got aboard Bond wagon with a gorgeous promo poster, which is now a ued collector's item.

Daylights* was not ignored by television. As the film represented nd's 25th year onscreen, a one hour documentary entitled "Happy niversary, 007", was telecast worldwide. The original broadcast ide the most of promoting the new James Bond. Subsequent leos of the show, while longer, delete a good deal of this material in ce of clips from earlier adventures.

Newspapers played up the anniversary, with both *Variety* and the llywood Reporter* devoting special sections to the history of 007 ns; including many witty and touching advertisements placed by nd alumni, to honor Cubby Broccoli. The press also played up a it by Prince Charles and Princess Diana to the set, highlighting a oto of the princess displaying some rather un-Royal behavior by

smashing a "break away" glass over her husband's head. The Eon team and the studio could breathe a sigh of relief when first week grosses for *Daylights* proved there was indeed a future in the 1990s for agent 007, and for his new offscreen *alter ego* Timothy Dalton.

Challenges emerged the moment the cameras started to roll on Dalton's second Bond epic. After many months of shooting, it was discovered that the film's shooting title "Licence Revoked" should be changed, when marketing studies indicated that U.S. audiences would relate the name of the film to the terminating of a driver's license – hardly a subject matter to induce audiences to wait in line at the box-office. Although considerable promotional material had been spent publicizing the original title, a campaign was launched immediately to focus on the new title *Licence to Kill*. No sooner did this occur, when it was discovered that "Licence" in the U.S. was spelled "License". As it would be prohibitively expensive to change the titles on every piece of promotional material, it was decided – after much debate – to stay with the Queen's English.

Not since *Dr. No* had a Bond film suffered marketing campaign frustrations to such a degree. MGM/United Artists – the film's distributor for the all-important American market – was in disarray with frequent changes in top management.

Although world class artists, like Bob Peak, had been employed to create a series of breathtaking teaser posters, the entire campaign was disposed of by the studio. A last minute poster was created "in house", and the results were less than impressive. A teaser poster was almost identical to the one used for *Daylights*, and the main ad campaign gave few clues that this was even a James Bond film. These factors, coupled with the release of the film at the height of summer competition, sank its chances of registering the traditional Bondian box-office figures in the U.S. This was truly disappointing as the film received better than average reviews, and benefited from a performance by Timothy Dalton that was truly remarkable.

Fortunately, a slightly more creative international campaign insured that the film did "socko" business in most other markets. Merchandise tie-ins included Polaroid Sunglasses, Olympus Cameras, good old Philips, and Bollinger Champagne. Various recordings of the title theme by Gladys Knight (bad news in the U.S., but a hit in the U.K.); a comic book adaptation of the story; Planter's Peanuts give-aways; and several lines of upscale clothing boosted returns. One inspired campaign touted James Bond nightclub events sponsored by Martini and Rossi. Three books helped promote the film: *The James Bond Girls*, *The James Bond 007 Fact File*, and a special adaptation of the screenplay in novel form by best-selling Bond writer, John Gardner.

Despite the fact that legal problems prevented a new James Bond film from being made for six years, during the early 1990s the series remained remarkably durable in terms of licensed properties. Among the more prominent collectors items were the series of plates manufactured by the Franklin Mint. The initial plate, a 30th anniversary tribute to *Goldfinger*, proved to be such a hit with collectors in America that shipments reserved for distribution in the U.K. were diverted to satisfy backorders in the U.S. market.

(Frustrated Brits eventually had the opportunity to purchase the plate in their homeland.) The second in the series, a 30th anniversary commemorative edition of *Thunderball* is released in 1995, with five more plates to follow.

Corgi continued its long relationship with the Bond films and produced another edition of the classic Aston Martin DB5 – this time with an Alpine backdrop on the packaging, designed to recall memories of *Goldfinger*. Other popular vehicle replicas were made by Doyusha of Japan. The kits produced in 1994 were superb models of the Aston Martin DB5 and the Toyota from *You Only Live Twice*. They became immediate worldwide sensations for Bond fans.

In 1994, Creation Entertainment – the company which pioneered the legendary Star Trek fan conventions – licensed the rights to hold official James Bond Conventions. The debut show in Los Angeles included a prestigious 30th anniversary "repremiere" of *Goldfinger* at the Academy of Motion Picture Arts and Sciences Theater. The screening was preceeded by a filmed tribute to Cubby Broccoli, who received the Ian Fleming Foundation's first *GoldenEye* Award. The award was presented by Pierce Brosnan and accepted on behalf of Cubby (who was recovering from surgery) by Michael G. Wilson. The convention itself was manna from heaven for 007 fans, who could spend their hard-earned money on vintage collectables and Creation's line of licensed products. Guests included Bruce Glover, Richard Kiel, Lynn Holly Johnson, Gloria Hendry, Martine Beswick, Bill Conti, and a reunion of George Lazenby and Peter Hunt. Many of the vintage props and vehicles were also on display.

The release of *GoldenEye* will see the largest advertising campaign ever undertaken for a Bond film, with MGM/UA budgeting over $20 million to launch the film in the U.S. alone. Two different teaser posters were created – one for the European market, and one for the U.S.. One hour T.V. specials for "prime time" were scheduled both countries, and in addition to the traditional British Ro Premiere, there will be a lavish U.S. premiere at Radio City Music H in New York City.

GoldenEye will also carry the most licensed products tied in tc Bond film in memory. Among items being produced: a ne *GoldenEye* pinball machine, a new Corgi Aston Martin DB5, Nintendo video game, GTE's phone debit cards, an entire line ladies cosmetics from Yves St. Laurent, a children's playset of clas Bond characters and vehicles from Galoob; Spy Guise's limit edition 30th anniversary poster of *Thunderball* and three promine books: *The Making of GoldenEye* by Garth Pearce, and updat versions of Graham Rye's *The James Bond Girls* and Dave Worra *The Most Famous Car in the World*.

GoldenEye will also feature the grand "unveiling" of BMW's newe sportscar for 1996 – the first time a prominent vehicle has ever be "premiered" in a motion picture. In addition to BMWs made for t mass market, there will also be a limited number of *GoldenEye* ca available for the more advanced Bond collectors. (Although BM' does not give advice about how to explain such an acquisition your wife!)

Additionally, MGM/UA Home Video will relaunch the enti James Bond series on video tape, with a marketing extravagar costing over $4 million. There will also be collector's editions on ta and laser disc featuring documentaries about the making of *Goldfing* and *Thunderball*. The lasers will also contain hundreds of rare st from the films, as well as collectables, posters, and rare featurette:

Although Bond fans have been frustrated over the last six yea with the absence of their hero from the screen, the marketing boc of 1995 proves that patience is a virtue, and that Bond is Back!

The classic Aston Martin DB5 figure prominently in the publicity for *GoldenEye*.

INTERVIEW WITH
PIERCE BROSNAN

The following interview was conducted with Pierce Brosnan in May, 1995 at Leavesden Studios in England. At the time, Mr. Brosnan was about to complete the filming of *GoldenEye*.

Q: What films influenced you as a young boy?
PB: In seeing *Goldfinger*, the seed was sown, as it were, to my becoming an actor. It wasn't that I consciously said "I want to become an actor ... I want to become James Bond". But, the magic of film certainly affected me with *Goldfinger*. The next night I went to see *Lawrence Of Arabia*. The thing that topped it off, really, was the Clint Eastwood movies - the ones he did with Leone. I was a young boy of 10, 11 or 12. I had seen Westerns in Ireland, but I had never seen a hero figure like Clint Eastwood. That really spurred me on, I think.

Q: How did it feel in 1986 to be so close to getting the Bond role in *The Living Daylights*, only to have it slip away due to your contractual obligations to Remington Steele?
PB: I felt very frustrated, very impotent because I was powerless to do anything. I had a contract with MTM. and they had 60 days in which to resell *Remington Steele*. ABC said "No." CBS. said "No". Near the end of the 60 days, NBC began to weaken. Cubby said, "You can have him for six episodes, but no more than six episodes." They said, "We'll think about it." They came back on the sixtieth day and said "We want the option of 22."

Q: That decision resulted in you losing the role of 007 to Timothy Dalton. In the ensuing years, have you ever seen *The Living Daylights*?
PB: I was sitting in a plane with my son, who at that time was about four or five. We were coming back from New York. And they said, "Today's film is *The Living Daylights*. So I couldn't walk out! (Laughs) I had to look. Then my son said, "Daddy, when are you coming on?" I said, "I didn't do the movie." At which point, I asked for a large Vodka. I didn't watch it, actually. I've never seen Timothy in his movies.

Q: You have specialized in playing urbane, sophisticated men. Did the other Bond actors have an influence on you in your early years in acting?
PB: Well, Connery was the Bond I was introduced to, so he is the man as far as I'm concerned. Having said that, nevertheless, I see what an amazing job Roger did, and I love Roger in the role because I feel he made it his own. He did it his way and was extremely successful.

Q: What was your reaction when you were told you finally got the role of Bond in GoldenEye? Were you surprised?
PB: No. Once you have been through the ringer, like I was in '86.... When Timothy left, I had a feeling it was going to come back around. People would tell me things from all around the world. Rumors began to happen. I just carried on working. Kept my head down.
   I met with Barbara (Broccoli), Michael (G. Wilson), and Martin Campbell. It was a very favorable meeting. About a week later, I was gearing up for my 41st birthday party. My girlfriend and secretary were in the house and a photographer, Greg Gorman, set up a photographic shoot. The phone rang and my secretary picked it up and broke the news to me. They started jumping up and down. I was sworn to secrecy, because that's part of the mystique of Bond. I said to the girls, "It's in the bag. I've got Bond. Let's rock 'n roll."

Q: What are you doing to personalize your interpretation of James Bond?
PB: That's a difficult question to answer. Just by virtue of my very presence within the piece, it's going to be different. The man is somebody who is very solitary. He is a man who is very passionate about what he does. His weakness is women. He is a man who is looking, searching for something in his life. But the job is everything. I would like to see a certain kind of vulnerability to him. That's a dangerous word to put in print, especially in the context of a Bond film. It's more about mood. It's more about style. For this movie, I'm really just trying to keep it as simple as possible.

All things come to those who wait – Pierce Brosnan making his debut as James Bond in *GoldenEye*.

A new face, a classic pose: Brosnan with Izabella Scorupco.

Q: *It's been said that for Bond to prosper in the 1990s, the character may have to succumb to the forces of political correctness. What are your thoughts on the matter, particularly as it pertains to Bond's relations with women?*
PB: I find the whole PC thing to be a certain form of censorship. I find it very boring and tiring, expecially when it comes down to a piece of entertainment such as Bond. For example, take the part of Xenia, played by Famke Janssen. Bond deals with her in his own way. She's messed with him and he'll mess with her. That's what turned people on in the first place. It's part of the mystique.

Q: *What is your reaction to the durability of the entire 007 phenomenon over the last 33 years?*
PB: I find it staggering. The thread of Bond has woven its way into the tapestry of my life in such a way that sometimes I stand back and say, "My God, where did this come from? For what purpose? For what reason?" I remember going home the day I stood there before the press of the world, making my announcement that I was going to be the next James Bond, feeling absolutely drained. Like the blood had been sucked out of me. I thought, "Have I made the biggest faux pas of my life? Was I too impetuous? Should I have thought about it a little bit more?" But this was like unfinished business in my life. I had to see this job done. I had to do it for my own satisfaction as an actor. And I had to do it for my wife, who really would have loved it all and was such a champion of mine and hung in there through all the dealings in 1986.

Q: *You have reportedly been doing many of your own stunts. Does this cause you or the producers any nervousness?*
PB: I can understand their concern. When I look back, I've done some really considerable things... with horses, hanging out of helicopters, coming out from underneath moving trains, climbing up the side of buildings in Hong Kong. There's a lot of money riding on this, but I like to be in there as much as possible. I think it behoves the character.

Q: *Let's talk about your late wife Cassie. She gave a memorable performance in* **For Your Eyes Only,** *and it's been said that from day one she was convinced you would ultimately portray Bond.*
PB: Yes. I think she would be absolutely over the moon about me getting the role. I think she would be a very happy woman for her guy, and to be able to share all of this. The role comes with its own burdens. But it allows me as an actor to hopefully do other work and create other characters. It also allows me to work for a better life for my family.

Q: *You've used your status as a public figure to work for charities devoted to women's health. How did you become involved with these causes?*
PB: I have been associated as a kind of ambassador toward women's health care since I lost Cassie. I was asked by the National Institute of Health to speak in front of Congress. At first I found it to be a very heavy undertaking. Then I began to find an articulation for my feelings and thoughts as a father and a man, and I went and spoke. Despite the sadness and the loss, my life somehow seems to be making sense once more. Good things are happening once more: my being in this part, which is hopefully going to be wonderful and entertaining for a whole new generation who are out there.

Q: *What is it like working in the family atmosphere of a Broccoli production?*
PB: I find it fascinating that this man – Cubby Broccoli – who is in his twilight is on the verge of a new beginning. We're doing this film in this old Rolls Royce factory [the first Bond film to be shot at Leavesden Studios] and there are no ghosts of Roger or Sean here. It's a fresh canvas. I enjoy this as a studio. I paint, and I feel very at home here.

Q: *When you were a young boy, you were impressed by Sean Connery's portrayal of James Bond. What do you hope that your young son brings away from your performance as 007?*
PB: Seeing a hero figure. Somebody who is a good man. A character who is a solid human being. And someone my son would say "I want to be like him. He's a cool guy."

GOLDENEYE

CAR CHASE
TRACKING IN FRONT of CARS - which weave back & forth - Bond trying to...

(Above) Original studio storyboard detailing the car chase between Bond and Xenia.

Roger Moore drops by the set at Leavesden to wish Pierce Brosnan and Michael G. Wilson success.

The years 1989 through 1994 were lean ones indeed for James Bond fans. Following the release of *Licence to Kill*, legal disputes arose between Danjaq, Inc and MGM/UA, which co-owns the series and distributes the films in America. Agent 007 remained in cinematic limbo. By the time a settlement was reached, 007 had been off the screen for the longest period of time since the series began in 1962.

In 1994, James Bond fans finally read the news they had eagerly awaited for so long: Danjaq and United Artists and the production company Eon Productions, were gearing up for production of the 17th official 007 epic. Screenwriter Michael France (*Cliffhanger*) had been hired to write an original screenplay. (France's qualifications were beyond dispute. As a teenager in the 1970's, he published a 007 fan magazine titled *Kiss Kiss Bang Bang!*). British writer Jeffrey Caine would be brought on board to co-author the script, and New York writer Bruce Feirstein would contribute to the final storyline.

The most obvious question became "Who will play James Bond?" when Timothy Dalton announced that, despite his affection for the films, he felt it was time to move on to new projects. While Dalton's parting was totally amicable, it meant that Eon would have to take immediate steps to find a suitable actor to fill 007's shoulder holster.

In July 1994, at a major press conference called by Eon in London, producers Michael G. Wilson and Barbara Broccoli announced who the new Agent 007 would be: Pierce Brosnan. Brosnan had lost the role in 1986 due to the demands of a TV contract to resume shooting episodes of *Remington Steele*. Now, fate had allowed him an unexpected opportunity to portray the world's most enduring screen hero. Brosnan's quick wit and sense of humor immediately endeared him to fans and press alike. During the press conference, it was also announced that the new film would be entitled *GoldenEye* (not coincidentally the name of Ian Fleming's house in Jamaica), and that a new director would be entering the Bond fold: Martin Campbell.

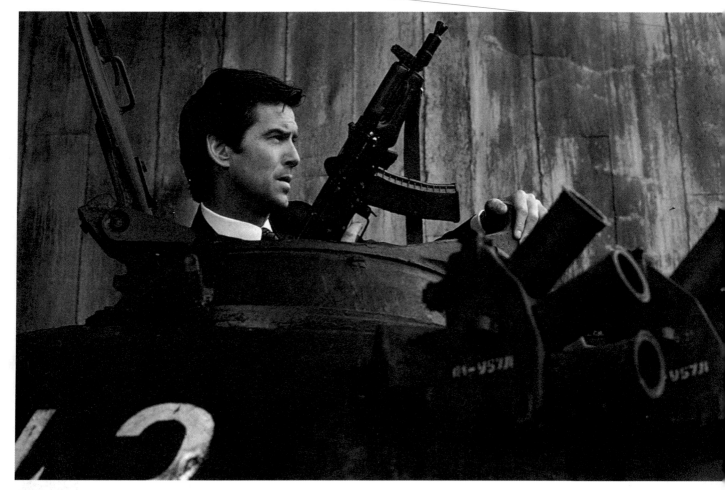

Filming of *GoldenEye* began in January, 1995 at Eon Production's new studio site at Leavesden Airfield, outside of London. Pinewood Studios, the traditional home of the 007 films, was unavailable due to other movies in production. Eon located the site at Leavesden, where an abandoned Rolls Royce aircraft engine facility once operated. In under six months, this area was transformed into one of the largest film studios in the world, with over 1.25 million square feet of interior stages and backlot facilities. It was here that production designer Peter Lamont, a veteran of the Bond films since *Goldfinger*, constructed some of the most magnificent sets ever to grace a 007 epic, including replicas of the city of St. Petersburg, Russia and the jungles of the Caribbean.

Once production began, the logistics of bringing the epic film to completion rivalled those of any previous Bond movie. A second unit team headed by Ian Sharp was shooting extensive footage on location in St. Petersburg, Russia while Martin Campbell directed extravagant action scenes at 'St. Petersburg' at Leavesden. Simultaneously, miniature effects supervisor Derek Meddings was creating other explosive sequences involving spectacular train

crashes, tank chases and the film's climatic battle atop a gigant satellite dish. Other location shooting was done in Puerto Ric Monte Carlo and the Nene Valley in the British countryside.

Key elements of the plot of *GoldenEye* are still being kept to secret as of this writing in May, 1995. Future editions of this book w critique the film in full detail. However, the following details can b told: the story opens during the Cold War years with James Bor and his friend and colleague Alexander Trevelyan, Agent 006 (Sea Bean) infiltrating a Soviet nerve gas facility. Their mission to destro the compound goes awry and Trevelyan is captured by the ruthle Soviet Army Commander Ourumov (Gottfried John). Bond is face with the moral dilemma of going through with the mission at th price of his friend's life, or aborting the plan and placing sentimer above duty. In the ensuing chaos, Ourumov executes Trevelya before Bond's eyes. Agent 007 makes a spectacular escape, but ove the years he is wracked by guilt over Trevelyan's death.

The action then jumps to the present day, with the former Sovie Union now a shaky conglomeration of independent states, each c which is in political chaos. Ourumov is now right hand man to Janu

CREDITS	
YEAR OF RELEASE	1995
CAST	Pierce Brosnan
	Sean Bean
	Izabella Scorupco
	Famke Janssen
	Joe Don Baker
	Robbie Coltrane
	Tcheky Karyo
	Gottfried John
	Alan Cumming
	Michael Kitchen
	Serena Gordon
	Desmond Llewelyn
	Samantha Bond
	Minnie Driver
	and Judi Dench as M
DIRECTOR	Martin Campbell
PRESENTED BY	Albert R. Broccoli
PRODUCERS	Michael G. Wilson and
	Barbara Broccoli
SCREENPLAY	Michael France and
	Jeffrey Caine
PRODUCTION DESIGNER	Peter Lamont
EDITOR	Terry Rawlings
MUSIC	Eric Serra

(facing page) Bond turns on the bad guys in the thrilling tank chase in St Petersberg.

(Above) The M for the 1990s: Dame Judi Dench makes her debut as Bond's superior.

(Below) A rare shot of the production team in St Petersburg.

a mysterious and unseen criminal mastermind who plans to use the stability of the former Soviet bloc to become the most powerful man in the world. Ourumov works with the sultry Xenia Onatopp (Famke Janssen) a stunning temptress with a penchant for constricting lovers to death during sex. They bluff their way into a key Russian satellite surveillance station near the Arctic Circle and slaughter the staff. They succeed in stealing the GoldenEye – a key to a satellite which has the power to render the world's defences useless as it unleashes a destructive force that is almost unimaginable. The goal of Janus is to use the GoldenEye as a threat to gain control over the financial fabric of every nation on earth.

In London, James Bond is assigned to crack the case by "M" (Judi Dench) who warns 007 not to allow the mission to become a way to revenge the death of Alec Trevelyan. Bond follows the trail to St. Petersburg, Russia where he hopes to use the local Mafia as a way of infiltrating the Janus organization. Among the friends and foes he encounters along the way are:

Natalya Simonova (Izabella Scorupco), a survivor of the massacre at the surveillance station. As the only witness who can identify Ourumov and Xenia as the murderers, she is being relentlessly pursued by the Janus organization.

(Below) Ourumov (Gottfried John) gets the drop on agent 006 (Sean Bean).

(Right) James Bond indulges in his favorite pastime.

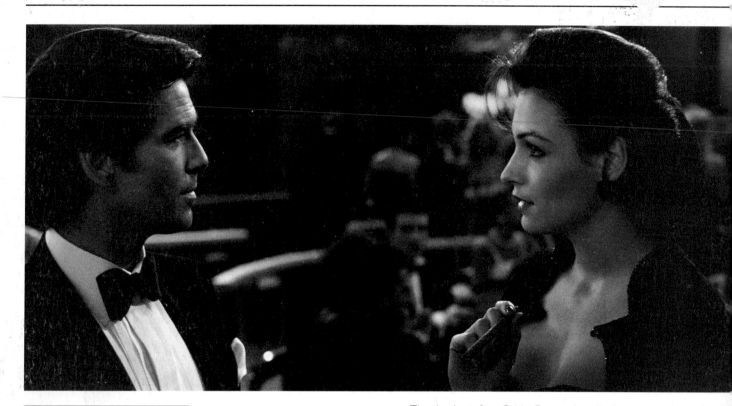

Bond's introduction to Xenia Onatopp (Famke Janssen) at the Monte Carlo casino.

Jack Wade (Joe Don Baker), Bond's CIA contact in Russia. A cynical, hard-boiled man who shows Bond the seedy side of the new Russia and helps him make important contacts in the Mafia.

Boris Grishenko (Alan Cumming), a rogue computer genius who has aligned himself with the Janus organization.

Valentin Zukovsky (Robbie Coltrane), a former KGB controller, of late a local weapons mogul on the St Petersburg black market. Bond is left in the unenviable position of needing Zukovsky's assistance despite the fact that he had almost mortally wounded him on a previous assignment.

Bond lets human emotion take over, and begins to anticipate revenge for Trevelyan's death. The trail to Janus leads from the streets of Russia to the Caribbean headquarters of the criminal mastermind. Here, Bond and Natalya have a face-to-face encounter with their prey. The shattering climax involves a fight to death atop a gigantic satellite dish hidden deep within the Caribbean jungle.

Although GoldenEye boasts a new James Bond and exciting young talent, there are also many veterans of the series who contributed to the latest 007 epic. Albert R. Broccoli has produced every Bond film since the series began with Dr. No in 1962. No other producer has ever been so identified with such a consistent body of work. Producers Michael G. Wilson and Barbara Broccoli have also been a driving creative force behind the series. GoldenEye features a new "M" (Judi Dench), and her scenes with Pierce Brosnan's Bond recall the grit and tension of the earlier Bernard Lee/Sean Connery scenes. This should quiet speculation about the suitability of a woman for the head of MI6. There is also a new Miss Moneypenny (Samantha Bond). Desmond Llewelyn makes a welcome return as the ill-tempered gadgets genius "Q".

The budget for GoldenEye makes it the most expensive 007 production to date. As stated previously, we cannot fully critique the film, because we have seen only about one hour of footage so far. However, this much can be said: GoldenEye appears to return Bond to his traditional roots in a number of ways. For the first time in many years, Bond is pitted against a larger-than-life villain with plans for world domination. There is also an emphasis on Bond's sexuality, and in this film he unapologetically indulges his appetite for beautiful women at every turn, whether friend or foe. Pierce Brosnan perfectly captures the right balance between being a killer and a lady killer. It is safe to say that with Brosnan onboard, the Bond legacy is in safe hands.

GoldenEye also boasts one of the strongest casts ever to grace a Bond film. Sean Bean is extremely impressive as Trevelyan and his scenes with Brosnan ring with real emotion. Izabella Scorupco is very convincing as Natalya, keeping alive the tradition of having Bond women who are strong, independent and self-reliant. She's also an extremely good actress. Famke Janssen ignites the screen with a sizzling performance as Xenia Onatopp, one of the most exciting of all Bond villains. Her portrayal of the sultry killer who takes orgasmic delight in eliminating the competition makes her the most memorable female Bond villain since Luciana Paluzzi's classic turn in Thunderball.

GoldenEye might well represent a renaissance period for the James Bond film. The absence of a 007 movie over the last six years seems to make this one more of an event, and the international media has been giving the production extraordinary coverage. Although the film has not opened as of this writing, and the box office receipts have therefore not been tallied, it is a safe bet that Cubby Broccoli will continue to make good on his longstanding promise to moviegoers...

"JAMES BOND WILL RETURN"